John Henry Parker

The Forum Romanum

John Henry Parker

The Forum Romanum

ISBN/EAN: 9783744746588

Printed in Europe, USA, Canada, Australia, Japan

Cover: Foto ©ninafisch / pixelio.de

More available books at **www.hansebooks.com**

THE
FORUM ROMANUM.

BY

JOHN HENRY PARKER, C.B.

Hon. M.A. Oxon., F.S.A. Lond.;
Keeper of the Ashmolean Museum of History and Antiquities
in the University of Oxford, etc.

OXFORD:
JAMES PARKER AND CO.

LONDON:
JOHN MURRAY, ALBEMARLE STREET.
1876.

PREFACE TO THE FORUM ROMANUM, &c.

THE great excavations that have been going on for many years, at intervals, in this most interesting part of the old City of Rome, are now so far completed that all the most important points are settled for ever, and are no longer matter of doubt, or dispute and discussion, but matter of fact, established by the most undoubted evidence,—the construction of the walls and the architectural details agreeing with the history long handed down, but hitherto only imperfectly understood. It seemed, therefore, necessary to change the plan of the publication of this work, and bring out as soon as possible a full explanation of all such important matters, making it the completion of this part of the work, and combining with it what would have been the eighth Regio, on the arrangement which had originally been begun. It is true that the eastern part of the Forum is still buried, and there must be a little uncertainty in that part; but this is very secondary, all the most important points are settled by the evidence of the construction, combined with the words of Augustus in his will, called the *Monumentum Ancyranum* [a].

The attempt, then, that is here made, is to give a concise account, clear and easy to understand, by arranging it in the form of a walk from the Capitolium, which included the Ærarium, Tabularium, Senaculum, and Municipium in one building, at the north end, to the steps up to the Via Sacra at the south. To this has been added a short account of the other objects in the eighth Regio, (including also the churches on this site,) and so incorporating the account of the Regio with the walk down the Forum.

These great excavations in the Forum were begun about 1812 by the Duchess of Devonshire, then resident in Rome, who excavated all the space between the Tabularium and the modern road, with the

---

[a] The *Monumentum Ancyranum* is of so much importance for the true history of the CITY OF ROME, and especially of the FORUM ROMANUM, that it has been thought expedient to reproduce a copy of it in Plates XXVIII. and XXIX. of the Forum, and add the explanations and completion of the words deficient, from the admirable work of Professor Mommsen, as the original is hardly intelligible to ordinary readers without this help.

consent of the French, who were then the governors of Rome[b]. On the return of the Pope to his temporal power, the work was suspended, and Prince Demidoff, then also residing in Rome during the winter season, offered to excavate the whole of the Via Sacra from the Forum to the Colosseum at his own expense, having been stimulated by the example of the Duchess. Pope Leo XII. at first gave him permission to do this, but in a few days retracted this permission, because some actors at his private theatricals had performed a piece supposed to have ridiculed the Pope[c]. The work was then suspended for about fifty years, and was not taken up again in earnest until the Italians took possession of Rome, and purchased the Farnese gardens of Napoleon III. These gardens happened to consist of the exact site of Roma Quadrata, with the foss on the southern side of it, and have been tolerably well excavated by Signor Rosa for the French Emperor, although, at the time he began, the excavations were made only in search of statues for the Paris museums; and it was after the example had been given by the British Archæological Society of Rome, of making excavations for historical objects only[d], that Napoleon III. decided on continuing the excavations on the Palatine for such objects also. Any well-informed Roman antiquary could have told him, in the first instance, that when the Farnese villa was built, and the Farnese gardens were made, in the seventeenth century, the great Farnese collection of statues, the finest collection in Europe, which is now in the Royal Museum at Naples, was chiefly found on this spot, where the great public palaces of the Cæsars had previously stood.

When the Italian Government bought this property, after the fall of the Emperor, it was on the understanding that these excavations for historical purposes should be continued; and Signor Rosa, who had been originally recommended to the Emperor by Dr. Henzen,

[b] Some idea of the enormous excavations that have been made in this part of Rome may be formed by comparing the view of the Forum in the seventeenth century (reproduced in Plate I.) with the view in 1874 (from a photograph) of Plate II.; and the view of the Temple of Saturn in 1812, reproduced from an official print of the French Government (in Plate VI.) with the same temple in 1874 (from a photograph) in Plate VII.

[c] This authentic anecdote is given in a contemporary work of good repute, the *Promenades dans Rome*, published under the fictitious name of Stendhal, now acknowledged as the work of Henry Beyle, many years French Consul at Civita Vecchia. (See vol. i. p. 321, edition of Paris, 1873, *seule édition complete*.)

[d] See the Plans and Views of the Porta Capena in the Supplement to the first volume of this work, originally published in the *Archæologia* of the Society of Antiquaries of London in 1869, taken from Mr. Parker's photographs. M. Viollet-le-Duc of Paris is a living witness that this influenced the Emperor to change his plan, to search for historical objects only on the Palatine, very much to his credit.

as superintendent of the work, was recommended to, and adopted by, the Italian Government for the same purpose: he had formed an excellent project for excavating the whole of the Palatine Hill, with the slopes round it, including the Via Sacra, the Forum Romanum, and the Colosseum. This project was adopted by the Italian Government, and is being gradually carried out as funds can be obtained. It was in pursuance of this plan that the great work in the Forum has been done. The whole of the western side of the Forum has now been excavated, and the platform of the great Basilica Julia[e], of the time of Augustus, has been cleared out from the Temple of Saturn, under the Tabularium[f], at the north end, to the Temple with the celebrated three columns at the south end[g]; which are therefore proved to have belonged to the Temple of Castor and Pollux, by the words of Augustus himself, who says "that he had enlarged this Basilica so much, that what had been the length became the breadth." It had been begun by Julius Cæsar himself, and much damaged by a great fire before it was completed. The excavations have brought to light walls and arches of travertine stone of the time of Julius Cæsar[h], running across from west to east at the north end of the great platform of Augustus, which occupies the whole of the western side of the Forum[i].

The general order given by Signor Rosa to his men in these excavations is, to continue till they come to the original pavement, or to water; a very good general order, but one which requires to be watched carefully, and carried out with discretion. This building was of two storeys, and great masses of the vault of the upper floor were lying on the original pavement when the excavations were first made, but were destroyed by the ignorant workmen in obedience to their general order, and sold to the builders as old materials. The same thing was done in 1873 and 1874, in the Thermæ of Caracalla, where, at that time, many hundred tons of the old vaulting could be seen cut up into blocks of a convenient size for building, and stacked ready to be carried away by the builders when convenient. In the Basilica Julia, after these fragments had been carried away, Signor Rosa rebuilt the bases of the brick arches, which had carried the vaults of the upper storey[j]; it had been rebuilt of brick after another great fire at the end of the third century, but Signor Rosa's restoration cannot have been strictly correct, for in several places he had to cut through the marble

[e] See Plates II., X., XVIII., XX.
[f] See Plates VII., VIII.
[g] See Plates XXI., XXII., XXIII.
[h] See Plate XVII.
[i] See Plate XVIII.
[j] See Plates II. and XVIII.

pavement of that period to insert the new brick bases of what he calls the restoration, as may still be seen by the modern stucco in the pavement round these bases. The raised steps of the platform remain all along the eastern side and southern end, the original pavement of the streets also remain at the south end in front of the temple, and the other down the centre of the Forum, which appears to have been a continuation of the Via Nova, parallel to the Via Sacra; this was on the eastern side of the Forum, going from the temple of Antoninus and Faustina[k] to the arch of Septimius Severus, and so joining on to the Clivus Capitolinus, (if, indeed, the name of Via Sacra was continued at all beyond that temple and the Regia opposite to it, for it appears to have been a short street full of temples, going from the Summa Sacra Via and Clivus Sacer to the Regia on the site of the present church of S. Maria Liberatrice).

On the eastern side of the central street is a row of brick constructions, about ten feet high and square[l], which are called by Signor Rosa the bases of the tall columns, with statues upon them, represented in the view of the Forum in the fourth century in a sculpture on the arch of Constantine; these structures are of that period, but they are hollow, and there is a door into each; they seem much more likely to have been the *tabernæ*[m] or wine-shops, and the view of the Forum, both on the marble walls of Hadrian in the Comitium, and on the Arch of Constantine, are taken from the south, looking north, with the Tabularium in the background[n]. The tall columns would then be on the line of the bank of earth on which the modern road is carried, and there is an enormous column that would correspond well with one of these still lying visible in an archway under the modern road[o].

At the south end of the Forum, at the western corner, is the temple of Castor and Pollux, before-mentioned, with the palace of Caligula, faced with the beautiful brickwork of his time[p],

---

[k] In the spring of 1876, the excavations made by the Italian Government have brought to light the pavement of the Via at the foot of the steps of the Temple of Antoninus and Faustina; the concrete foundations of the seven lower steps remain, the upper ones have been destroyed, and the whole of the marble has been carried away. Palladio states that there were twenty-one steps in his time, and the measurements agree with this. The temple stands on the high bank by the side of the foss-way, and the steps led down to the original pavement of the Via Sacra, which appears to have gone straight down the eastern side of the Forum to the Arch of Septimius Severus.

[l] See Plate XIX., the lower view.

[m] *Tabernæ* are shops of any kind, including wine-shops, and as this Latin word is the origin of the English name for a wine-shop or tavern, this was evidently a common use of the word.

[n] See Plate XVI.

[o] See Photograph, No. 3167.

[p] See Plates XXI., XXII., XXIII. The walls of the Palace are much concealed by modern buildings.

within the boundary of the old Palatine fortress, but on the same level as the Forum; and so close to it that a doorway might be made from it to the temple, which we are told by Suetonius was used by Caligula as a vestibule to his palace. Opposite to this, at the southeast corner of the Forum, are the remains of the Rostrum[q] and temple of Julius Cæsar; and between the two a small oval fountain, with a shallow channel for water cut in marble round it, of the time of Augustus, which could only be the fountain of Juturna[r], according to the legend of the miraculous horsemen, who watered their horses at this spot, on the southern bank of the Curtian lake, formed by the meeting of three streams from the Palatine, the Capitol, and the Quirinal, which was drained by the Cloaca Maxima[s]. Close to the remains of this fountain a fragment of the Fasti, of the time of Augustus, was found, beginning with the words, ROMULUS FILIUS MARTIS[t]; this was at first preserved on the spot where it was found, it has since been removed to the Capitoline Museum, where other parts of the same set of Fasti previously found near the same spot are preserved. Just to the south of the fountain are two steps going up to the Via Sacra, which was on rather a higher level than the Forum, and not a road for horses and carriages in that part; a pavement passed under the temple of Antoninus and Faustina on the eastern side, and another probably passed under the cliff of the Palatine on the western side, but has not yet been excavated. A few yards from the Forum, but on the higher level, is the *podium* of the round temple of Vesta[u]; the temple built between the two hills, when they were united in one city, and enclosed by one wall, as we are told by Dionysius. This round temple stands immediately in front of the modern Church of S. Maria Liberatrice[x], which is proved by the clearest evidence to be on the site of the Regia. This had been given to the Pontifex Maximus for his abode during the whole time of the Republic; but when Augustus, as emperor, was also appointed Pontifex Maximus, he refused to give up the House of Hortensius which he had previously bought on the Palatine above, and in which he resided for forty years; and he gave the Regia to the Vestal virgins for their abode, because it was close to their temple. When the present church was built in the seventeenth century, a number of inscriptions were found, with the names of Vestal

---

[q] See Plate XX.
[r] See Plate XXIII., and Photograph, No. 3158.
[s] See Plate XIX.
[t] See Photograph, No. 2729.
[u] See Plate XXIII., and Photograph, No. 3149.
[x] See Plates XXI. and XXIII.

virgins upon them, clearly proving that this had long been their habitation. The construction of the basements, both of the temple of Vesta and of that of Castor and Pollux, is of the time of the Kings[7], and thus the whole history hangs together; the construction and the legends confirm each other.

The Via Sacra has so long been considered as part of the Forum Romanum, and is so treated in such a number of works of good repute, that it is difficult to separate them, although it is now made evident by the excavations of 1875, that the Forum properly speaking terminated with the steps in a line with the Rostrum and Temple of Julius Cæsar, and the Temple of Castor and Pollux at the southern end, and did not include the *Regia*, which was within the boundary of the Palatine. The Temple of Antoninus and Faustina is just to the south of this line, and that is recorded as being on the Via Sacra. The Clivus Sacer begins in front of the church of SS. Cosmas and Damian, and goes up to the steps of the Porticus Liviæ on the Summa Sacra Via. The great Basilica of Constantine stands partly on the slope; the upper part of the pavement of the slope was excavated in the time of the French, about 1812, but this interesting excavation has not been continued up to 1876. On the right hand, or south-western side of the Summa Sacra Via, important excavations were made by Signor Rosa, for the Italian Government, in 1874-75, and these brought to light the Lavacrum of Heliogabalus, with the church of S. Maria Antiqua made in it. The descent from the Arch of Titus to that of Constantine must have been the Clivus Triumphalis, or line of the triumphal procession of the army, as this line passes under these two triumphal arches.

[7] See Photograph, No. 3157.

CONTENTS.—FORUM ROMANUM.

	PAGE.	PLATE.
THE excavations have thrown an entirely new light on the historical topography of the Forum	3	III.
———— These were absolutely necessary to understand it	ib.	
———— Photography also is of great use for explaining the remains by comparison	ib.	
Arrangement of this chapter, in a walk, from the north-east end to the south-west	ib.	
The FORUM ROMANUM belongs to the earliest period of Roman history	ib.	
———— Length, 671 ft.; breadth, 202 ft. at north end, and 117 at south	4	
The name of Forum has a double meaning: one general, for all the market-places in Regio VIII.; the other special, for the "Great Forum" only	ib.	
Part of the site has been the Curtian Gulf, which was formed by the meeting of three streams without any sufficient outlet	ib.	
———— This was drained by the Cloaca Maxima	ib.	
At the north end stands the great public building called the CAPITOLIUM, which included the Ærarium, Tabularium, Senaculum or Curia, and the Municipium	5	III.
———— This great building stands on the southern slope of the Hill of Saturn; the foss of that hill, when it was a separate fortress (afterwards paved and made into a street), was the true northern boundary of the Forum	ib.	
The Temples of Concord, of Saturn, the Dei Consentes, and the Schola Xanthi, were strictly within the limits of the Capitoline fortress, and are sometimes mentioned as in the Capitol in that sense	ib.	
The foundation of the old wall and of the PORTA SATURNI can be traced	ib.	III.
———— The ground within this line is on a higher level	ib.	
———— But the wall was destroyed at an early period, and these temples were then commonly reckoned as in the Forum	ib.	

	PAGE.	PLATE.
THE TEMPLE OF CONCORD was founded B.C. 303, rebuilt B.C. 216, and again A.D. 11	5	IV.
———— there are remains of all three periods	ib.	
———— the back wall touches the Ærarium under the Tabularium	ib.	
The original AREA OF SATURN included this site	6	
THE GATE OF SATURN was a double gate; the foundations of the wall between the two gates remain	ib.	
———— The pavement of the CLIVUS CAPITOLINUS, of the time of the Republic, passes on one side of the wall, and that of the street of the Empire on the other side	ib.	
THE TEMPLE OF CONCORD was called the Senate House	ib.	III.
———— But the space is not large enough for the Senate to assemble	ib.	
———— There is a passage under the *podium* of the temple	ib.	
THE SENATE HOUSE, or Curia, was behind it, in the eastern part of the Capitolium	ib.	V.
———— The Temple of Concord served as a vestibule to it, and the decrees were read from the steps	ib.	XXV.
———— This large hall behind the Tabularium can be traced by the substructures. The upper part was destroyed by Michael Angelo, when the Municipium over it was built of stone instead of wood	7	
THE SENATE HOUSE, or hall for the Senate to meet in, could only have been on that site	ib.	
———— It is above the level of the GRÆCO-STASIS, as Varro says	ib.	V.
———— This hall was 60 ft. long and 30 wide	ib.	
———— The mention of it by Cicero in his second Philippic agrees with this	ib.	
———— (A translation of the passage is given)	ib.	
———— The Emperor Pertinax sat down in the Temple of Concord to wait for the key of the Senate House	8	
THE GRÆCO-STASIS was on a platform at the east end of the temple; the site is now covered over by the sloping path of Michael Angelo	ib.	
———— This space is exactly suited for the purpose of hearing the decrees read	9	
THE TEMPLE OF SATURN	ib.	VI.
———— This is the one that touches the Ærarium, close to that of Concord	ib.	
———— Both were within the wall of the fortress	ib.	
———— This temple was called the ÆRARIUM, or Treasury, because it was the vestibule of it	10	VII.
———— Behind the *podium* is a doorway to a steep flight of steps, for the clerks of the Treasury to ascend to their offices	ib.	VIII.
———— These steps are mentioned by Cicero	ib.	

CONTENTS.

	PAGE.	PLATE.

The SCHOLA XANTHI is on the lower level, under the Temple of the DEI CONSENTES . . . . . . 10 IX.

——— These were discovered in the sixteenth century, with the inscriptions on them . . . . . . *ib.*

——— The colonnade was restored by Canina . . . 11

THE CLIVUS CAPITOLINUS passes in front of it . . . *ib.*

THE TEMPLE OF VESPASIAN is on the outer side of the pavement of this street, on the site of the foss, and not within the fortress . *ib.* X.

——— There is no place for a Treasury under it . . *ib.*

Three Rostra in the Forum, one by the side of the Arch of Septimius Severus . . . . *ib.* XI.

——— Another at the south-east corner, near the Temple of Antoninus; this was that of Julius Cæsar, excavated in 1874. The third is not yet excavated . . . . . . 12 XX.

A Rostrum in the Forum is represented in sculpture on the Arch of Constantine . . . . *ib.*

The buildings in the background of that sculpture are the Tabularium, with the Temples of Concord and Saturn . . *ib.*

THE ROSTRAL COLUMNS 13

——— that of Duillius, A.D. 14, is represented on a medal . *ib.*

The MILLIARIUM AUREUM and UMBILICUM URBIS . . *ib.* XI.

——— The streets of Rome measured from it, but not the roads . 14

A Church of SS. Sergius and Bacchus was built in A.D. 790 against the Arch of Septimius Severus, and was destroyed in 1540 . *ib.* XII.

An arch under the modern road, with foundations of a temple, and a gigantic marble column . . . . . *ib.*

COLUMN OF THE EMPEROR PHOCAS . . . . *ib.* XIII.

THE COMITIUM, the open space for the Comitia, or assemblies of the people . . . . *ib.*

TWO SCREEN WALLS OF MARBLE, with fine sculpture of the time of Hadrian, in the Comitium . . . . 15 XIV.

——— On the inner side of each wall are the *suovetaurilia* . 16 XV.

——— On the outer side are groups of figures, &c. . . *ib.*

——— On both, the figure of Marsyas, or Silvanus, and the fig-tree *ib.*

——— The same subject is represented on coins of Hadrian . 17

——— Pliny mentions the fig-tree and the figure of Silvanus as near this site . . . . *ib.*

The sculpture of the Forum, on the Arch of Constantine, has a row of tall columns . . . . 18 XVI.

——— A row of brick structures down the middle of the Forum, said to be the bases of these columns, are more likely to be wine-shops of the third century . . . . *ib.*

There were two temples of MARS ULTOR: the round one was in the Forum . . . . *ib.*

	PAGE.	PLATE.

ATRUM LIBERTATIS, the site now occupied by the churches of S. Martina and S. Hadriana 19

Base of an equestrian statue . . . . . . *ib.*

BASILICA JULIA OF JULIUS CÆSAR . . . *ib.* XVII.

———— Æmilia (?) . . . . . . *ib.* XXV.

BASILICA JULIA OF AUGUSTUS . . . . 20 II.

———— Early buildings on this site . . . *ib.* XVIII.

———— That of Augustus had the Temple of Saturn at one end (the north), and that of Castor and Pollux at the other end (the south) *ib.*

———— The celebrated Three Columns belonged to this . *ib.*

———— The construction of the early part is travertine, of the time of Julius Cæsar 21

———— This agrees with the Monumentum Ancyranum . *ib.*

FOUNTAIN OF THE DIOSCURI . . . . . 22 XXI.

TEMPLE OF CASTOR AND POLLUX 23

PALACE OF CALIGULA . . . . *ib.* XXII.

LAKE OF CURTIUS 24

CLOACA MAXIMA . . . . *ib.*

———— The three springs which formed and supplied the lake . *ib.*

Steps up from the south end of the Forum . . . 25

Fountain of Juturna . . . . *ib.*

TEMPLE OF VESTA . . . . . . *ib.* XXVII.

Fragment of Fasti Consulares . . . . . *ib.*

Probable restorations 26

The private house of Trajan, on the Aventine; and of Hadrian, near the Thermæ of Caracalla . . . . . *ib.*

The history of the Forum usually received is based on conjectures only, the principal objects of interest were so long all buried . 27

The Palaces of the Cæsars, on the Palatine, were chiefly public offices after the first century . . . . . *ib.*

———— Extent of the Forum greatly exaggerated by these conjectures . . . . *ib.*

The present Arcus Quadrifrons, or Arch of Janus, stands in the Velabrum . . . . *ib.*

———— A Janus had originally two faces, afterwards four . 28

———— One kind of Janus was made of bronze . . *ib.* XXVII.

———— There was a Janus in each of the fourteen Regionaries of Rome 29

———— These were small structures of bronze . . *ib.*

———— One at the junction of the four principal Forums . 30

CONTENTS.

	PAGE.	PLATE.
TEMPLE OF JUPITER CAPITOLINUS	31	XXVII.
———— This stood on the top of the Tarpeian rock . .	ib.	
———— A description of this temple	32	
———— Remains of it	ib.	
———— This temple is considered by many to have been on the site of the Church of Ara Cœli, but the evidence on the other side is strong	33	
———— The statue of Marforio, or Mars . . .	ib.	
Pavement of the Piazza del Campidoglio has been much raised above the original level	ib.	
The statue of Marcus Aurelius	ib.	
AQUEDUCTS in the Forums—the Appia, Marcia and Julia, Anio Vetus and Novus, Claudia and Argentina, or di S. Giorgio .	34	
———— The lines by which they were brought . . .	ib.	
———— Tunnel through the rock of the Palatine still visible .	35	
———— Passed over the bridge of Caligula to the Capitol .	ib.	
———— Remains at the foot of the Capitoline Hill . .	ib.	
———— The western part of the Ærarium turned into a reservoir of water	ib.	
———— This made in the third century, in the time of Al. Severus	ib.	
———— Remains of the bridge of Caligula . .	ib.	
THE OTHER FORUMS	36—43	
Forum Olitorium, or vegetable-market—remains of it .	36	
———— Piscatorium, or fish-market . . .	ib.	
———— Suarium, or pig-market	ib.	
———— Pistorium, or of the Bakers . . .	ib.	
———— of Cupid, on the upper Via Sacra; perhaps the same as the Forum Rusticorum	ib.	
———— Sallustii, near the House of Sallust . .	ib.	
———— of Julius Cæsar	37	
———— of Augustus, and Temple of Mars Ultor . .	39	
———— of Nerva, or Transitorium . . .	40	
———————— Figure of Pallas or Minerva there .	ib.	
———— of Vespasian, or Forum Pacis . .	41	
———— Boarium, or cattle-market . .	42	
———— of Trajan	ib.	
Monumentum Ancyranum	53	XXVIII.
CHURCHES IN THE FORUM ROMANUM, &c.	53—64	XXIX.
———— S. Martina and S. Luca .	54	
———— S. Hadrian, or Adrian .	55	

	PAGE	PLATE

Church of S. George and S. Sebastian, or S. Georgio in Velabro   55

———— ———— Classical portico of the thirteenth century   56

———— ———— Campanile   *ib.*

———— S. Theodorus   58

———— Ara Cœli, on the Capitol   59

———— ———— Long a favourite burying-place; curious inscriptions on the tombs   60

———— ———— South Porch—Mosaic Pictures   *ib.*

———— ———— Tombs of the Savelli, A.D. 1306; of Honorius IV., A.D. 1286   61

———— ———— Relics of S. Helena   *ib.*

———— ———— Ambones—Cosmati-work   62

———— ———— The Convent was built or rebuilt A.D. 1250   *ib.*

REGIONARY CATALOGUE OF REGIO VIII.

	PAGE.	PLATE.
FORUM ROMANUM MAGNUM *Continet*	44—48	XIX.
Rostra tria	11	
Genium Populi Romani aureum	46	
Et equum Constantini	19	
Senatum	6	IV.
Atrium Minervæ	40	
Forum Cæsaris	36	
——— Augusti	39	
——— Nervæ	40	
Cohortem vi. Vigilum	46	
Basilicam Argentariam	ib.	
Templum Concordiæ	5	V.
Umbilicum Romæ	13	XI.
Templum Saturni	6	III.
——— Vespasiani et Titi	11	X.
Capitolium	5	III.
Milliarium Aureum	13	XI.
Basilicam Juliam	20	II.
Templum Castorum et Minervæ	23	XVIII.
Græco-stadium	7	
Vestam	49	XXVII.
Horrea, Germanica et Agrippinæ	ib.	
Aquam Cerneutem, quatuor Scauros (Scaros), sub ædem	ib.	
Atrium Caci	ib.	
Vicum Jugarium et unguentarium	47	
Porticum Margaritarium	ib.	
Elefantum Herbarium	ib.	
Vici XXXIIII. Ædiculæ XXXIIII.	ib.	
Insulæ MDCCCLXXX. Domus CXXX.	48	
Horrea XVIII. Balnea CLXXXV. Lacos CXX. Pistrinæ XX.	ib.	
Regio VIII. continet pedes M.XIIII.LXVII.	ib.	

LIST OF PLATES.

FORUM ROMANUM.

PLATE
I. THE FORUM ROMANUM IN 1650, at the Time of the Jubilee.
II. GENERAL VIEW OF THE FORUM IN 1874.—Temple of Castor and Pollux.—The Basilica Julia, &c.
III. TEMPLE OF CONCORD, Tabularium, and Ærarium.—Pavement of the Time of the Republic. (See p. 5.)
IV. ——————— Senate-house.—A. Plan of the Hall of Meeting, a little above the level of the Tabularium, behind the east end of it. B. Plan of the Substructure, above the level of the Ærarium. (See p. 7.)
V. ——————— Senate-house.—Senaculum, or Curia, in the Capitolium.—Sections.
VI. THE TEMPLE OF SATURN IN 1810.
VII. ——————— in 1874. (See p. 9.)
VIII. ——————— The Podium, or Basement, and Doorway of the Ærarium (the head of which is seen over the *podium*).
IX. PORTICO OF THE DEI CONSENTES, and School of Xanthus. (See p. 10.)
X. TEMPLE OF VESPASIAN IN 1874. (See p. 11.)
XI. MILLIARIUM AND ROSTRUM. (See p. 13.)
XII. ARCH OF SEPTIMIUS SEVERUS &c., in 1874. (See p. 11.)
XIII. COLUMN OF PHOCAS, Arch of Septimius Severus, &c. (See p. 13.)
XIV. One Side of one of the WALLS (OR SCREENS) IN THE COMITIUM, in fragments, as it was found in 1872, before it was put together.
XV. THE TWO MARBLE WALLS IN THE COMITIUM. (See p. 16.)
XVI. 1. One Side of one of the MARBLE WALLS OR SCREENS IN THE COMITIUM.
2. Sculpture from the Arch of Constantine.—VIEW OF THE FORUM.
XVII. BASILICA JULIA. (See p. 19.)
XVIII. ——————— Temple of Castor and Pollux, &c. (See p. 21.)
XIX. 1. Cloaca Maxima, (B.C. 615; Livii Hist., i. 38).
2. *Podium* or Base of an Equestrian Statue.
XX. ROSTRUM AND TEMPLE OF JULIUS CÆSAR. (See p. 25.)
XXI. NORTH-EAST CORNER OF THE PALATINE.
A. Remains of the Palace of Caligula.
B. Modern Church of S. Maria Liberatrice, on the Site of the REGIA.
C. The Temple of Castor and Pollux, or of the Dioscuri, with the celebrated Three Columns.

PLATE
XXII. Probable Restoration of the TEMPLE OF CASTOR AND POLLUX, &c.
  A. Temple, north side.
  B. Part of the Palace of Caligula, joining on to the Temple.
  C. Pier of the Bridge of Caligula, with the springing of the Arches that went across at the west end of the Forum.
  D. Part of the Bridge and of the Palace.

XXIII. Probable Restoration of the Temple of Castor and Pollux, &c.
  A. Part of the Palace of Hadrian.
  B. The *podium* or Basement of the round Temple of Vesta, excavated in 1874; behind it is seen in outline,
  C. The modern Church of S. Maria Liberatrice.
  D. Some remains of steps leading up to the Palatine.
  E. Front Portico of the Temple of Castor and Pollux, restored.
  F. A continuation of the Bridge of Caligula.

XXIV. Probable Restoration of the PALACE AND BRIDGE OF CALIGULA, looking west.
  A. NORTH-EAST CORNER OF THE PALATINE, with part of the Palace of the time of Hadrian.
  B and C. Part of the Palace and Bridge of Caligula. (See p. 23.)
  D—D. Probable Restoration of the Bridge.

XXV. COINS OR MEDALS, with Representations of Buildings and Sculptures in the Forum.
  1. The Temple of Concord.
  2. The Basilica Æmilia.
  3. Hadrian addressing the Roman people, A.D. 119.
  4. The Lictor setting fire to the bonds of the public debt.

XXVI. COINS OR MEDALS, with Representations of other Buildings and Sculptures in the Forum.
  1. Temple of Venus, *temp.* Hadrian.
  2. ——————— Roma.
  3. Tomb of Maximianus.
  4. Circular Temple of Mars Ultor, *temp.* Augustus.
  5. ——————————— Augustus.
  6. Temple of Antoninus and Faustina.

XXVII. COINS OR MEDALS, with Representations of other Buildings and Sculptures in the Forum.
  1. Temple of Jupiter Feretrius.
  2. ——————— Janus.
  3. ——————— Jupiter Capitolinus.
  4. ——————— Trajan.
  5. ——————— Jupiter Ultor.
  6. ——————— Vesta.

XXVIII., XXIX. INSCRIPTION OF AUGUSTUS, now at Ancyra, called the *Monumentum Ancyranum.* (See p. 53.)

VIA SACRA.

PLATE
- XXX. CHURCH OF SS. COSMAS AND DAMIAN. Longitudinal Section.
- XXXI. ——————————————— Plans.
- XXXII. TEMPLE OF ANTONINUS AND FAUSTINA, and Church of S. Lorenzo in Miranda. Section and Plan. (See p. 65.)
- XXXIII. BASILICA OF CONSTANTINE. Front View. (See p. 82.)
- XXXIV. ——————————————— Back View, and Interior of Apse.
- XXXV. ——————————————— Sections. A—B. Longitudinal. C—D. Transverse.
- XXXVI. ——————————————— Plan.
- XXXVII. SUMMA SACRA VIA.—1. Apse, now in the Monastery of S. Francesca Romana, from the north, with the Colosseum in the distance.
  2. The same double Apse from the south, with the Monastery and Campanile in the background, and the Substructure of the Platform in the foreground.
- XXXVIII. PORTICUS LIVIÆ and Colossus of Nero. Restoration. (See p. 86.) The Platform on the Summa Sacra Via, looking east, with steps up to it at the north end, and a substructure at the south end, agreeing with the Plan of the Porticus Liviæ, in the Marble Plan of Rome of the third century, with a probable restoration of it.
- XXXIX. SUMMA SACRA VIA. Church of S. Maria Antiqua, excavated in 1874.
- XL. Church of S. Maria Antiqua, A.D. 847—855. Plan. (See p. 92.)
- XLI. THE ARCH OF TITUS.
- XLII. THE ARCH OF CONSTANTINE.
- XLIII. East Wall of the TEMPLUM URBIS ROMÆ, on which the Marble Plan was fixed. (See p. 74.)
- XLIV. DETAILS OF THE WALL OF THE MARBLE PLAN, with remains of the Metal Hooks by which the Slabs of Marble, with the Plan engraved upon them, were attached to the wall. The lower part of the Plate shews a Fragment of a Cornice of the third century, with Brick-stamps of the same period, with Fragments of the Marble Plan then found,—the Porticus Liviæ, with that name upon it.
- XLV. TEMPLE OF ANTONINUS AND FAUSTINA, as Excavated in May, 1876.

PLAN OF THE SUMMA SACRA VIA, ON THE SUB-VELIA.

THE FORUM ROMANUM.

FORUM ROMANUM.

This account of the FORUM ROMANUM has been kept back some years, with other portions of the present work, in consequence of the great excavations that have been going on, and are still being continued,—yet what has already been done, has thrown so much new light on the very important subject of *the true history of the City of Rome, that it ought not to be kept back any longer.* In this work, the endeavour always is to make a *demonstration* of what is stated, so that no one can deny it when shewn all the facts demonstrated [a]. This could never be done before these excavations were made, nor without the use of photography. With the help of these, some important points which have hitherto been subjects of conjecture only can be made clear, and although other objects remain buried, this is not a sufficient reason for keeping back what can now be demonstrated.

In order to understand properly what has been recently done, it is necessary to recapitulate to some extent what has been done before—from the north end of the Forum Romanum to the southern extremity of that forum,—thence along the Via Sacra from north to south,—up the Clivus Sacer,—through the Summa Via Sacra,—and down the Clivus Victoriæ to the Colosseum,—along the whole of this line excavations have been going on, at intervals, from 1812 to 1874.

The Forum Romanum belongs to the very earliest period of Roman history; it occupies part of the level space between the Palatine and the Capitol, and it was on this ground that the battle between the Romans and the Sabines took place, in the fifth year after the foundation of Rome, when the Sabine women rushed between their fathers and brothers and their husbands, and made peace between them, according to the legend related by Livy [b]. The direction of the Forum is nearly from north to south, trending a little from north-east to south-west; it is wider at the northern end under the Tabularium in front of the Capitol, 202 ft., including the *clivus*, than

---

[a] I have also endeavoured to make each part of the work complete in itself as far as possible, so that the results of my investigations may not be entirely lost, should I not live to complete the whole.

[b] "Mettus Curtius ab Sabinis princeps ab arce decurrerat, et effusos egerat Romanos, *toto quantum foro spatium est*; nec procul jam a porta Palatii erat," &c. (Livii Hist., lib. i. c. 12.)

at the southern, between the church of Lorenzo in Miranda or temple of Antoninus and Faustina, and the opposite corner of the Palatine, 117 ft.; its greatest length is 671 ft.[c] The old valley and the trenches in it of the fortified Hill of Saturn, and the swamp between that and the Palatine Hill Fortress, was made into the Forum Romanum when "these two hills were united in one city and enclosed with one wall." The custom of decorating the market-place with trophies seems to have been begun by Camillus, who hung the silver-gilt shields of the Samnites there[d], [B.C. 307].

The Forum Romanum was the most celebrated of all the Regiones in Rome; the name, like many other names, had a double signification, one general, the other special. In its general sense it included all the Capitoline Hill and the Forums round the base of it; those of Julius Cæsar, Augustus, Nerva, and Trajan, as well as the original one, between the Capitoline and the Palatine Hill, which is its special and limited sense. To begin with the latter, which is usually called "The Great Forum," and is so called by Dio Cassius in the second century[e]. The gulf into which Curtius leaped was in the middle of the Forum Romanum, as we are told by Dionysius (ii. 42), and it appears to have been in the same spot as the pool into which the Emperor Commodus was thrown from his palanquin. The early sculpture of the time of the Republic representing this event, now preserved in the Capitoline Museum, is said to have been thrown into the gulf; it was found under the church of S. Maria Liberatrice, at the foot of the Palatine. It therefore remained a pool or swamp, called a lake, for some centuries, and the Cloaca Maxima was not deep enough to drain it entirely. The stream of water from the upper part of the Palatine, near the Arch of Titus, now subterranean, may have passed close round the corner of the hill, and so formed part of the gulf or lake. Three streams meet at this point; the one from the Palatine, the second spring now rises under a shop behind the church of S. Hadrian, the third rises at the foot of the Capitoline Hill, in the lower chamber of what is called the Prison of S. Peter.

Beginning at the north end with the great public building originally called the Capitolium, which contained on the ground-floor, and partly

---

[c] See the Plan at the end of this part or chapter, and Plates I. and II.

[d] "Dictator ex senatus consulto triumphavit: cujus triumpho longe maximam speciem captiva arma præbuere. Tantum magnificentiæ visum in iis, ut arata scuta dominis argentariarum ad forum ornandum dividerentur. Inde nutum initium dicitur fori ornandi ab ædilibus, quæ in tensæ ducerentur." (Ibid., lib. ix. c. 40.)

[e] Dionis. Cassii Hist. Rom., lib. xliii. c. 22.

cut out of the rock, the Ærarium, or Public Treasury; and over it the Tabularium, or Public Record-office (the records of Rome having been kept upon bronze *tabulæ* or tablets); and behind that, at the east end, the Senaculum or Senate-house; and over all, the Municipium or Public-offices of the Municipality [f]. This great building is usually considered as the north end of the Forum. Strictly speaking, the Forum did not begin until the outer or south side of the wall of the old Capitoline fortress, with the Porta Saturni, or gate of Saturn, in it; this was the true northern gate into the Forum. The temples of Concord and of Saturn, and the *porticus* of the Dei Consentes with the Schola Xantha under it, being within the wall of the Capitol, were not properly in the Forum, but were usually so considered, because the wall of partition was destroyed at an early period. The division between the two is now marked by the paved street made in the foss of the Kings (as were many of the streets of Rome in the time of the Republic); but there are slight remains of the old wall and the old gate. The foundations of the wall between the double gate are visible, and the construction is the same as the wall of the Ærarium and Tabularium, which Varro says was considered in his time to have belonged to the city of the Sabines, before the arrival of the Romans; this is probably going a little too far, but it shews that it was an old building in his time, and he wrote about fifty years before the Christian era, according to the legends *then* current. It is more probable that it was built at the time of the union of the Sabines, on the hill of Saturn, with the Romans on the Palatine, when they might well have foreseen the future greatness of Rome, and provided public buildings accordingly.

The buildings in the Forum, usually so called, naturally begin with the TEMPLE OF CONCORD [g] at the north-east corner. Of this we have only the *podium* or basement remaining [h], but this is about fifteen feet high. This temple has been several times rebuilt; it was first built in the year 303 B.C., rebuilt about a century afterwards in 216 B.C., and again in A.D. 11, and remains of all these three periods can be found in this basement; the outer wall, of large squared stones of travertine, is of the latter period, and the back wall touches that of the Ærarium. The small narrow space between that and the Temple of Saturn [i], is said to be part of

[f] See Solini Collectanea, ed. Mommsen. Berolini, 1864, p. 38; see also part iii., Construction, p. 35, and the set of Plates of the Capitolium.

[g] This temple is represented on a coin. See Donaldson's Coins and Medals, and Photos., Nos. 492 B.

[h] See Plates III., IV., V., and Photograph 3156; also part iii., Construction, p. 45.

[i] This is visible in the photograph, No. 3156; see also Plates IX. and X.

the area of Saturn, which was, however, of considerable extent, as the church of S. Hadrian stood in it. On the outside of the wall the pavement of the Clivus Capitolinus, of the time of the Republic, passes on the western side of the wall of the gate of Saturn [k], which was a double gate, as were many of the other gates of Rome. Another pavement of the time of Septimius Severus passes on the eastern side of the same wall. Under the *podium*, at this point, we see the entrance to a subterranean passage, which was excavated in 1873 [l]. The walls of this passage are faced with reticulated-work of the time of the Republic; but it is stopped abruptly at the further end by a wall belonging to the rebuilding in A.D. 11, another entrance having then been made into the Senaculum behind it. On the surface of the raised platform of the temple we have walls with distinct remains of a thin veneer of marble [m]. The Temple of Concord was often called the Senate-house, but the space is not large enough for the Roman senate to have assembled within the walls of the temple (that space was also largely filled with statues), although the decrees were given out from the steps of that temple. There must have been a passage and a door from that temple to the senate-house behind it, but this was not seen by the people, and this accounts for the name being given to the temple itself. Dio Cassius, himself a Roman senator, says that "the senate assembled in the building *near* the Temple of Concord [n]."

The Senate-house of the Regionary Catalogue can be no other than the one in the great building already described [o], and called by so many names. Neither the Municipium, the Curia, the Ærarium, nor the Tabularium are mentioned in the Regionary Catalogue, and yet as all of these were in the Regio, they must all be included in the general name of Capitolium, being all in that one great building. The Senatum is frequently considered as identical with the Temple of Concord, from the steps of which its decrees were announced; but it is here mentioned separately, and this has led some antiquaries to conjecture a building for meetings of the Senate on the site of the Church of S. Martina, but that was the site

---

[k] This is also visible in the photograph, No. 3147.

[l] It is shewn also in Plate XVII.; more distinctly in another photograph, No. 3146.

[m] See Plate XVIII., and photograph, No. 3145.

[n] Dionis. Cass., Hist., lib. lviii. chap. 11.; see also the series of Plates of the Capitolium, &c., in Part III. "Senaculum supra Græcostasin ubi ædes Concordiæ et basilica Opimia. Senaculum vocatum ubi Senatus aut ubi seniores consisterent." (Varro, de Ling. Lat., c. xxxii. p. 155.)

[o] See the Appendix to the Chapter on the Construction of Walls, p. 45, at the end of vol. i. of this work.

of the bronze Janus between the Fora, and it is too distant from the steps of the Temple of Concord. The senators would in that case have marched in procession through the crowd from the place of meeting to the steps. It is far more probable that their place of assembly for debate was in the great building behind the temple, which was over the entrance to it, as we have said. The difficulty remains that it is mentioned separately, but we cannot see where else it could be placed near to the temple; the Græcostasis and the great prison were evidently to the east of it, and to the west was the Temple of Saturn, in front the Comitium. There seems no possible place for the Senatum, but the space behind the temple in the Capitolium, and Varro says that it was *above* the Græcostasis. It might possibly have been on the site of the great hall now occupied by the municipality, on the northern side of the building, facing the open place in the centre of the hill, with a passage through from the top of the stairs, that led up from the doorway behind the temple under the level of the platform, and through the basement of it. But this is not probable; the marble steps lead up from the passage behind the platform of the Temple of Concord to another large hall behind the Tabularium, and on the eastern side of the Capitolium; the upper part of this has been destroyed, when Michael Angelo rebuilt the east end, and two brick arches have been built across the old hall; but there are remains of the early wall at the south end, the substructure remains, and the steps plainly led up to a door at the east end of that wall, now destroyed, because Michael Angelo rebuilt the east wall, and left a passage of six feet wide between the old wall, (the lower part of which remains,) and his modern wall.

The place for the senators to assemble was on the slope of the hill, behind the portico, a space sixty feet long by thirty wide, in which there was room for the senators to be seated on the benches mentioned by Cicero, between which the soldiers stood on a certain occasion. The celebrated speech of Cicero in his second Philippic, in which he mentions the Senate-house as on the Capitoline slope, agrees perfectly with this site; he calls it also *the Cell of the Temple of Concord*:—

" Have you so entirely lost all shame as well as chastity, that you could dare to say in this temple, in which, while I was advising that senate which formerly, in flourishing times, presided over the whole world, you placed round it armed men of the basest character? You have dared to say even (What is there that you would not dare?) that I, as consul, was surrounded by armed slaves. . . . What Roman knight is there? What youth of noble blood except yourself? What man of any station, who remembered that he was a citizen of Rome, who was not *on the slope of the Capitol* when the senate was assembled in this temple. Who was there who did not give in his name? although there were not scribes enough to write them, nor tables enough to contain their names. . . . But now what an act it is, I will not say of audacity, for he wishes to be audacious, but of folly, (in which he surpasses all men,) . . . . to make mention of *the slope of the Capitol* when armed men are actually between our benches? Here, in this Cell of Concord! Oh, ye immortal gods! in which I, as consul, gave that wise advice by which to this day we live :—

"ARMS MUST YIELD TO THE GOWN P."

When the Emperor Pertinax (A.D. 193) wanted to go into the senate-house at night, he ordered the *Cell of the Curia* to be opened, and while his attendants were searching for the keeper with the key, he seated himself in the Temple of Concord q. This makes it evident that the temple was not the *Senatum*, nor the *Curia*, but the way to the great hall, called indifferently by these two names.

THE GRÆCOSTASIS.

The GRÆCOSTASIS was the place of waiting for the ambassadors of Greece and other countries, at the foot of the steps of the Temple of Concord, from which the decrees of the Senate were given out. A part of this site is visible, but it is much covered over by the modern path made by Michael Angelo, when he built in stone the upper part of the Capitolium, and made great changes in the approaches to it. The foundations of the eastern wall of the temple are visible, and form the western side of this level space, which must be the exact site of the Græcostasis. There is just sufficient level space for this between the east side of the platform of the temple and the great prison (now the Church of the Crucifixion in this part); the ground here is on a higher level than the Forum, which also agrees with the history we have of it. Part of the ground has been cut away in making the sloping path and the steps, as may be seen by the foundations of the Tabularium at that end being undermined. There is no room for it anywhere else; on the north side the wall of the temple touches that of the Capitolium, on the south side the steps descend to the paved street, called Clivus Capitolinus, on the west side there is only a narrow space between this temple and that of Saturn. The steps went in three directions, east, west, and south; but the only

---

p Cicero, in his second Philippic, c. 7, 8; see the Latin text, in vol. i. p. 47 of Appendix to Construction.

q "Factus est autem sexagenario major imperator pridie kal. Januarii, de castris nocte cum ad Senatum venisset et cellam curiæ jussisset aperiri neque inveniretur ædituus, in templo Concordiæ resedit." (Julii Capitolini Pertinax, c. 4, ap. Script. Hist. Aug.)

place where the ambassadors could have stood to hear the decree read was on this level space, which is exactly suited for the purpose. Pliny mentions it as near the Rostra and the Curia, "Where from the Curia you see the sun between the Rostra and the Græcostasis [r]," that is, looking from the windows of the Curia, or law-courts, over the Tabularium (which looked nearly due south), between the Rostra on the west and the Græcostasis on the east, or due south, exactly over where the Arch of Septimius Severus now stands, which was not built until after the time of Pliny. He also states that it was on a higher level than the Comitium, and that a small bronze temple(?) (or figure with a canopy?) of Concord was erected in it [s].

THE TEMPLE OF SATURN [t].

This must be the other temple, close to that of Concord, of which we have the remains, including not only the *podium* or basement, built against the wall of the Ærarium, but three columns, with their entablature and part of the inscription; because Varro [u] implies that the Temple of Saturn was within the wall of that fortress; he also mentions the gate of Saturn along with it, and the remains of that are close to this temple, in the line of the wall of the old fortress outside of that temple. We are also

---

[r] ". . . cum a Curia inter Rostra et Græcostasin prospexisset Solem." (Plinii Nat. Hist., lib. vii. c. 60.)

[s] ". . . ædiculam aeream fecit in Græcostasi, quæ tunc supra comitium erat." (Ibid., lib. xxxiii. c. 6.)

[t] See No. 929. This temple has been called by many names at different periods; at the time of the great excavations in 1812, it went by the name of Jupiter Tonans. This is now considered to have been a small temple with a bell, in that part of the Capitoline Hill called Monte Caprino, at the entrance to the large temple of Jupiter Capitolinus, on the top of the Tarpeian rock. The name now usually given to this one under the Tabularium and Ærarium is the Temple of Vespasian, because a passage of the Einsiedlin Itinerary is understood to mean that the inscription is on that temple. But the evidence that it was connected with the Ærarium behind it seems decisive that this must have been originally called after Saturn; but in the time of Alexander Severus, when the temples in the Forum were nearly all rebuilt, the public treasury seems to have been removed from the old vaults under the Tabularium, in which some of the vaults were then turned into a reservoir of water supplied by an aqueduct; of this the *specus* remains visible at the east end, and a man can go into it.

[u] "Europæ loca multæ incolunt nationes, ea fere nominata aut translatio nomine, aut ab hominibus. Sunt et nomina ab tot montibus quos postea urbs mureis comprehendit: e queis Capitolium dictum, quod heic cum fondamenta foderentur ædis Jovis, caput humanum inventum dicitur. Hic mons ante Tarpejus dictus, a virgine Vestali Tarpeja, quæ ibi ab Sabinis necata armis *est sepulta*; ejus nominis monimentum relictum, quod etiam nunc ejus rupem Tarpejum appellatum saxum. Hunc antea montem Saturnium appellatum prodiderunt, et ab eo late Saturniam terram, ut etiam Ennius, appellat. Antiquum oppidum in hoc fuisse Saturniam scribitur. Ejus vestigia etiam nunc manent tria: quod *Saturni fanum* in faucibus, quod Saturnia porta, quam Junius scribit quam nunc vocant Pandanam, quod post ædem Saturni, in ædificiorum legibus parietes postici muri sunt scripti." (Varro de Ling. Lat., lib. iv. c. 5.)

told by Macrobius in the Saturnalia (c. viii.) that the Romans "would have the Temple of Saturn for their treasury." Solinus (c. ii.) also says that "the building which had been the treasury of Saturn was consecrated as a temple" in his honour. And Plutarch (*in Publicola*) repeats that the treasury of Saturn was made into a temple, which remained in his time. The real meaning of this was the same as in the case of the Temple of Concord, there was a doorway in the wall of the Ærarium at the back under the *podium* of the temple. This doorway still exists, and the head of it is now visible[x]. But when this temple was rebuilt in the third century by Septimius Severus, this doorway was blocked up, and the *podium* built up against it, as we now see. This doorway opened at the foot of a very steep flight of steps, long unknown, because buried until it was excavated by Canina in 1868. The steep steps of the Ærarium are mentioned by Cicero (*pro Fonteio*, i. 4), who jocularly compares going up them to climbing the Alps.

Beyond the Temple of Saturn, in the north-west corner of the Forum, but included within the wall of the Capitol, as shewn by the paved street in front of it, which was part of the Clivus Capitolinus, are two buildings on different levels, one called the SCHOLA XANTHI[y], on the lower level, which looks more like a row of shops; the other on the higher level, called the Porticus of the DEI CONSENTES[z], close under the Tabularium, with a colonnade of eight small columns with Corinthian capitals. The name of this was ascertained by an inscription on the cornice, found when it was partly excavated in the seventeenth century. These chambers were first discovered in the sixteenth century. The marble facing then remained, with Doric pilasters, and two inscriptions on the architrave, all of which have disappeared, but they are printed in Gruter's Inscriptions[a]. This building is called Schola in that inscription, which also gives the names of Xanthus and of Trosius, at whose expense it was restored[b]. They also state that they were for the use of the scribes

[x] It is seen in the photograph, No. 3148, and in Plate X.

[y] Named after Aulus Fabius Xanthus, curator, who built the shops for the copyists of books, and the trumpeters or cryers in the Ædiles Curules, as recorded on an inscription found in the fifteenth century, and reproduced by Lucius Faunus in his work on Roman Antiquities, c. 20: see Plate XXII.

[z] See Photos., Nos. 913, 914, 2325.

[a] C. AVILIVS . LICINIVS . TROSIVS . CVRATOR | SCHOLAM . DE . SVO . FECIT | BEBRYX . AVG. L. DRVSIANVS . A . FABIVS . XANTHVS . CVR . SCRIBIS . LIBRARIIS . ET . PRAECONIBVS . AED . CVR . SCHOLAM | AB . INCHOATO . REFECERVNT . MARMORIBVS . ORNAVERVNT . VICTORIAM . AVGVSTAM . ET . SEDES . AENEAS . ET . CETERA . ORNAMENTA . DE . SVA . PECVNIA . FECERVNT.

[b] See Plate XI.

or clerks who kept the registers of the Roman conquests. The colonnade was cleverly restored from fragments by Canina about 1830; but the columns are not all alike, they have belonged to two different porticoes, they are not in a straight line, but meet at an obtuse angle. Strictly speaking, this building is not in the Forum (as has been shewn); it was within the wall of the Capitoline fortress, which can be clearly traced, and the foundations of the gate of it, called the Porta Saturni, can be seen nearly between the temples of Saturn and of Concord, but a little in front of the line, as those two temples were also in the Capitol, and not in the Forum. The paved road of the time of the Empire passes in front of the line of the wall, and was originally made in the foss. The clivus, or sloping road up to the place, in the centre of the Capitoline Hill, is interrupted by the bank that carries the modern road just behind this building. The clivus was originally a zig-zag road, going on in a direct line to Monte Caprino, and probably to the entrance of the Temple of Jupiter Capitolinus, now in the garden of the Palazzo Caffarelli, before it turned to the right at a sharp angle to the central place. There are remains of the old wall on the left-hand side of the road or street over Monte Caprino, but the whole space is so covered by modern houses that it is difficult to trace the original plan.

On the other side of the paved street is a temple with eight columns, usually called the Temple of Saturn, but it must be the Temple of Vespasian, as there is no place for a public treasury under it[c]. Both these temples were rebuilt by Septimius Severus; the construction, therefore, does not help us; but the historical evidence, when properly understood, appears to be decisive. The old *clivus Capitolinus*, or sloping road from the Capitol, descends through the Arch of Septimius Severus[d]—we find on the right hand of it, in going down, slight remains of one of the Rostra.

There were three *rostra* in the Forum Romanum. Of these three one was this, near the north-east corner of which there are remains consisting of the round end, which has evidently been cased with marble; this is close to the western side of the well-known arch of Septimius Severus, and appears to have been rebuilt at the same

[c] See Plate XII., and Nos. 897, 1076.
[d] See Plate XIII., and No. 1209. Flaminius Vacca (ap. Fea Miscellanea, Nos. 67—69) relates that in excavations made in his time near this arch, some inscriptions of the fourth century were found, and were placed at the entrance to the Farnese gardens. With these were panels of sculpture in bas-relief, which had belonged to the Arch of Marcus Aurelius, and are now fixed in the wall of the staircase in the Palazzo del Conservatori. This was found in the church of S. Martina, and the statue of Marforia was by the side of it.

time. That of Julius Cæsar was at the opposite end of the Forum, and remains of it were brought to light by the excavations in 1874, just opposite to the Temple of Castor and Pollux, and nearly under that of Antoninus and Faustina, beyond the line of the south end of the Basilica Julia. His temple stands close behind it in that corner of the Forum, and the round end of this *rostrum* almost touches the temple. It is evident from this that the orator stood on the flat side of the *rostrum*, not on the round end, as has been commonly supposed. This is also shewn from another representation of a *rostrum* of the time of Constantine, from the sculptures on his arch [e].

The flat side of the *rostrum* is represented with the crowd; there is an open space in the middle for the orator to stand and speak from, and a platform on each side for the councillors to stand and hear him, somewhat in the nature of a modern jury-box in a court of justice [f]. The one represented on the Arch of Constantine seems to have stood near the marble screen in the Comitium, or about the middle of the Forum. In front of each platform is a *cancellus* or *transenna*, or pierced marble parapet, about two feet high. Behind each platform is an idol, one of which is evidently Jupiter or Jove.

The buildings in the background appear to be the arcade of the Tabularium, with its Tuscan columns, and the temples of Concord and of Saturn, and the Arch of Tiberius between them, on the site of the Porta Saturni, which is in accordance with probability and with other evidence. Of the third *rostrum* no remains have yet been found, but the western side of the Forum Romanum has not yet been excavated. There is another representation of the Forum Romanum in sculpture, of the time of the Emperor Hadrian, upon the two walls of marble which are believed to have been screens in the Comitium, the place of meeting and voting-place for the consuls.

Pliny mentions the three Rostra in the Forum [g]. There were also attached to the Rostra, columns ornamented with beaks or prows of galleys, called *Rostral columns*, one of which is called *aureum*, which probably means of bronze gilt, not of gold, as in the case of the *milliarium aureum*, which also was gilt, not of gold. One is described by Ulpianus [h], and Suetonius [i], and by Servius in his commentary on the Æneid of Virgil, in his comment of the line—

"Ac navali surgentes ære columnas."

[e] See Plate XVIII., and Photos., No. 918.
[f] If this was intended for *two* rostra, there would have been two places for the orator to stand.

[g] "Equidem et Sybillæ juxta rostra esse non minor, tres sint licet." (Plinii Nat. Hist., xxxiv. 11.)
[h] "Denique eum quoque qui in foro eodem agat, si circa columnas atque

Julius Cæsar erected rostral columns for the naval victories over the Carthaginians, one of which, in a Rostrum, was found in the Forum, with the famous Archaic inscription upon it relating to C. Duillius, but greatly shattered; it is now in the Capitoline Museum. It is very minute in its details of the spoils taken in the fight, and recites the number of ships with their crews, the triremes, quinqueremes, and septiremes captured or sunk, the quantity of gold and silver money, and the weight of the brass, all deposited in the public treasury. It also recites the number of captives led in triumph. Cato mentions his remembering to have frequently seen in his youth Duillius returning from a supper preceded by pipe-players, to attract notice and recall attention to the conqueror of the Carthaginians.

The Rostral Column of Duillius is represented on a medal of Augustus, A.D. 14 [k]. The figure stands upon a tall pedestal, or short Doric column, ornamented with the prows of vessels and anchors. The column was erected in the Forum Romanum to commemorate the victory over the Carthaginians gained by C. Duillius, mentioned by Pliny [l], Quintilian [m], and Servius [n]. It is obvious that the Rostra were originally of wood, and perhaps the earliest were those of the ships of Antium, which were placed in the Forum or market-place as a trophy of the great naval victory, B.C. 334, as recorded by Livy [o]. They were afterwards made of bronze and of marble.

In the Regionary Catalogue, a golden or gilt image of the Genius Populi Romani on the Rostrum is mentioned. This was erected by Aurelian [p]. The horse of Constantine is mentioned along with it, as if the two were near together.

The MILLIARIUM AUREUM [q], that is, the golden or gilt mile-stone, was placed in the centre of Rome by Augustus, B.C. 28, and was also called *Umbillicus Urbis*. The two are usually considered as the same, but both are mentioned in the *Curiosum Urbis*, which is not likely to have been done if they were identical; though they must have been close together, as both are mentioned as the centre

---

stationes se occultet videri latitare veteres responderunt." (Ulpianus, Falcinius i.)

[l] "Salvidieno Orphido objectum est, quod tabernas tres de domo sua circa forum civitatibus ad stationem locasset." (Suetonius in Nerone, c. 37.)

"Romanum Forum est ubi nunc rostra sunt." (Servius in Virgil, Æneid, lib. viii. 361.)

[k] Donaldson, Coins, 53; Photos., No. 405 A.

[l] Plinii Nat. Hist., lib. xxxiv. c. 5.

[m] Lib. i. c 7.

[n] Servii Com. in Georgic. iii.

[o] "Naves Antiatium partim in navalia Romæ subductæ, partim incensæ, *rostrisque* earum suggestum, in foro exstructum, adornari placuit: *Rostraque* id templum appellatum." (Livii Hist., lib. viii. c. 14.)

[p] "Aurelianus Genium Populi Romani aureum in Rostra posuit." (Catalog. Imperator. ap. Eccardum.)

[q] Dio Cass., lib. liv. c. 8; see Plate XXIV., and Nos. 916, 917.

of Rome. A round brick pedestal near the Arch of Septimius Severus may have been one of them, and a fragment of marble that appears to have been part of a mile-stone, with holes in it as for fixing bronze plates upon it, was found near this spot. The mile-stones were not measured from that point, some were measured from the gates in the wall of *the City*, others from the gate in the outer wall or *mœnia*, as appears from the treatises on the aqueducts by Frontinus, written in the first century, and by inscriptions on the Porta Maggiore, in which the length of the aqueducts *from that point* is recorded. The mile-stones in the Via Latina were measured from the Porta Latina. It is said to have been the design of the great Emperor to have had all the miles on the Roman roads measured from this stone, but the design was never carried out; probably it was not found practicable, as mile-stones had long been placed on all the roads, and to have changed them all would certainly have been very difficult. This stone is mentioned by Tacitus[r] as under the Temple of Saturn; it is the same distance from the temple of which three columns remain, close to the Ærarium, and from the one on the outer side of the paved street made in the foss of the old fortress called the Clivus Capitolinus, of which eight columns remain, and which we have shewn to be that of Vespasian. It is mentioned in the same manner by Suetonius in the life of the emperor Otho, and by Pliny, as the centre of the streets of Rome leading to the thirty-seven gates, in a passage long considered as inexplicable, but which we have shewn to be readily explained by an examination of the ground [s].

The church of SS. Sergius and Bacchus, martyrs, was founded (?) or restored (?) in the time of Pope Hadrian I., A.D. 790, by Antistes [t], *præsagus*, which is, literally, a prophet, but was then the title of an officer of the Church. It was "situated near the boundary of the temples," according to the same historian, that is, on the eastern

---

[r] "Inde ad Milliarium aureum sub ædem Saturni pergit." (Taciti Hist., lib. i. c. 27.)

"Ergo destinata die, præmonitis consciis, ut se in foro sub æde Saturni ad Milliarium aureum opperirentur." (Suetonius in Othone, c. 6.)

"Ejusdem spatium, mensura currente a Milliario in Capite Romani fori statuto, ad singulas portas, quæ sunt hodie numero triginta septem, ita ut duodecim semel numerentur, prætereanturque ex veteribus, septem, quæ esse desierunt, offert passuum per directum xxx.

M DCC LXV." (Plinii Hist. Nat., lib. iii. c. 5, s. 9.)

[s] See part ii. sect. 2, of this work, on the Walls and Gates of the Empire.

[t] "Item Diaconiam SS. Sergii et Bacchi ejusdem Diaconiæ dispensator propter metam templi, quod situm super eas videbatur, evertens super eandem ecclesiarum, a fundamentis ipsam basilicam exterminavit, quam restaurare minime valens, misericordia motus ab eorum martyrum amore, hic præsagus Antistes a fundamentis in ampliorem restauravit." (Anastas., 854.)

side of that part of the Forum Romanum that is full of temples, against the Arch of Septimius Severus, between that and the Mamertine Prison. It was destroyed by Pope Paul III., A.D. 1540, at the time of the visit of the Emperor Charles V. to Rome, when a number of old buildings were destroyed in that part of Rome to make the open space, called in ridicule by the wags of that period, *Campo Vaccino*, or 'the cattle pasture,' a name it still retains.

Passing through the arch [u] to the low level, we then go under the modern road by a passage made through the bank. Here we see what appear to be foundations of another temple, but the stones used for these foundations are large tufa blocks of the time of the Kings, taken from the outer wall of the old fortress, probably destroyed in the time of Titus [v]. The wall was standing in the time of Varro, who mentions a gate in it, as we have said. In the same passage with this basement is a gigantic marble column lying horizontally, which is quite four feet in diameter [x].

Emerging from this subterranean passage, we arrive at the Column of the Emperor Phocas [y], erected A.D. 608. This column stands upon a lofty base, and that upon a flight of steps constructed of old materials from other buildings. All this was buried up to the foot of the column until the year 1813, and the name was not known until it was then found upon an inscription on the base. It was called by Byron the *Nameless Column*.

The Comitium was a certain space in the Forum Romanum near the foot of the steps of the Temple of Concord, in which the Comitia, or public meetings for the election of the consuls, were held from the earliest period.

"[Romulus] erecting a tribunal, where he sat in judgment, in the most conspicuous part of the Forum, with the most formidable appearance from the soldiers who attended him, *being three hundred in number*, and the rods and axes borne by twelve lictors, who whipped those *in the Forum* whose offences deserved it [z]," &c.

Very near to the column of Phocas, in the north-east corner of the recent excavations, are remains of two marble walls in the

---

[u] See Plate XIV.
[v] See No. 3167. A temple of Titus is mentioned along with these in the *Curiosum*, but not in the *Notitia*. This has evidently been cased with marble. At first sight it appears much older than the time of Titus, the tufa blocks of the wall being evidently of the time of the early Kings.

[x] This is probably one of the great columns with statues or images on the top, shewn in the view of the Forum from the Arch of Constantine, Plate XXII.
[y] See No. 2288, and Plate XV.
[z] Dionysius Hal., Ant. Rom., b. ii. c. 29.

Comitium, covered with fine sculpture on both sides[a]. These two walls have on one side of each, the three animals prepared for sacrifice,—the bull, the ram, and the boar, hung with garlands as usual, called the *suovetaurilia*. On the other side of each wall are groups of figures; one is a procession of persons carrying books or tablets, which they are throwing into a heap to be burnt. They are supposed to represent the books of the taxes which the Emperor Hadrian[b] had cancelled, as is recorded by Spartianus in his life of that emperor[c]. At one end of the other wall is an orator standing on a rostrum and addressing the emperor, who is seated in state on a throne, surrounded by his officers. Behind him is the sculpture of the celebrated fig-tree and the image of Marsyas[d], or, as some say, Silvanus[e], which are also repeated at the end of the other wall. In the background is seen, in the sculpture, the upper part of the Tabularium, with one of the temples, and an arch or gateway at the north end of the Forum, as it then appeared from that spot. These two marble walls stand upon a basement of stone of the time of the Republic, and the partitions are believed to have been originally of wood and covered with a roof, until they were rebuilt of marble in the time of Hadrian.

That this great act was recorded on sculpture at the time we

[a] These walls were found in fragments in 1872, buried twenty feet deep, and were cleverly put together by Signor Rosa, under a shed prepared for the purpose, which is shewn in the photograph of the Column of Phocas—see Nos. 2959, 2960, 2961, 2962, 3160, and Plates XVI., XVII., XVIII.

[b] It seems probable that Hadrian carried out and completed what Trajan had begun; the debts cancelled are said to have amounted to some millions of pounds sterling.

[c] Hist. Aug. Script. Spartianus in Hadriano, c. 8.

[d] "Marsyas in Concordia delubrio religatus. Verum de quo delubrio intelligit, incertum est, ut propter commendatorem, qui ait Marsyam fuisse pro rostris est veris cansonum hoc delubrium fuisse ad Comitium quo coibant litum causa (teste Varrone), putat ad Curiam hostiliam, antiquam rostra ex hostibus capta fixa fuerunt in Græcostasi, sub dextra Comitii supra quam Senatum, quod ibi seniores consisterent, ubi ædes Concordiæ (ut habet Varro) quæ in Græcostasi sita fuit (ut scribit Plinius)." (Scholia Ant. in Horatii Sat., lib. iv. sat. 6, edit. Lugd. Bat. 1596, p. 382.)

"Comitium ab eo quod coibant eo Comitiis curiatis et litium causæ." (Varro, de Ling. Lat., c. xxxii. p. 154.)

"Curiæ duorum generum, nam et ibi curarent sacerdotes res divinas et curiæ veteres, et ubi senatus humanas ut curia Hostilia, quod primas ædificavit Hostilius Rex."

"Ante hanc Rostra quo jus ad vocabulum, ea hostibus capta fixa sunt rostra. Sub dextra lux jus a Comitio locus substructus, ubi nationum subsisterent legati qui ad senatum essent missi is Græcostasis appellatus, a parti et multa." (Ibid., p. 155.)

Horatii Satiræ, lib. i. Sat. 6; Martialis, Epig., lib. ii. ep. 54.

[e] "Ruminalem arborem in Comitio." (Taciti Annal., xiii. 58.)

"Colitur ficus arbor in foro ipso ac Comitio Romæ nata, sacro fulguribus ibi conditis. . . . Fuit et ante Saturni ædem . . . sacro a Vestalibus facto, cum Silvani simulacrum subverteret. Eadem fortuito satu vivit in medio foro, qua . . . ostento fatali Curtius . . . expleverat." (Plinii Nat. Hist., xv. 20.)

have a notice, and that it was placed in the Forum (of Trajan) is said also, but that seems to be a mistake. The procession is headed by an orator who stands on a rostrum, and addresses the emperor, who is seated on his throne, and surrounded by his officers of state. The same buildings in the background are represented here as on the one from the arch of Constantine. The scene represented on the marble walls is evidently intended as the view from the Comitium itself, just where the walls stand in the Forum. The steps have not yet been found, but the level is so much below that of the pavement under the Arch of Septimius Severus, that there must have been steps down to it, probably under the bank of earth on which the modern road is carried.

The same subject that is represented on the walls in the Comitium — the great donation of the Emperor Hadrian to the Roman people, and the burning of the deeds in order to cancel their debt — is also represented on four of the coins of that Emperor, with slight variations[f].

The account given by Pliny of the celebrated fig-tree in the Comitium and in the middle of the Forum, confirms distinctly the view that these marble walls are in the Comitium; they are said to have been for the purpose of keeping off the pressure of the mob from the persons going up to vote for the consuls. The basement is high enough from the pavement to have served for seats, when the partition was of wood only. The excavations on the eastern side of the Forum itself remain to be made at present, (in 1875); the great bank of earth on which a modern road is carried, and which is from fifteen to twenty feet deep, conceals everything; some years must probably pass before this can be removed, as it involves great changes in all that part of the city. Pliny says that the fig-tree named in the Forum and in the Comitium, was sacred to lightning, and was before the Temple of Saturn — that it sprang up of its own

---

[f] These are described in the excellent work of Cohen on the Roman Numismatics; the first is No. 1046, with this legend --

RELIQVA VETERA II. S. NOVIES MILL. A ROSTRA S. C.

The obverse is a head of Hadrian. The reverse has on the left a lictor setting fire to a heap of papers, and holding in his hand a fusee and a hatchet.

No. 1047 has on the obverse the same head, with a different legend, RELIQVA VETERUM RISTINTOVIQ. NOVIES. MILLIES ABOLITVR. Reverse, the same figure of a lictor burning papers, and two citizens standing in front of him.

No. 1048, Obverse, the same head and inscription. Reverse, the same figure also, with *two* figures as in 1047.

No. 1049, Obverse, as before. Reverse, same lictor, but *three* figures of citizens lifting up their hands in acclamation.

This is the only one of this subject that is engraved in Cohen, but he enumerates and describes eleven hundred and sixty-nine (!) coins of the Emperor Hadrian, or Adrien as the French call him.

accord, on land that had been part of the Curtian lake, and had been made sacred to the Vestal Virgins, and had an image of Silvanus under it. At the end of each part of the procession on the sculpture is the fig-tree, with the image of Silvanus, evidently to identify the spot. The base of a gigantic column of the time of Constantius, A.D. 353, which has the same three *suovetaurilia* carved upon it, was found in the Forum, and is now placed at the entrance to the palaces of the Cæsars [g].

On the Arch of Constantine, on a sculpture of his time, is another representation of a rostrum in the Forum Romanum near this site, with the buildings in the background as they then appeared, differing somewhat from what it was in the time of Hadrian, but still sufficiently like to be recognised as the same place, and the comparison of the two is interesting [h]. In this is represented a row of tall columns, with an image on each of them; these are of the end of the third century, and therefore could not be represented in the time of Hadrian. Down the Middle of the Forum is a row of square brick buildings, called by the Roman antiquaries the bases of these columns, but they are hollow, and appear to have been shops. The tall columns, with images on the top of them, are more likely to have been at the north end, where the modern road up to the Capitol is carried on a bank of earth, with a passage under it, in which one of the large columns is lying. The building in the background is more likely to have been the Tabularium than the Basilica Julia, which is the modern Roman theory.

A Temple of Mars Ultor is also mentioned in the inscription of Augustus, sometimes called his will, but now generally called the Monumentum Ancyranum [i]. There were two temples of Mars Ultor, one in the Forum of Augustus, a large oblong temple, of which there are considerable remains; the other small and round, known from the coin [k] only: but an inscription [l] which was over the door of the old church of S. Martina, at the north-east corner of the Forum, and which is printed by Nibby, seems to shew that this was the site. It appears to have been originally in the Atrium Caci, which is supposed to have been the same with the Atrium

---

[g] See Photos., No. 2971.

[h] See Plate XVII., and the description of it also, and Photos., No. 3168.

[i] EA . AVTEM . SIGNA . IN . PENETRALI . QVOD . EST . IN . TEMPLO . MARTIS . VLTORIS . REPOSVI. There is nothing to shew which of the two temples is here intended, but it must be the round one.

[k] See Photos., No. 491 C.

[l] MARTYRII GESTANS VIRGO MARTINA CORONAM, EIECTO HINC MARTIS NVMINE, TEMPLA TENES.

Libertatis, mentioned by Cicero in his letters to Atticus, and by Servius[m], then an open space on which now stand the two churches of S. Martina and S. Hadrianus. Inscriptions mentioning it have been found in both these churches[n]. The latter seems to shew that it was rebuilt by Valentinian towards the end of the fourth century.

On the opposite side of the Forum, in the north-west corner of the excavations, are remains of the Walls of the original BASILICA JULIA, built of travertine[o] in the time of Julius Cæsar, crossing the Forum from east to west; this building was damaged by fire before it was completed; it was then taken up and finished by Augustus, who enlarged it so much that what had been the length became the breadth[p]. We now see the raised platform of this great basilica, as rebuilt by Augustus, extending from north to south the whole length of the Forum, with steps up to it from the paved street, which went down the middle[q]. It should be mentioned that the brick bases now seen on the platform of the Basilica Julia are entirely modern, built by Signor Rosa in imitation of what he believed to have been the *original plan*, but he had in several places to cut through the marble pavement of the third century to insert them[r].

On the eastern side of the Forum, at this end, was the Basilica Æmilia, which probably extended along the greater part of the eastern side of the Forum, in the same manner as that of Julia did on the western side. Some slight remains, supposed to have belonged to it, were found in making a drain in front of those two churches in the year 1869[s]. Farther to the south, on the eastern side of the Forum, is the basement or *podium* of a gigantic equestrian statue, commonly said to be that of Domitian, but more likely to have been that of the Horse of Constantine, which is given in

---

[m] "Alii atria magnas ædes et capacissimas dictas tradunt; unde Atria Licinia et Atrium Libertatis." (Servius in .En. i. 726.)

[n] In S. Martina :—
SENATVS . POPVLVSQVE . ROmanus
LIBERTATI. (Ap. Gruter, xcix. n. 11.)
In S. Hadrian :—
SALVIS . DOMINO . NOSTRO . ZENONE .
AVGVSTO . GLORIOSISSIMO . REGE .
THEODORICO . VALENTINIANO V.C. ET
INL. EX. COM. DOMESTICO . SACRI .
PALATII . IN . ATRIO . LIBERTATIS . . .
QVÆ VETVSTATE . . . VE . CONFECIT.
(Ap. Maii, Script. Vet., v. 327.)

[o] See Nos. 2731, 3163, and Plate XIX.

[p] FORVM IVLIVM ET BASILICAM QVÆ
FVIT INTER ÆDEM CASTORIS ET ÆDEM
SATVRNI CŒPTA PROFLIGATAQVE OPERA
A PATRE MEO PERFECI ET EANDEM
BASILICAM CONSVMPTAM INCENDIO
AMPLIATO EIVS SOLO SVB TITVLO NOMINIS FILIORVM MEORVM INCHOAVI
ET SI VIVVS NON PERFECISSEM PERFICI AB HEREDIBVS MEIS IVSSI.

[q] See Photos., No. 3229.

[r] See Nos. 2726, 3229. This pavement may possibly be later, but in any case it should have been let alone.

[s] This is shewn in another photograph, No. 190.

the Regionary Catalogue as in Regio VIII.; that of Domitian is not there mentioned. The brickwork of the base is of the fourth century, and the very thick casing of yellow marble, called Giallo Antico[t], lying near to it, is not likely to have been of an early period. Marble was scarce in Rome in the first century, but was superabundant in the third, as was seen by the great number of large blocks of valuable marble left on the landing-place and buried in the mud of the Tiber for sixteen hundred years, until they were discovered in 1867-68.

The Basilica Julia[u] of Augustus[v]. This great building, and the Basilica Æmilia, before mentioned, not yet excavated, were only a carrying out of the plan, and rebuilding on the same sites, as in the time of the Kings, according to the legends given by Livy[w] that Tarquinius Priscus built arcades (*porticus*), probably double arcades, one over the other, as in the Forum of Trajan, and shops, and separated the private dwellings from the public offices. That king also administered justice in the Forum, and spake to the people there, and ornamented the shops of the merchants and the smiths, as we are also told by Dionysius[x]. At a later period, Plutarch mentions in the life of the emperor Galba that the people rushed to the Forum, not in flight, but to occupy the arcades (*porticus*) and the eating-houses as a theatre. Dio Cassius also says that the senators and their wives assembled in the Forum in funeral attire, and seated themselves in the arcades (*in porticibus*), perhaps in the upper storey[y]. There were at one period seven of these shops, which, after a fire, were reduced to five, as is recorded by Livy[z]. He also mentions some of these shops as schools, in speaking of Virginia[a]. Some games were played in the Forum at night with lamps. Julius Cæsar and Octavia, a sister of Augustus, assisted at these games, as we are told by Pliny[b], and Suetonius[c]; an enormous number of statues were placed in the Forum, as is mentioned by Pliny and various other authors. The emperor Constantius, on his celebrated visit to Rome, is said by Ammianus Marcellinus[d] to have been quite amazed and stupified by the number.

Returning now to the western side of the Forum. It has been

---

[t] See No. 3169.
[u] Suetonii Octavianus, c. 29, et in Caligula, c. 37; Plinii Epist., lib. v. Epist. 21, lib. vi. Epist. 23.
[v] See Plate XX.
[w] "Ibi . . . rex Romanus vicit." (Livii Hist., i. 15.)
[x] Dionys. Halicarnas., Ant., lib. 3.

[y] Dio Cassius, lib. 74.
[z] Livii Hist., xxvii. 14.
[a] Ibid., iii. 44.
[b] Plinii Nat. Hist., xix. 6.
[c] Suetonius, Julius Cæsar, 39.
[d] Ammianus Marcellinus, lib. xvi. c. 10, s. 13.

mentioned that the Basilica Julia extended along the whole of this side of the Forum, from the Temple of Saturn at one end, to that of Castor and Pollux at the other end; this we are distinctly told in the inscription of Augustus[e]. This therefore identifies the celebrated three columns, respecting the name of which volumes of conjectures have been written, as THE TEMPLE OF CASTOR AND POLLUX[f].

The old part of the Basilica that remains is of travertine, and extremely plain; very much of the same character as the Arch of Dolabella on the Cœlian, which is dated by an inscription, A.D. 10. These arches are part of a great market-hall, or Basilica, and therefore are probably of the time of the founder, Julius Cæsar. These are all towards the northern end, and near the Temple of Saturn. Large additions have been made to them in brick, of a debased period, not earlier than the fourth century, and perhaps later. In addition to the arches that remain, there is one original base, rather further to the south; this is of travertine, and to this Signor Rosa has added forty-seven others, of bad brickwork, in imitation of the same debased character as the additions before mentioned. The inscription called the Monumentum Ancyranum states clearly that the Basilica Julia of Augustus extended from the Temple of Saturn at one end (of the site of which there can be no doubt, as it was connected with the ancient Treasury or Ærarium under the Tabularium) to the Temple of Castor at the other end. This must have been the temple at the south-west angle of the Palatine, to which the celebrated three columns belonged, the real name of which was so long much disputed. The Arch of Fabianus is also distinctly said to have been in the Via Sacra[g], near to this and the Temple of Faustina. This great Basilica is stated to have been built in the area of the Comitium, which was the lowest ground in the Forum, below the level of the Græcostadium, and to have been begun by Julius Cæsar, but damaged by fire before it was completed, and then restored and finished by Augustus; this is recorded on the inscription before cited. It is also said that he enlarged it so

---

[e] See Plates XXII., XXIII.

[f] See Nos. 911, 2289.

[g] "Fornix Fabianus arcus juxta Regiam in Sacra Via a Fabio Consule constructus, qui Devictis Allebrogibus Allobrox cognominatus est, ibique statua ejus posita propterea est." (Asconius in Cicero ad Verrem, art. i. c. 7.)

And again, Trebellius Pollio, in his comment on these words of Cicero :—

"Videt ad ipsum fornicem Fabianum in turba Verrem."

"Fuit denique hactenus statua in pede montis Romulei hoc est ante Sacram Viam inter templum Faustinæ ac Vestæ ad arcum Fabianum, quæ haberet inscriptam Gallieno minori, Salonino additum, ex quo nomen ejus intelligi poterit." (Trebellius Pollio in Saloninno Gallieno.)

"SENATORES ad Puteal Scribonis Licinii, quod est in porticu Julia ad Fabianum arcum consistere solebant." (Scholiast. Persii, Sat. iv. v. 49.)

much, that what had been the length became the width, and that the whole area of the Comitium was then covered over.

This Basilica was burnt at the end of the third century, with other public buildings, under Carinus and Numerianus, and rebuilt under Diocletian and Maximianus [h]. This is further confirmed by an inscription given by Gruter [i], and said to have been found on the spot. It had been on the base of a statue, which was placed as an ornament in the Basilica Julia, then newly repaired. On the side of this base was another inscription, damaged, but giving the names of the Consuls under Septimius Severus (A.D. 199). Other inscriptions shew that there were shops in or round the Basilica; one of a money-changer [k] was found in a tomb in the Via Labicana, near the Tor Pignatara, or Mausoleum of S. Helena.

Dionysius of Halicarnassus relates a legend of the apparition of the Dioscuri, Castor and Pollux, to Postumius, in the attack on the army of the Latins. They appeared on horseback, and

"charged at the head of the Roman horse, wounding with their spears all they encountered, and driving the Latins before them. After the battle was over, they appeared in the Roman Forum, at the beginning of night . . . they then dismounted, and washed themselves in the stream, which rises near to the Temple of Vesta [l]. . . . Of this extraordinary and wonderful apparition there are many memorials in Rome, as the Temple of Castor and Pollux, which the Roman people erected in the Forum where they appeared, and the stream near it, said to be dedicated to them," &c. [The fountain, of which there are remains, was built on this spot.]

This temple was rebuilt by Tiberius [m], and the columns are of his time; but although the temple was rebuilt *from the foundations*, the foundations themselves were not rebuilt, and the solid basement or *podium* of it is of the time of the Kings, of the second period, built of the large blocks of tufa, each of a ton weight, which made as good a foundation as any architect could require [n].

The first distinct notice we have of a Temple of Castor in Rome is in the year 256 (B.C. 487), when the Dictator Postumius, in the war with the Latins and family of the Tarquins, vowed to build one [o]. This vow was fulfilled by his son, and the temple was dedicated in the year of Rome 274 (B.C. 479), but no exact site is mentioned for

---

[h] "... Operæ publicæ fabricatur sunt, Senatum, Forum Cæsaris, Basilica Julia," &c. (Catalog. Imp. Eccardi.)

[i] GABINUS VETITIUS PROBIANUS, V. C. PRAEF. URB STATUAM QUAE BASILICAE JULIAE A SE NOVITER REPARATAE ORNAMENTO ESSET ADIECIT.

[k] L. MARII FORTUNATI NUMMULARI DE BASILICA JULIA.

[l] This description agrees with the site of this ruin. The Temple of Vesta was in front of the church of S. Maria Liberatrice, close to this spot.

[m] Dion. Cass. Hist., lib. lv. c. 27.

[n] See No. 3157.

[o] Livii Hist., lib. ii. c. 20.

this[p]. The next notice of it is, that a bronze plate was fixed there in A.U.C. 415 (B.C. 337), to commemorate the conquest of the Latins[q]. The next and the last notice of it in Livy, is that an equestrian statue of Marcius was ordered to be placed in the Forum, in front of the Temple of Castor[r], to commemorate his triumph over the Hernicians. This is also mentioned by Cicero[s] as a statue in the Forum before Castor. Aurelius Victor mentions the Temple of Castor at the lake of Juturna, which agrees with this site. This temple was rebuilt by Augustus, and dedicated by Tiberius[t], in A.U.C. 759, A.D. 6, on the 27th of January, as mentioned by Ovid[u], who also mentions it as near the lake of Juturna[v].

In the Regionary Catalogue the dedication is given as to Castor and Minerva, *Templum Castoris et Minervæ*. This is a singular deviation from the usual account of the dedication of the temple to Castor and *Pollux*, for which it is not easy to account, but it can hardly mean two temples.

The Temple of Castor and Pollux being thus ascertained, we are thereby enabled to fix another point hitherto doubtful. Suetonius mentions that Caligula used this temple as a vestibule to his palace. The great brick building of the time of Caligula which stands close to it, on the same level, and is only separated from it by the pavement of the street, must therefore be the Palace of Caligula, which has hitherto been placed on the Palatine Hill, fifty feet above it. The remains of this palace are much concealed by modern houses built up against it, but at the west end of it remains of the bridge can be made out; two of the tall brick piers of which remain visible above the houses, and in the outer one the springing of an arch for a continuation of the bridge can be distinctly seen[x].

The palace at the north-east corner of the Palatine, usually called of Caligula, is really of the time of Trajan and Hadrian, as is shewn by a comparison of the construction with that of the Villa of Hadrian at Tivoli[y]. The tall brick piers which carry a lofty vault over the paved sloping road in that part are also of the time of Hadrian, built against the wall of the Palace of Trajan; the straight vertical

---

[p] Livii Hist., lib. ii. c. 42.
[q] Ibid., lib. viii. c. 11.
[r] Ibid., lib. ix. c. 43.

[s] Cicero Philipp., vi. c. 5.
[t] Suetonius in Tiberio, c. 20; Dion. Cassius, lib. lv. c. 27.
[u] "Fratribus illa deis fratres de gente deorum
Circa Juturnæ composuere lacus."
(Ovid. Fast., lib. i. 707.)
also the basin of a fountain.

[v] The English word *lake* does not convey the true meaning of the Latin word *lacus*, which certainly means sometimes the loch of a canal, and probably

[x] See Nos. 1447, 1451, 1757, 3170, and Plate XXVI. of Forum.
[y] See Nos. 899, 2973.

joint between them is distinctly visible, and is in places a couple of inches wide[f]. But a narrow passage corbelled out upon the wall of another palace, faced with a piece of pierced marble parapet (called Transenna or Cancelli), and resting upon a rich stucco vault supported by the corbels, leads straight to the bridge of Caligula, and may be of his time[a].

The lake or swamp commonly called "the Curtian lake" (from the legend of the celebrated leap into it in the earliest days of Roman history, but also called the lake of Servitius[b]), was close to the western side of this, and the Vicus Jugarius began at this point, on the northern side of the lake, going from the Forum Romanum to the Forum Boarium. Part of the ground-plan of it is represented in a fragment of the marble plan of Rome[c].

The Cloaca Maxima passes under the south end of the platform of the Basilica Julia, and the construction of it is of the character called Etruscan, the vault of it being semi-hexagonal instead of the usual semicircular form[d]. This agrees exactly with the subterranean passage connected with the great Prison of the Kings, which was discovered a few years since, and both are attributed to the same period by Livy, that is, the second period of the Kings, the time of Ancus Martius.

There are very abundant natural springs gushing out under the tufa rock at the north-west corner of the Palatine, in the Lupercal, which is in the Velabrum, and so far agrees with the inscription[e]; it is entered in the Catalogue as in Regio X., having been within the line of the outer wall of the Palatine fortress. Another abundant spring coming from the Quirinal, can now be seen under a shop behind the church of S. Hadrian. This must have been under some temple or building in the time of the early Empire, at the date of the Regionary Catalogue. It was in this Regio, and although it was a short stream, and soon carried into the

---

[f] See Nos. 2253, 2972.

[a] See No. 2255, and Plate XVI. of Supplement to vol. i.

[b] "Servitius lacus appellatur ea qui cum faciendum curaverat in principio vici Jugarii, *continens Basilicam Juliæ*, in quo loco fuit effigies hydræ posita de M. Agrippa." (Festus in voce Servilii lacus.)

[c] Canina, in his Plan of Rome, has added another fragment to this with much ingenuity; but unfortunately the other fragment is on a different scale, and the two could not possibly have been intended to be put together. There are three different scales in the Marble Plan.

[d] See No. 3164, and Plate XXI.

[e] C. CLODIVS C. L. EVPHERVS
NEGOTIATOR PENORIS
ET VINORVM
DE VELABRO A. IIII SCARIS
ARAM POSVIT SIBI
CONSECRAVIT
DEDICAVITQVE
LIBERISQVE SVIS
POSTERISQVE EORVM.

The corrections indicated in the text are those of Dr. Henzen, and are obviously true.

Cloaca Maxima, a portion of it may have been left open expressly to serve as a fish-pond for the delicate fish called Scarus. The stream now runs in a drain on the eastern side of the Forum Romanum, at a higher level than the Cloaca Maxima, into which it is afterwards conveyed. In the year 1873 both streams were brought to light by the excavations, one running from east to west, near the middle of the Forum, the other running in the same direction but further to the south, under the south end of the platform of the Basilica Julia, at a considerable depth; the vault of the first is mediæval, that of the second very early, of the date of the original Cloaca Maxima. Scarus is the name of a fish of a particular kind, some say what we call a *bream*, considered a great delicacy by the ancient Romans, and of which four are supposed to have been carved on the wall of the cave in which this water came out. Clodius Eupherus, who had placed an altar here, was a wine-merchant, and he is supposed to have been also the keeper of an eating-house (a dealer in victuals and drink).

Returning to the south end of the Forum, there are two steps up from it to another platform on a higher level, which proves that this was the end. Here are some slight remains of the Fountain of Juturna, which had an oval basin with a shallow channel for the water to run round, of which some portions remain visible [f]. This fountain stood half-way between the Temple of Castor and Pollux and the Rostrum and Temple of Julius Cæsar, which was also excavated in 1873. The curved wall of the rostrum, with the base of the temple behind it, and a paved platform for an audience, are visible [g]. A little to the south of this, and on the western side of the Via Sacra, just at the south of the fountain, is the circular basement or *podium* of the Temple of Vesta, which is also of the time of the Kings, of the second period [h]. Both of these temples, that is, of Castor and of Vesta, are mentioned by Dionysius [i] as having been built "when the two hills were united in one city and inclosed in one wall."

ROMULUS . MARTIS . F. REX . ANN . . . . .
DE . CAENINENSIBUS . K. MAI . . . .
. . . . MARTIS . F. REX . II.

The above commencement of the Fasti Consulares was found on the twentieth of April, 1872, in the Forum Romanum, close to the Rostrum of Julius Cæsar, and is placed by Signor Rosa near the spot where it was found. It is believed to belong to the same set

[f] See No. 3158, and the Plan.
[g] See No. 3159, and Plate XXII.
[h] See No. 3149.
[i] Dionys., Ant., ii. 50.

of Fasti of which other fragments are preserved in the Palace of the Conservator, on the Capitoline Hill.

Having now arrived at the south end of the Forum, and ascertained beyond all question the real history of several buildings which have for centuries been subjects of controversy from conjectures only, probable restorations have been made upon paper, of some of the most important of them, which will make the existing remains better understood [k]. So much of the basement of the great Temple of Castor and Pollux remains in its place, that there can be no doubt that the celebrated three columns were part of a portico of ten columns, which have accordingly been placed on a probable restoration, in a drawing by Signor Cicconetti [l]. In the same manner, enough remains of the palace and bridge of Caligula to shew what it must have been. It is probable that the bridge served more than one purpose; it carried the *specus* of an aqueduct from the Palatine to the Capitol, with a road for horses by the side of it, as was usual in the aqueduct-bridges, as at the Ponte Lupo near Poli, which crosses a narrow gorge, and is of great height, quite as high as this bridge of Caligula. It may also have served to connect the principal part of the palace on the level of the Forum with another part of the palace on the hill above, at the back of that of Trajan and Hadrian before mentioned, which may have been built up against it. Those emperors had each their private residence in other parts of Rome, that of Trajan on the Aventine connected with the Thermæ of Sura [m], who was his cousin, and it is probable that all that part of the Aventine was the residence of the family to which Trajan belonged. The private house of Hadrian was near the Thermæ of Caracalla; there are considerable remains of it, (miscalled the Villa of Asinius Pollio [n]). The great public buildings called the Palaces of the Cæsars, seem to have become in the second or third century merely public offices, (much in the same manner as Somerset House in the Strand, —originally a great palace, is now entirely devoted to public offices). On the Palatine, the different parts of these great buildings were named after the emperors in whose time each part was built, but there are no divisions between them.

The usually received history of the Palatine and of the Forum, as of other parts of Rome, is based entirely on the works of the great scholars of the seventeenth century, chiefly Panvinius and his school,

[k] See Plates XXIII., XXIV. engravings of them, Plates XXV., XXVI. 1747.   [n] See Nos. 630, 631.

[l] See No. 3195, and the Photo-
[m] See Nos. 789, 833.

some of the most learned men of their day. They had collected all the passages of the classical authors—called in Rome *texts*—relating to the City of Rome, and explained them to the best of their ability, and they were clever men, and well read; but when the greater part of the buildings of the City were buried from fifteen to twenty feet deep, it was impossible for any one to decide with any certainty the exact site of each building. For instance, the extent of the Forum Romanum has long been a matter of discussion: some made it extend to the west as far as the Arcus Quadrifrons, or Arch of Janus, which was thought by them to be the connection between the Forum Romanum and the Forum Boarium; others made it extend to the south as far as the Summa Sacra Via, and almost to the Colosseum. The exact length of it has now been ascertained beyond all question, and it is found to be much smaller than was expected. The Temples of Concord and of Saturn under the Tabularium and Ærarium, are at the north end of it; the exact north point is the Church of S. Giuseppe, over the Prison of S. Peter, just to the east of the Arch of Septimius Severus. The Temple of Antoninus and Faustina is on the east side of the south end; this temple was in the Via Sacra, not in the Forum. The Temple of Castor and Pollux is at the south-west corner, and formed the vestibule to the palace of Caligula, which was not in the Forum. The Basilica Julia extends down the whole length on the western side; the width of this Forum has not yet been ascertained, but it is believed that the part now excavated is about two-thirds of the whole width.

The ARCUS QUADRIFRONS, commonly called the Arch of Janus[o], still stands at the junction of the Aqua Argentina, from the Lupercal on the south, and another stream from the north, which passes under it, and falls into the main stream in the Cloaca Maxima. At this site there would be originally a draw-bridge between the two fortresses, one on the Palatine, the other on the hill of Saturn; and hence the custom of closing it in time of war, or leaving it open in time of peace. And this structure was sometimes called a temple: it probably had an altar under it. The original Janus of the legendary history was built by Quirinus, or Romulus, as mentioned by Macrobius[p].

Suetonius mentions that the Janus Quirinus was closed for the third time by Augustus, having been previously closed by Numa and by T. Manlius Torquatus[q].

[o] Photos., No. 197.
[p] Macrobii Saturn., c. ix.
[q] Suetonius Oct., c. xxii.; Horatii Carmina, lib. iv. Ode 15; Virgilii Æneid., vii. 607; Donaldson's Coins, No. 12; Photos., No. 496 A.

This marble arch stood in the Argiletum, a bed of clay which had been also the Velabrum, and which extended as far as the Forum Olitorium. This is stated by Livy[r], who says that the Janus in the lowest part of the Argiletum was opened in time of peace, and closed in time of war. Servius[s] attributes it to the time of Numa Pompilius, and calls it a *sacrarium*, or holy place, at the bottom of the Argiletum, and near the theatre of Marcellus. The shops of the booksellers seem to have been especially in this district, which Martial[t] mentions in speaking of his own book. Livy[u] also mentions the Porta Carmentalis as near to it, and the small stream which here runs into the other larger stream, in the Cloaca Maxima, is there called the Cremera; it comes from the north, near the Pantheon (as before mentioned).

Servius[x] goes on to shew that a change took place in the form of the Janus; they had originally two faces only, but were afterwards altered to four, after the conquest of the Etruscan city of Faliscus; on this occasion the Sacrarium, or holy place, in which the gate was closed in time of peace, was transferred to the Forum Transitorium, probably because the chief traffic of the city, which had been originally from the Palatine to the Capitol, passing under that Janus, had been transferred to the thoroughfare from the city of the two hills on the east, to the western side of Rome. This new Janus was of bronze; of what material the original one was we have no evidence; but a wall of the Kings has been found leading from it to the Palatine, so that it was one of the gates of THE CITY of the two hills. The present marble arch is of the

[r] "Janum ad infimum Argiletum indicem pacis, bellique fecit . . . sunt geminæ belli portæ." (Livii Hist., i. 19.)

[s] "Sacrarium hoc Numo Pompilius fecerat circa imum Argiletum, juxta theatrum Marcelli; quod fuit in duobus brevissimis templis. *Duobus* autem propter Janum bifrontem." (Servii in Virgilii Æneid, lib. vii. 607, edit. H. A. Lion, Cottengæ, 1827.)

[t] "Argiletanas mavis habitare tabernas,
Cum tibi parve liber scrinia nostra vacent."
(Martialis, lib. i. epig. 4.)

[u] "Infelici via dextro Jano portæ Carmentalis profecti, ad Cremeram flumen perveniunt." (Livii Hist., ii. 49.)

[x] "Postea captis Phaleris (Faliscis) civitate Tusciæ inventum est simulacrum Jani cum frontibus quattuor. Propter quod in foro transitorio constitutum est illi sacrarium aliud, quod novimus hodieque quattuor portas habere (al. Unde quod Numa instituerat, translatum est ad Forum transitorium, et quattuor portarum unum templum est institutum).

Janum sane apud aliquos bifrontem, apud aliquos quadrifrontem esse non mirum est. Nam alii eum diei dominum [vel auctorem] volunt, in quo ortus est et occasus. Horatius (Serm. 2. 6, 20): *Matutine pater, seu Jane libentius audis*. Alii anni totius, quem in quattuor tempora constat esse divisum. Anni autem esse deum illa res probat, quod ab eo prima pars anni nominatur. [Nam ab Jano *Januarius* dictus est.]" (Servii in Virgilii Æneid, lib. vii. 607.)

third century, and there is no appearance of any earlier stone or marble building.

Another kind of Janus was much smaller, and made of bronze, not of stone or marble; and it must have been one of the latter kind that was placed at this meeting-point of the four Forums. One of these is clearly described by Procopius [1]:—

"There was a Janus in the Forum in front of the Curia, a little above the figure of the three Fates, or Parcæ (sometimes called also Sybils). This temple was made entirely of bronze, and of a square form; it was hardly large enough to hold the figure of Janus. The bronze image was four cubits long (3 feet 9 inches), in other respects like a man, but that it had two faces, one looking towards the sun, or the east, the other towards the west. There were bronze doors in each face."

In the Ordo Romanus of A.D. 1143, the procession is said to have passed under the triumphal arch of Septimius Severus, and behind the temple of Concord and the temple of the Fates. It therefore went up the eastern side of the Capitolium, and the temple of the Sybil or the Fates may have been on the site now occupied by the Church of S. Joseph, under which is that of the Crucifixion, and under that is what is now called the Prison of S. Peter; that is, just on the other side of the path that passes on the east of the temple of Concord. But that path is modern; the Janus may therefore have stood on the site of the other modern church of S. Martina on the opposite side of the road, which would also be at the junction of the four Forums (Romanum, Julius Cæsar, Augustus, and Nerva). It had one face to each forum. A Janus is represented on a coin of Nero, in perspective, shewing one side and one end of a cella, square or oblong, with pilasters at the angles, in either side of a large door which occupies the whole end. In the time of Domitian a Janus was erected in each of the fourteen Regiones of Rome; but they were probably all of bronze, excepting the one at the entrance to the Forum Boarium. Suetonius [2] records them among the works of Domitian, and says there was upon each a *quadriga*, and the Trophies of the Triumphs. A bronze Janus is represented on a coin of Commodus, A.D. 187.

The author of what is now called *the spurious* Regionary Catalogue, who took the name of Publius Victor, and whose compilation (if such it is) generally shews great learning, says, in the summary at the end, there were thirty-six Jani in Rome. They

---

[1] Procopius de bello Gothico, c. 25.
[2] "Janus arcusque cum quadrigis et insignibus triumphorum per Regiones tantis ac tot extruxit, ut quidem Græci inscriptum est ἀρχει." (Suetonii Domitianus, c. 13.)

were certainly numerous, and for the most part small structures of bronze (as has been said above [a]). The Scholiast on Horace says there were three of these in the Forum Romanum [b]: one at each end, and one in the middle, near the Basilica of Paulus Æmilius and the rostra, which was the resort of the usurers, or money-lenders, to whom Horace alludes when he says that his bank is broken [c].

Two of these bronze Jani [d] stood near the north-east corner of the Forum Romanum, in front of the Basilica Pauli Æmilii, and are probably those intended by Ovid in the Fasti, when he speaks of the number of Jani, and especially of two at the junction of two Fora [e]. Martial, in his Epigrams, speaks of the junction of four Fora [f]: and two at the Arch of Fabianus, one above, the other below. These seem to be referred to by Horace: "This upper Janus leads from below [g]," &c. Cicero mentions the Janus sometimes as the place of meeting of debtors and creditors, and for collecting money; and that some of the best of men were seen sitting in the middle of the Janus, as if they had been philosophers disputing in a school [h].

---

[a] Although the later Catalogue attributed to Rufus and Victor are considered by Preller, who is followed by modern scholars, to be spurious, only a compilation, and therefore of no authority; the objects mentioned are frequently supported by the existing remains in a remarkable manner, and if they are forgeries they are very clever ones. The opinion of the local antiquaries of the Roman school that this Catalogue was made for the use of the local magistrates of each Regio, and was added to from time to time as was found necessary, seems a fair explanation of the variations in it.

[b] "... et forum porticibus tabernisque claudendum, et Janos tres faciendos." (Livii Hist., xli. 27, A.U.C. 278, B.C. 475.)

[c] "Duo Jani ante basilicam Pauli steterunt ubi locus erat freneratorum, Janus dicebatur locus." (Scholiast in Horatii, lib. ii. ep. 1.)

"Janui autem tres erant, una in ingressu fori, altera in media, ubi erat ejus templum prope basilicam Pauli, vel pro Rostris: huc concurrebant et potissimum stationes suas habebant frenatores, alii ad reddendum frenus, alii ad accipiendum: tertia autem statua erat ad exitum fori." (Scholiast in Horatio, lib. ii. Sat. 3, v. 18.)

[d] Photos., No. 490 A, from a coin.

[e] "Quum tot sint Jani, cur stas sacratus in uno
Ilic ubi juncta foris, templa duobus habes."
(Ovidii Fast., lib. i. 257.)

[f] "Sed nec Marcelli, Pompeianumque, nec illic
Sunt triplices thermæ; nec fora juncta quater."
(Martialis Epigr., lib. x. epist. 51.)

[g] "... Hæc Janus summus ab imo Perducet," &c.
(Horatii Epist., lib. i. 54.)

[h] Cicero de Officiis, lib. ii. c. 25; and Philippica, c. 51.

TEMPLE OF JUPITER CAPITOLINUS.

An account of the original temple on the top of the Tarpeian rock has been given in the appendix to the first volume of this work. This appears evidently to have been the one excavated by the Chevalier Bunsen, when he was Ambassador in Rome for the Prussian Government, and still left open for view in the gardens of the Caffarelli Palace, now the residence of the ambassador of the German Empire. Ammianus Marcellinus mentions this temple by the name of JOVIS TARPEI, and as preceding all others [i].

This had long been treated as foundations only for the great temple of the Empire on the same site; but we still have considerable remains of the outer wall of the sacred enclosure of the original temple, and the fact of so large a space having been given up to it within the arx, or pretorium, the keep of the castle, and residence of the chief officer, shews that great importance was attached to it. The great temple of the Empire, which had been rebuilt in the most sumptuous manner in the time of Vespasian and Domitian, seems to have been *entirely* destroyed. Half of the roof was carried away by the Goths under Genseric, as Procopius relates:—

"Genseric, for no other reason than because he hoped for treasure, sailed with a large fleet to Italy; and ascending (the Tiber) to Rome, as no one offered any resistance, he became master of the palaces.... But Genseric carried away captive Eudoxia, along with the young Eudocia, and Placidia, children of Valentinian; and loading the ships with a great amount of gold and silver, and other property of the Emperor, he sailed to Carthage, having spared neither brass (or bronze), nor anything else in the palaces. For he stripped the Temple of Jupiter Capitolinus, and carried away half of the roof. This roof was formed of the best bronze, and overlaid with gold in abundance, so that it appeared splendid in the highest degree, and worthy of much admiration [k]."

So valuable a material as gilt bronze was not likely to be suffered to remain, when for centuries all these fine ruins were looked upon only as quarries of building material. The representation of the temple on a coin gives the best idea of what it was; but all this rich ornament being portable, was sure to disappear. It is represented on a coin as a Corinthian temple on three steps,

---

[i] "Jovis Tarpei delubra quantum, terrenis divina præcellunt." (Ammianus Marcellinus, xvi. 10. 13.)

[k] Procopius de Bell. Vand., lib. i. c. 5. This roof is said to have cost a sum equivalent to two millions sterling.

with six columns and figures between them, a tympanum enriched with sculpture, and figures standing on the roof of two chariots and horses, and two eagles.

That there was a quadriga (or chariot on four wheels) made of terra cotta, on the summit of this temple, is mentioned by Festus incidentally under the word Ratumena. He also says that it was of Etruscan workmanship, and placed there by the Romans of Veii, after the inhabitants of that city were transferred to Rome. His account of it shews that it was a conspicuous object to any one coming towards the Capitoline Hill from the north, as it was the first object seen by the charioteer whose horses had ran away with him from Veii [m]. This also shews the use of terra cotta ornaments on the buildings of Rome at that period.

The marble walls were used in the Middle Ages, to make the great flight of steps up to the church of Ara Cœli, as recorded on an inscription; and the marble columns not being useful for that purpose, were thrown over the rock by the workmen, and the remains of broken columns were found buried at the foot of that rock by Vacca. This was nearly the same spot where Livy relates that a great mass of the rock fell over in B.C. 192 [n]. A number of other columns in fragments were found buried behind the Palazzo del Conservatore [o], and under the Caffarelli Palace, which had not been thrown over the rock, but thrown aside as useless, and used probably for foundations to the mediæval palace.

The accounts of the different witnesses as to what each has seen, collected in Fea's *Miscellanea*, are, however, contradictory on some points, and difficult to explain. In another place Vacca [p] states that—

"I remember that under the Tarpeian rock, on the side near the Church della Consolazione, when Muzio de Leis and Agrippa Mace were building, many fragments were found on the slope of the hill, all square work fallen from that height."

"Near the arch above-mentioned was the statue of Marforio; and the Romans, wishing to decorate the fountain in the Piazza Navona, had the statue taken as far

[m] "Ratumena porta a nomine ejus appellata est, qui ludicro certamine quadrigis victor Etrusci generis juvenis Veiis consternatis equis excussus Romæ periit: qui equi feruntur non ante constitisse, quam pervenirent in Capitolium, conspectamque fictilium quadrigarum, quæ erant in fastigio Jovis templi, quas faciendas locaverant Romani Vejenti cuidam artis figulinæ prudenti, quæ bello sunt reciperatæ: quia in fornace adeo creverant, ut eximi nequirent: idque prodigium protendere videbatur, in qua civitate eæ fuissent, omnium eam futuram potentissimam." (Festus de Verb. Sign., lib. xvi.)

[n] Livii Hist., xxxv. 21.

[o] Vacca, Memorie, M. 64.

[p] Ibid., ap. Fea, M., pp. lxxxi. and lxxxii.

as S. Mark's; but repenting, had it taken back to the Capitol, where it now serves as a river for the fountain in that Piazza [q]. In moving the statue from its place, they found that large basin [r] of granite which is now a horse-trough in the middle of the Forum Romanum, where the market is [s]."

This temple is still considered by many scholars to have been on the site of the church of Ara Cœli, notwithstanding the strong case that has been made out on the other side. The great public building called the Capitolium must always have been of the same height that it is now, although the upper part was of wood until the time of Michael Angelo, who rebuilt it in stone, but did not make it any higher than it had been originally. This stands directly between this church and the forum, and almost entirely blocks out the view of the one from the other; whereas Cicero [t] appeals to the statue in front of it as then standing and overlooking the forum. The bridge of Caligula was made to connect his palace on the Palatine, or rather at the foot of it, with this temple; and there are remains of this bridge pointing directly to the temple on the Caffarella height [u]. When Cicero says that the statue of Jupiter overlooked the Curia and the Forum, he must mean that part of it where the Basilica Julia was afterwards built. Probably one of the law courts was always held on that site. Dion Cassius [v] also quotes the passage from Cicero, and confirms that the statue was made to turn towards the east, to overlook the Forum and detect the conspiracy.

From the observations of Vacca [w], and his record of what he remembers to have seen in a deep pit, which he calls a gulf, dug in the Piazza del Campidoglio, it is evident that this fine square of Michael Angelo has the pavement of it at a much higher level than what it had been before his time. Vacca says (No. 19) that his master, Vincenzo de Rossi, descended into this abyss, and there saw a fine sculpture of a woman seated on a bull; that is to say, the mythological legend of Jupiter and Europa, in bas-relief on a wall.

The fine bronze statue of Marcus Aurelius on horseback, which now stands in the centre of the Piazza del Campidoglio, was found

---

[q] It is now in the courtyard of the Capitoline Museum; it was engraved by Signor Bottari, tom. iii. of that museum, tav. i., where he relates the opinions of the other antiquaries as to the subject represented; he believes it to be Oceanus. But Marforio was another name for Mars, that name occurs in the fragments of the early part of Dion Cassius, xi. edit. Reimar, vol. i. p. 6.

[r] This large basin, of red granite, has been destined for the fountain to be made in front of the Obelisk of the Quirinal.

[s] F. Vacca, Memorie, lxxxiii. 69.

[t] Ciceronis Orat. in Catilina, c. ix. § 19, 20, 22.

[u] See Plate XXII., and the plan of the Forum.

[v] Dionis. Cass., Hist., xxxvii. 34.

[w] F. Vacca, Memorie, 19, ap. Fea Misc., page lxix.

in the time of Sixtus IV.[x], c. A.D. 1480, in a vineyard belonging to the Lateran convent, near the Scala Santa. It is said by the Roman antiquaries to have stood originally in the Forum Romanum, and to have been removed to the Lateran by Clement III., c. A.D. 1190, and to have been left there, neglected, for about 300 years, until Sixtus IV. removed it. It was long supposed to be the horse of Constantine, and was placed in the Piazza del Laterano. It was removed to its present situation by Paul III., c. A.D. 1540. The marble base for it was made by Michael Angelo; and as it was difficult to find a piece of marble sufficiently large for the purpose ready cut, the Pope gave him a piece of the frieze (?), or cornice (?), of the temple of Trajan. The likeness of the head of the statue to that of Marcus Aurelius, as shewn on his coins, cannot be mistaken.

Aqueducts.

The eighth Regio was supplied with water, according to Frontinus, by the Aqua Appia, the Anio Vetus, the Marcia, and the Julia; the Claudia and the Anio Novus united being afterwards added on the upper level as usual[y]. The Aqua Argentina, or the S. Giorgio, also rises in or near this Regio, and runs in its course through a part of it. This Regio of open places for public meetings and markets, must have been very abundantly supplied with water. The course by which these different streams were conveyed to this Regio from their entrances into Rome remains to be traced. The Appia probably came along under the Cœlian on the same line as the arches of Nero, but at a much lower level, to the great subterranean reservoir near the Arch of Dolabella, and thence along the branch to the Colosseum, then under the lower Via Sacra.

A branch of the Anio Vetus was probably brought from the Porta Maggiore, along the valley between the Cœlian and the Esquiline, to the great reservoir near the Colosseum, and thence also under the Via Sacra.

The Marcia and the Julia were probably brought over the Esquiline and the Quirinal, as those Regiones were also supplied with the same water. The Claudia and the Anio Novus being distributed in all the Regiones, were conveyed in the *specus* that was carried on the arches of Nero, continued by Domitian and Trajan from the central reservoir over the Arch of Dolabella[z], down the side of the Clivus Scauri, and on the arches from the Cœlian to the Pala-

---

[x] F. Vacca, M. 18, ap. Fea, p. lxii. [y] See the Chapter on the Aqueducts, and the Photographs of them, and the Plates to that chapter.
[z] See Photos., Nos. 72, 305.

tine, the lower parts of which remain. There was a tunnel cut through the rock of the Palatine, and this remains visible at the north end, behind the church of S. Theodore, where the rock has been cut away, and it there makes another angle [a], turning towards the east in the direction of the bridge of Caligula. The later aqueducts always followed nearly the same line as the earlier ones; and there are remains of a reservoir and *specus* both cut out of the rock at the foot of the Capitoline Hill, nearly in a line with the north end of the bridge of Caligula; it is a little to the west of the steps that lead up to the municipal offices, and now under a wine-shop in the cellars at the back below the level of the street. This could only have belonged to the Anio Vetus; but the Anio Novus would be carried on the same line as a general rule, but with some deviation; they enter Rome in parallel lines, but the Anio Vetus on the northern side of the Porta Maggiore, and the great reservoir for it is on the line of the cliffs of the Esquiline Hill, not of the Cœlian; it is in that part nearly under the arches of the Marcia, not of the Anio Novus and Claudia. The great porticus of Nero, a mile long, against the cliff of the Esquiline, probably had the *specus* of the Marcia upon it, and that of the Anio Vetus under it. The Marcia supplied the thermæ of Titus, and with a branch to the Colosseum. The Anio Vetus was at too low a level for the reservoir in the gallery there, and went straight on under the Via Sacra to the Forum, and supplied the reservoir now under the wine-shop, where the *specus* also remains in a tunnel. The western part of the Ærarium, under the Tabularium, was turned into a reservoir for the water from an aqueduct in the third century, the time of Alexander Severus, when the temples in the Forum were rebuilt, and great changes were made. The public treasury had been transferred to some other place before this time.

The water of the Anio Novus could only have been brought on the high level, in the usual manner, into this Regio, by means of a lofty bridge from the Palatine Hill, and the bridge of the time of Caligula [b] seems to have been really built for this purpose; but as it passed close to the Basilica Julia on the western side of the Forum Romanum, this offended the people, and to pacify them the story of the Emperor going to consult Jupiter Capitolinus was invented; but the people were not satisfied, and the bridge was soon destroyed, excepting that part of it which forms the western part of the palace of Caligula, remains of which are still standing.

This completes the Forum Romanum properly so called, as far

[a] Photos., No. 3182.   [b] See Plate XXIV. of Forum.

as yet excavated; the eastern side is still buried (1875) under the modern road, and the houses, including the churches of S. Hadrian and S. Martina; the paved street turns right and left; there are two steps up to the Via Sacra (as has been said).

THE OTHER FORUMS.

It will be convenient under this head to enumerate all the other Forums or market-places of which we have any notice. In the Regionary Catalogue[c] eleven only are given, of these the six most important are the Forum Romanum, those of Julius Cæsar, Augustus, Nerva, Trajan, and Boarium. The remaining five are of secondary importance, and some of them are scarcely known by any other notice of them. On the other hand, some are omitted which are well known in other ways. The Forum Olitorium, or vegetable-market, was at the foot of the Capitoline Hill, towards the northwest, and there are remains of it near the theatre of Marcellus. The Forum Piscatorium, or fish-market, was probably always held on the same site that it is now, in the colonnade of the Porticus of Philippus, just outside of the Porta Triumphalis, the state entrance into THE CITY, which also separates the colonnade of Philippus, outside the City, from that of Octavia within it. The Forum Pacis of Vespasian, with the Temples of Peace and Rome facing to it, must have been of some importance. Yet of these only the Forum Boarium is mentioned, and others are introduced of which little is known, such as Forum Athenobarbi, which is supposed to have been on the Pincian Hill; Forum Suarium, or pig-market, is known by an inscription found by Panvinius in the seventeenth century, and by the Church of S. Nicolas in Porcibus, now of the Lucchesi, in the Via Lata; the Forum Pistorium, or of the Bakers, is known to have been on the Aventine. Those of the Gauls, Forum Gallorum, and of the country people, Forum Rusticorum, are only guessed at. The Forum of Cupid is mentioned by Varro near the Macellum, or meat-market, on the upper Via Sacra, and it is also mentioned by Terence; it was a market for country produce, such as apples and honey, perhaps the same as the Forum Rusticorum.

The Forum Sallustii was near his house, and garden, and Circus, between the Porta Collina and Porta Salaria, outside of THE CITY, but within the outer wall of Rome, in the part frequently called the Pomerium. The Forum Archemorium is said to have been

---

[c] That is, in the *Curiosum Urbis* and the *Notitia de Regionibus*; the Catalogue is in fact one, with slight variations.

under the Quirinal: the Forum Diocletiani—near his Thermæ: the Forum Exquilinum to have been the same as the Macellum Livianum, or meat-market of Livia, near the Arch of Gallienus.

The FORUM OF JULIUS CÆSAR. We are told by Dio Cassius that—

"the Forum of Julius Cæsar was built by that emperor. The Forum and the Temple of Venus, which he also founded, he consecrated in the year of Rome 708 (B.C. 45), with much splendour and many shows. On that occasion he built a wooden theatre called an amphitheatre, fit for the wild-beast shows and the gladiators who were exhibited. On that occasion the animal called a camel-leopard was first exhibited in Rome, having been brought to Rome by Cæsar for that purpose. Other games and races, both horse and foot, were exhibited in the circus on that occasion. According to the custom of the Romans, forty elephants with men on them also fought."

The Forum of Julius Cæsar was the one next adjoining to the Forum Romanum to the north-east[d], and therefore on the eastern side of the great Prison of the Kings, popularly called the Mamertine Prison; a massive building, which is mentioned by Vitruvius as forming an ornament to the north end of the Forum, along with the Capitolium and the Tabularium, of which it must have formed a sort of continuation. The prison was rebuilt in the time of Tiberius, as recorded on an inscription on the front, still *in situ;* but the subterranean chambers being very massively built, were not rebuilt, but treated as foundations only[e]. On the eastern side of the prison are remains of an arcade, or porticus, rebuilt of the old materials, the large blocks of tufa of the time of Servius Tullius, but each arch rests upon a block of travertine inserted in the time of the Early Empire. This porticus probably formed the western side of the Forum of Julius Cæsar. It is in a small court called the Vicolo del Ghettarello, and the whole space of the Forum is covered with modern houses and streets. It had the Forum of Augustus on the east, that of Trajan to the north, and that of Nerva to the south, but the only part now remaining visible is the building just before mentioned. The place called by Winckelmann *Spolia Christi*, from a church of that name, at the beginning of the Via Alessandrina, is believed to have been in this Forum, and on this spot the statue of Julius Cæsar, now in the Capitoline Museum, was found[f]. He also

---

[d] The land in this part of Rome was so valuable at that period, that Julius Cæsar is recorded to have paid an enormous sum for the site of his Forum, equal to upwards of eight hundred thousand pounds sterling. This is related by Suetonius, Julius Cæsar, c. 26.

[e] See Part I. of this work, Appendix, pp. 103–112; also Photos., Nos. 777, 778, 848, 849, and Plates VI., VII.

[f] Winckelmann ap. Fea Miscellanea, No. 18.

says that the tomb of a woman called Rufina, and the inscription upon it, was found there[g]; but there seems to be some mistake about this, unless this space was not included in the City of the two hills, which is possible. In that case, the tomb must be a very early one, and an inscription of this period is not probable, unless it was Etruscan. Remains of the Arch of Trajan, at the entrance of his Forum from the south, are also said to have been found on this site, with a number of marble tablets in bas-relief, one representing Trajan on horseback crossing a river, and figures of horsemen, similar to those on the Arch of Constantine[h].

An equestrian statue of Julius Cæsar stood in his Forum; it was of bronze gilt, and the horse was a remarkable work of art, said to have been the work of the celebrated Greek sculptor, Lysippus, and brought to Rome from Alexandria by Cæsar. Statius[i] sings the praises of this horse, and describes it as standing in the Forum of Cæsar. Donatus considers it to have been the horse of Domitian that was intended.

Of this once splendid Forum we have no remains visible, it is all built over by poor modern houses; all that we know is, that the east front of the great Prison of the Kings must have faced towards it, and the porticus, or double arcade, of which we have remains, formed the west side of that Forum. The southern front faced to the Forum Romanum, and its massive character is mentioned by Vitruvius as an ornament to the north end of the Forum, along with the Ærarium and the Curia. The Temple of Venus, in the Forum of Julius Cæsar, is also mentioned by Vitruvius as of the species called *Pychnostylis*[k]. Suetonius mentions the ceremonies at the dedication of the Forum[l]. Pliny mentions[m] that the roots of a lotus-tree, which grew in the area of Vulcan, extended into the Forum of Cæsar, passing by the Municipium.

---

[g] Winckelmann ap. Fea Miscellanea, No. 23.   [h] Ibid., No. 4.

[i] "Cedat equus, Latiæ qui contra templa Dionis
Cæsarei stat æde Fori. Quem tradere est ausus
Pellæ, Lysippe Duci, mox Cæsaris ora
Aurata cervice tulit . . ." (Statius, Silvæ, lib. i. 84.)

[k] Vitruvius de Architectura, v. 2. Remains of a temple found by Palladio on this spot are believed to have belonged to the Temple of Venus. Palladio says that these remains were found in his time opposite to the church of S. Martina (which he thought was the site of the Temple of Mars Ultor). He calls the district after the statue of Marforio, and a particular part of it he calls Pantano. He mentions also that the foundations of a temple remained, with a quantity of marble finely carved, with dolphins on a cornice, and a trident, which made him call it a temple of Neptune, but the same attributes belong to Venus also.

[l] Suetonius, Julius Cæsar, c. 26.
[m] Plinii Nat. Hist., xvi. 86.

FORUM OF AUGUSTUS. Of this Forum the eastern wall remains; it is a very fine and lofty wall, built of old materials, taken from the great wall of the time of the early Kings, which formed the second wall of Rome, and enclosed the two hills in one City; but it has been rebuilt with a cornice or corbel-table added, and plain strings of travertine inserted at intervals in the tufa wall. An arch has been made in it of the stone from Gabii, called *Sperone*, which was generally used in the time of the Republic. At the south end of this lofty wall, part of one of the old round towers of the time of the Kings has escaped by accident, by not falling in with the plan of the Forum, and has not been rebuilt. On the inner side of the wall of the Forum of Augustus are niches for statues[n], but these terminate with the wall that was rebuilt, and are not continued in the part which belonged to the old tower, that has not been rebuilt. This is now in the workshop of a stone-mason on the southern side of the arch. The other side of the old tower, with the travertine wall inserted into it, is also visible behind the houses, at the corner of the next street, in which the image of Pallas stands, but at the opposite end, and on the opposite side of the street[o].

Pliny mentions the Forum of Augustus among the great works of his time, along with the Basilica of Paulus Æmilius on the eastern side of the Forum Romanum, of which we have a representation on a coin[p] of A.D. 14, and the Pantheon of Agrippa, which he calls after Jupiter the Avenger.

The Temple of Mars Ultor is mentioned in the *Monumentum Ancyranum* as being in this Forum, and there are considerable remains of it against the east wall of it, which evidently stood there when the temple was built, for the cornice at that end rests upon the wall. The fine columns of which the upper part is visible, are only a small portion of it; that portico had eight columns, of which only four remain visible. The substructures and bases remain in the cellars of the monastery, and are shewn in Signor Cicconetti's plan of this Forum[q].

---

[n] These niches were obviously for the statues, mentioned by Suetonius (in Octavianus, c. 31), by Tacitus (Annal. ii. 67), and by Augustus himself in the *Monumentum Ancyranum*—

ET . IN . FORO . AVGVSTO . SVB . QVADRAGIS . QVAE . MIHI . EX . S . C . POSITAE . SVNT.

[o] The best way to see it is to pass through the "Caffè del Palladio," or from a balcony at the back of a house on the Via del Grillo. See the "Second Wall of Rome," in Plates VI., VII., VIII., of Supplement, and Photos. Nos. 853, 881, 3153, 3154.

[p] Photos., No. 490 n. "Nonne inter magnifica basilicam Pauli columnis e Phrygibus mirabilem, FORUMQUE DIVI AUGUSTI, et templum Pacis Vespasiani Imperatoris, Augusti, pulcherrima operum, quae unquam: Pantheon Jovi Ultori ab Agrippa factum, cum theatrum ante texerit Romae Valerius Ostiensis architectus ludis Libonis." (Plinii Nat. Hist., lib. xxxvi. c. 24.)

[q] See Plate VIII. of Supplement.

Forum of Nerva.

The Forum Transitorium was also called Palladium, from the figure of Pallas or Minerva, which still stands in the cornice over the site of a wayside altar dedicated to that goddess, which was at the entrance from the Forum to an open area between that and the Forum Romanum, called the area of Minerva. Martial [r] calls this Forum by the name of Palladium, and at the same time mentions the Forum Pacis in such a manner as to shew they were close together. This Forum was ornamented with colossal statues of the Emperors in marble, and columns of bronze by Alexander Severus, in imitation of Augustus, who had placed similar ornaments in his Forum; of this we are told by Lampridius [s]. This Forum was begun by Domitian, and finished by Nerva, as we are told by Suetonius [t]. It was also called Pervium, as Aurelius Victor mentions in his "Lives of the Cæsars [u]," and Martial in his Epigrams [v]. In the time of Pope Paul V., A.D. 1610, a temple was destroyed, which had stood here till that time; the marble was wanted for the great fountain that he made in the Janiculum, above the church of S. Pietro in Montorio [x].

An inscription of the time of the Emperor Nerva was on the marble casing under the figure of Pallas. It was carried to the fountain on the Janiculum, which was made by Palladio for the Pope, who gave him the marble of this temple or altar as building material. The old tufa wall was covered with marble, and had marble columns in front of it, three of which remain still, with the fine cornice and the figure of Pallas or Minerva. Palladio had some respect for antiquities, which his employers had not; and he preserved as much as he could of the old buildings given to him for materials, and made careful drawings of them, which are published in the fourth book of his work on architecture. The old tufa wall has the arch of a gate in it, filled up with old materials, but distinctly visible; and it is easy to see that the old tufa wall stood

---

[r] " Libertum docti Linensis quære secundi
Limina post Pacis Palladiumque Forum."
(Martialis Epigr., i. 3.)

[s] "Statuas colossas vel pedestres nudas vel equestres divis imperatoribus in foro divi Nervæ quod transitorium dicitur locavit, omnibus cum titulis et columnis aereis quæ gestorum ordinem continerent, exemplo Augusti qui summorum virorum statuas in foro suo e marmore collocavit additis gestis." (Script. Hist. Aug., Lampridius, Alexander Severus, c. 28.)

[t] Suetonius in Domitiano, c. 5.
[u] Aurel. Victor de Cæsar., c. 12.
[v] Martialis Epigr., x. 28.
[x] This inscription, then removed, was long visible on the wall of the fountain:—
IMP. NERVAE . CAES. AVG. PONT. MAX.
TRIB. POT. II. IMP. II. PROCOS.
Palladio has preserved drawings of it, which are engraved in his works.

there before, and was merely made use of, and cased with marble,—not erected for this temple or altar. This was more probably one of the wayside altars which were numerous in Rome, than a temple; there was a temple opposite to it, on the other side of the street.

The FORUM OF VESPASIAN, called also Forum Pacis, is not mentioned in the Regionary Catalogue, but must have been in the fourth Regio, which is named after the Templum Pacis, and joined on to the other market-places. It is mentioned by Symmachus by the name of Forum Vespasiani[y], and it is placed by Nardini in the third Regio, the Esquiline. The boundaries of the Regiones III. and IV. are very uncertain, the plans of these and others are entirely conjectural, and though generally correct, they cannot be depended on, upon doubtful points, on the boundary lines.

The architect of the Forum Pacis is said to have been Apollodorus, who directed most of the works of Trajan, and was considered the first architect of his day; and it is stated to have been built with great regularity and symmetry, and richly ornamented—so much so as to excite the warmest admiration from Constantius, as we are told by Ammianus Marcellinus[z]. It has been entirely built over with modern houses, and the exact site was not known until the beginning of the present century, when it was ascertained by excavations, and its principal direction traced, but many parts are still concealed by modern buildings.

This was a large Forum, and appears to have been made in part of the great foss of the second wall of Rome, with the cliff of the Velia faced by a wall at the south end, and that part of the old wall which still exists at the north end, with the ancient tower on which the Tor de Conti is built at the north-east corner, and the gate against which the marble columns and cornice, with the figure of Pallas or Minerva are placed, but on the opposite side, at the northwest; that wall separated the Forum of Vespasian from that of Nerva. It had the great temple of Rome on the western side, and the back of the temple of Antoninus and Faustina, the cell of which is built of the large tufa blocks taken from part of the second wall of Rome, which passed near them. These great blocks, of a ton weight, were not often carried far.

Procopius, writing in the sixth century, and describing what he saw, says that—

"a drove of oxen, driven from the fields round Rome, passed through the market-

---

[y] "... et quum ad Forum Vespasiani tam ego, quam vir spectabilis vicarius perurgente populo fuissemus ingressi ut quietem utriusque partis multitudini suaderemus," &c. (Symmachi Epist., lib. x. ep. 78, ed. 1617.)

[z] Ammianus Marcellinus, xvi. 10.

place, which the Romans call the Forum Pacis, because the Temple of Peace is in it. In front of the Forum is a certain old fountain, consisting of an ox of bronze, which I believe to be the work of Phidias, or of Lysippus the Athenian [a]."

The FORUM BOARIUM was the cattle-market or Smithfield of ancient Rome, and was connected with the Forum Romanum by the arch erected in honour of Septimius Severus by the silversmiths, who resided in that quarter, and are believed to have had their own market-place, called the Forum Argentarium. This is supposed to be implied by the inscription on the arch, which was erected at the expense of the merchants in the Forum Boarium and Argentarium. The Aqua Argentina runs into the Cloaca Maxima close to that arch: this was at the north-east corner of the Forum Boarium; the river Tiber formed the western side; its south end extended nearly to the cliff of the Aventine. Several temples stood in this Forum: the one best known is that usually called the Temple of Vesta, but was that of Hercules, as stated by Livy [b]. The principal temple of the Vestal Virgins was on the other side of the Palatine Hill, at the entrance to the Via Sacra, as before mentioned; one is mentioned to have been liable to be flooded by a high inundation of the Tiber, but such a flood may have reached the Forum Romanum. The church of S. Maria in Cosmedin is made out of two temples, one of which was probably that of Mater Matuta. The celebrated Bocca della Verita stands in the porch of this church. That mask of white marble with the mouth in it is of great antiquity, and the upper lip is cut in such a manner that it would slip up and down, so that a priest behind with a winch could fix the hand of any one whom he suspected of taking a false oath.

The FORUM OF TRAJAN is so closely connected with his other magnificent buildings, that it is impossible to separate them. They were all made in what had been originally the great foss of the Capitoline fortress, on the eastern side, in which was the road as usual; but this being too narrow for the purpose the great emperor had in view, he enlarged it on its eastern side by cutting away as much as was necessary of the tufa rock of that part of the Quirinal Hill. This is recorded on the base of the column, in an inscription which says that the rock cut away was of the same height as the top of the column, and we see the Tor delle Milizie now standing on the rock at that level. Under this, at the corner, is the east side of the Forum,

---

[a] Procopius de bello Gothico, lib. iv. c. 21.

[b] "Forum Boarium, or cattle-market, ... the chapel of patrician chastity which stands in the cattle-market, near the Round Temple of Hercules." (Livy, book x. c. 23.)

with a double row of shops, one on the level of the market-place, of which the old pavement remains in front of them, the other on a ledge of the rock behind and above them. This peculiar arrangement of the double row of shops round the market-place at different levels was followed by the Romans in the city of Chester in England on the border of Wales[e]. The triumphal arch of Trajan was at the entrance to his Forum from the south, that is, from the Forum of Augustus. Beyond the Forum northwards are the remains of the Basilica Ulpia, of which we see the bases of the columns, and part of the columns themselves, magnificent masses of granite, some of which, lying flat, were used as foundations for the Palazzo Valentini, which is on the site of the Temple of Trajan, on the other side of his celebrated column on which is carved, in a beautiful winding series of bassi-relievi, the whole history of his Dacian war. On the western side of his Forum, against the foot of the Palatine, the curve is visible in the line of houses, but the only remains are in the cellars.

But these great works of Trajan afford quite material enough for another volume, and cannot conveniently be added to the Forum Romanum; topographically also they lie to the north of it, and the southern line—along the Via Sacra, up the Clivus Sacer, and again along the Summa Sacra Via—is the line on which the great excavations have been made during the last two or three years, leading on to the Colosseum, where equally important excavations are still going on [in 1875]. The Forum of Trajan will probably follow in a few years, and then will be the better time to publish an account of them.

---

[e] The remains of these ancient shops are now, in part, public property, and the key of the yard in which they stand is now kept by a keeper near the spot, who shews also the Column of Trajan. Another part of the second series of these shops is in the garden of a palace, and not open to the public, but can be clearly seen from the garret-windows at the back of the houses in the Via del Grillo. A third series of shops, at a still higher level, can be traced on the summit of the rock, and at the foot of the Tor delle Milizie, now in a barrack-yard, to which access is easily obtained.

REGIONARY CATALOGUE.

Preface.

The plan on which this work was commenced in 1865, was to divide Rome into the fourteen Regiones of the time of Augustus and of the fourth century, and endeavour to give some account of all the objects mentioned in the Regionary Catalogue, and of the churches and other buildings on the same site; at the same time to investigate the line of the aqueducts, with Frontinus for a guide, and to trace their course through the city and the suburbs, which we saw would throw light on many other objects of interest; and to examine the Catacombs so closely connected with the history of the churches, that one would not be complete without the other. After a considerable part of the work had been prepared in this manner, the great excavations that were going on began to upset so many of the ideas usually entertained, that it was necessary to wait and watch them.

The number of pits that we had dug in various parts of Rome in searching for the Walls of the Kings, and the line of the subterranean and other aqueducts, especially about the Porta Capena, excited a good deal of attention, and led Napoleon III. to carry on his great excavation in the Farnese gardens, on the Palatine, for *historical objects*, and not only in search of statues, as he had begun. Then came the enormous excavations for THE NEW CITY on the hills, on the site of the city of the Kings and of the Empire, which are hardly yet terminated, and the Italian Government going on with their great work in the Forum Romanum, the Via Sacra, and the Colosseum. All this has compelled us to change our plan, and make use of the materials we had collected in another form, as here presented to our readers.

But the Regionary Catalogue can still be used as an index to this portion of the work. By the Regionary Catalogue is understood that of the *Notitia de Regionibus* and the *Curiosum Urbis* combined; they are the same catalogue, with slight variations. Nearly all the objects mentioned in this catalogue for the eighth Regio are described in the previous part of the present chapter, and the Regionary Catalogue may now be used as a sort of index to it, adding notices of such things as are not already included. In most instances a reference to the page where it is described is sufficient, but in few instances, where no remains have been found, notes are here added, following the Catalogue.

Regio VIII.

Forum Romanum Magnum.

Continet:

	Page		Page
Rostra tria	11 and 25	Templum—Castorum	9
Genium Populi Romani auream	13 and 46	———— Minervæ	22
Equum Constantini [a]	19	———— Vestam	46
Senatum	7	Horrea Germaniciana et Agrippiana	,,
Atrium Minervæ	40		
Forum—Cæsaris	37	Aquam cernentem	,,
———— Augusti	39	Quatuor Scauros (or Scaros)	,,
———— Nervæ	40	Sub æde (ædem)	,,
———— Trajani	43	Atrium Caci	,,
Templum Divi Trajani		Vicum Jugarium [c]	47
Columnam cochlidem altam pedes cxxviii semis, Tradus intus habet clxxxv, Fenestras xlv.		Porticum Margaritarium	,,
		Elefantum Herbarium	,,
		Vici xxxiv.	,,
Cohortem sextam Vigilum	46	Ædiculæ xxxiv.	,,
Basilicam Argentariam	,,	Vicomagistri xlviii.	48
Templum Concordiæ	8	Curatores ii.	,,
———— Saturni.		Insulæ iiicccclxxx.	,,
———— Vespasiani	9	Domus cxxx.	,,
———— et Titi [b]	15	Horrea xviii.	,,
Umbilicum Romæ	13	Balnea lxxxvi.	,,
Capitolium	4	Lacos cxx.	,,
Miliarium aureum	13	Pistrina xx.	,,
Græcostadium	8	Pedes xiii. lxvii.—Curiosum tredecim milia lxvii.—Notitia.	
Basilicam Juliam	19		

[a] Equum Constantini is in the *Notitia* only.
[b] et Titi occurs in the *Notitia* only, not in the *Curiosum Urbis*.
[c] Vicum Jugarii also occurs in the *Curiosum* only.

To the mention of the Genius Populi Romani, the second object mentioned in the catalogue after the Rostra, and which stood in the centre of Rome, near the Arch of Septimius Severus, as is mentioned on page 13, it should be added that an inscription was found on that site, on which had probably been the base of the statue [d].

Cohors VI. *Vigilum.* Where this great barrack of the sixth corps of the *Vigili*, or night guards, was situated, has not yet been discovered; a probable place for it seems to be in the valley between the Palatine and the Capitol, nearly opposite to the Church of S. Theodore, where Pius IX. built a large sort of barrack for the reception of the numerous foreign missionary bishops who were brought back to Rome from South America and other parts, to vote for the doctrine of the Infallibility of the Pope being made an article of the Faith in 1872.

The Basilica Argentaria is supposed to have stood near the smaller Arch of Septimius Severus, erected by the (*Argentarii*) or silversmiths, to the honour of that emperor.

The Temple of Vesta was not actually in the Forum, but so close to it that it is often so mentioned, and is included in this Regio. The remains of it were found in 1874, and an account of it is given in our section on the Via Sacra, in which it actually stands within a few yards of the Forum, but a step higher.

Horrea, &c. Where these great barns or warehouses were situated has not yet been ascertained.

Aquam Cernentem, &c. It has been conjectured that a fish-pond for this rare fish was made from the subterranean stream that still rises behind the Church of S. Hadrian, and which now falls into the Cloaca Maxima in the Forum. It may have been under a temple, if *ædem* is the correct reading of the word.

Atrium Caci. Of this no account is given, and no remains found; it may be conjectured to have been a small court, with an image of that mythical personage. Some have proposed to read *antrum*, and make this the Cave of Cacus, but the legend certainly

---

[d] GENIO . EXERCITVS
QVI . EXTINGVENDIS . SAEVISSIMIS . LATRONIB
FIDE . ET . DEVOTIONE . ROM . EXSPECTAT
VOTIS . OMNIVM . SATISFECIT.
This is given by Gruter, p. cix. num. 3, and copied by Nardini.

places that cave on the Aventine, where a cave exists, which fits the legend; there is no such cave in this Regio.

Vicus Jugarius. This was the street that led from the Forum Romanum to the Porta Carmentalis, under the Capitoline hill on the northern side. It is mentioned by Livy in describing the entry of two white cows into THE CITY from the Temple of Apollo in the suburbs; they came through that gate along the Vicus Jugarius to the Forum [e]. This Temple of Apollo was in the Flaminian meadow [f]. Also, on the occasion of the great fire, which lasted two days and nights (B.C. 213), it burnt everything between the *Salinæ*, or salt-wharf, in this part of Rome, and the Porta Carmentalis, with the streets of Aquimaelius and Jugarius.

Porticus Margaritarius. This has been conjectured by Nibby to be a portico or colonnade in the small court where the statue of Mars or Marforius was placed, in front of the great prison, but no authority for this conjecture has been found.

Elefantus Herbarius. According to some authors this was a statue of an elephant, erected by Augustus; according to others it was a yew-tree, or perhaps a box-tree, or a cedar, cut into that form, which seems more probable from the name. The situation of it is shewn by the Ordo Romanus, or bull of Anocletus II., as being in the street under the Capitoline hill, on its northern side, made in the old foss, called in its eastern part Via della Pedacchia, and in the western Via di Tor de' Specchi [g].

Vici xxxiv.

Ædiculæ xxxiv. It will be observed that the number of Ædiculæ is always the same as the number of streets in each Regio. These are believed to have been *way-side altars* at the corners of the streets, and that the one remaining of Pallas or Minerva, at the corner of the Forum Transitorium, is an example. But it is probable that they were generally small structures of bronze, of the same kind as the Jani. The level of the streets of Rome has been raised at least fifteen feet in many parts, and more in some, and it is certain that the same line was not *always* followed for the streets, though it often was; it seems, therefore, useless to trace the thirty-four streets in this Regio, which include those on the

---

[e] "A porta, Jugario vico, in forum venere." (Livii Hist., xxvii. 37.)
[f] "Solo aequata omnia inter Salinas ac portam Carmentalem cum Æquimaelio Jugarioque vico." (Ibid., xxiv. 47.)

[g] "Ab alio latere via publica, quae ducit sub Capitolium . . . usque in templum majus, quod respicit super elephantum. A tertio latere," &c. (Ordo Romanus.)

Capitoline hill, and on the slopes, and at the foot of it, and on all sides of it. The number may be traced on the map without much difficulty, but there can be no certainty that the lines are the same: there are usually two streets meeting at each gate, and forking off from it on each side, and there were several gates in this Regio.

The *Vico-Magistri, Curatores,* and *Denuntiatores* are official persons, not places.

Insulæ, 3480. These could only have been the dwellings of the people, one for each family, what the French call an *appartement*,— the Scotch, a flat,—and the English, chambers or lodgings,—*insulated* from the rest of the house, and which the Romans of this day call *a house*. It is not possible to place the number on the ground in any other manner.—Another meaning of the word is an insulated block of houses with streets on all sides, but that signification is not applicable here. The marble plan of Rome shews a number of *insulæ* along the sides of the streets everywhere. The shops that remain in the Forum of Trajan, with a room above, or behind, or both, is an *insula*[h].

Domus, 130. These are what are now called in Rome "palaces," the residence of some great family.

Horrea, 18. Large barns, or public warehouses.

Balnea, 86. Bath chambers.

Lacos, 120. Cisterns, or reservoirs of water, of any size, called also Castella Aquæ.

Pistrina, 20. Bake-houses.

Continet pedes, 1467. This probably means the number of superficial feet in the Regio, although Victor reads it *in ambitu*, or in circuit; the number of feet will not agree on the latter plan.

[h] The following inscription can hardly be reconciled with the *insulæ* being blocks of buildings.
INSVLAS AD PRISTINVM STATVM SVVM SECVNDVM LEGES PRINCIPVM PRIORVM IMPP. L. SEPTIMI SEVERI ET AVR. ANTONINI RESTAVRARI ATQVE ADORNARI . . . PROVIDIT. (Gruter, 1090. 19.)

TEMPLE OF VESTA.

The excavations in 1875 extended rather beyond the limits of the Forum Romanum strictly so called, and into the Via Sacra; the circular Temple of Vesta [1] was in that street, and not in the Forum; the podium or basement of this temple, of the time of the Kings, was cleared out, and a passage made round it on the level of the original pavement. It stands just in front of the modern church of S. Maria Liberatrice [2], which is recorded to have been on the site of the Regia, or royal palace of the Kings. This, during the whole period of the Republic, was the residence of the Pontifex Maximus, as the real head of the State as well as the Church. When Augustus was made Pontifex Maximus, he refused to leave the house of Hortensius, which he had previously bought, and where he then resided, and gave the Regia to the Vestal Virgins as their residence, because it was close to their temple; and when the church was built on this site in the seventeenth century, a number of inscriptions with the names of Vestal Virgins upon them, were found, on what had evidently been the bases of statues; this thoroughly identifies the site. But the Regia was always considered as on the Palatine, because, although it stood on the level ground, it was within the original wall of that fortress, or fortified hill, to which the line of the Via Sacra was the ditch or foss. The piece of sculpture of the time of the Republic, representing Mettius Curtius [k] on horseback, leaping into the gulf near the spot, was also found on the site of this church. This is now preserved by being built into the wall on the staircase of the Palazzo del Conservatore in the Piazza del Campidoglio.

The first mention of this temple is by Dionysius [l], as belonging to the earliest period of Roman history; and the construction of the wall of the basement, or *podium*, of it, excavated in 1874-75, is as rude and early-looking as it well could be [m].

"Numa, after his accession to the government, did not remove the particular temples belonging to the curiæ, but erected one temple common to them all between the Capitoline and Palatine hills. For both these hills had already been

---

[1] Photos., No. 3149.
[2] Photos., No. 3195 *.
[k] Photos., No. 1658. The witness of this finding is Flaminius Vacca, in his *Memorie*, or Memoranda of what he had seen; printed by Fea in his Miscellanea, No. III.   [l] Book ii. c. 66.
[m] See the plan of the Via Sacra for the exact site, and Photos., No. 3249, for the aspect of the podium.

encompassed with one wall; the Forum, in which this temple was built, lying between them. He also enacted that the keeping of the holy things, according to the custom established among the Latins, should be committed to virgins."

Cicero [n] also mentions a mysterious voice being heard from this temple, warning the people of the approaching capture of the city by the Gauls, and says it was at the foot of the Palatine, and on the slope towards the Nova Via; from this it appears that there was another street close under the Palatine, then called "the New Street," parallel to the Via Sacra, on the opposite side of the valley.

Horace [o], in a well-known passage, speaks of a great flood of the Tiber extending to the Regia and the temple of Vesta, as something marvellous. In the great flood of 1870 the water again rose as high as that point, but such instances are very rare; it must be a very extraordinary flood to reach so high.

Livy [p] relates the legend of the mysterious voice of warning of the capture of the city by the Gauls. In all these passages he also speaks of this temple as being in the Nova Via; the words of Augustus place it in front of the Regia, the site of which is identified (as we have shewn), and it follows that the Nova Via, or new road, in this part of Rome, was on the western side of this valley of the Palatine, and close under the north-east corner of that hill. Yet the modern Romans now place the legend of the mysterious warning voice at the altar at the north-west corner, close to the church of S. Anastasia on the Germalus, near the Velabrum.

THE REGIA.—This well-known historical building is on the Palatine: that is, it was within the line of the outer wall of the ancient fortress; but again, it is so close to the Forum, and so nearly connected with it, that it seems more natural and more convenient to give some account of it here. The site has been identified (as has been said) by the inscriptions found there, A.D. 1556, when the church of S. Maria Liberatrice was built, and the site agrees with all the passages relating to it in the classical authors.

Solinus [q] says that :—

"Numa resided first on the Quirinal hill (doubtless in the Capitolium Vetus of the Regionaries), then near the temple of Vesta in the Regia, as it is still called."

[n] "Nam non multo ante Urbem captam exaudita vox est a luco Vestæ, qui a Palatii radice in novam viam devexus est." (Cicero de Divinationes, lib. i. c. 45.)

[o] "Vidimus flavum Tiberim, retortis Litore Etrusco violenter undis, Ire dejectum monimenta regis Templaque Vestæ." (Horatii lib. i. ode 2.)

[p] Livii Hist., lib. v. c. 32—50, and 52.

[q] Solinus, c. 1.

Temple of Vesta.

Virgil alludes to it in his account of the settlement of Evander, and Servius[r], in his commentary on the passage, exclaims:—

"Who is ignorant that Numa dwelt in the Regia at the foot of the Palatine, near the Forum Romanum."

Ovid[s] speaks of

"the narrow space that held the courts of Vesta, where had been the great Regia of the bearded Numa."

Aulus Gellius[t] mentions

"Vestal virgins having been caught and taken to the courts of Vesta, and given up to the pontiff."

In another passage Servius[u] repeats that

"The court of Vesta was in the Regia of Numa Pompilius, and to be near this temple, and that this was not consecrated to the augurs, nor yet a place of assembly for the senate, but the virgins were there."

That temple is not mentioned as in the Via Sacra, although it is on the same line as that of Antoninus, and above the steps at the south end of the Forum; it is therefore included in our account of the Forum. It appears to have stood in the Via Nova, mentioned by Cicero as a new road in his time, or at least so called, and this must have been parallel to the Via Sacra, but close under the cliff of the Palatine; and the arch of Titus must have been upon it, at the southern end, while the north end of the Via Nova must be the paved street down the middle of the Forum, with the steps of the Basilica Julia on the western side of it. The continuation of the Via Sacra must have been parallel to this, nearly on the line of the present road, but twenty feet below the level of it, and passing under the arch of Septimius Severus into the capitol, on the eastern side of the Porta Saturni of Varro, while the Via Nova entered the old Capitoline fortress on the western side of the wall of partition between the double gate, which remains *in situ*. It had been observed that the pavement on that side was of the time of the Republic, while that on the other side is of the time of the early Empire. So that the Via Sacra and the continuation of it had been re-paved at that time, and the Via Sacra had not.

---

[r] Servii in Virgil. Æneid., lib. viii. p. 263.

[s] Ovidii Fasti, lib. vi. c. 263.

[t] "Virgo autem Vestalis simul est capta atque in atrium Vestæ deducta et pontificibus tradita [est]: eo statim tempore sine emancipatione ac sine capitis minutione e patris potestate exit et jus testamenti faciundi adipiscitur. De more autem ritu quæ capiunde virginis literæ quidem antiquiores non exstant, nisi, quæ capta prima est, a Numa rege esse captam." (Aulus Gellius, lib. i. c. 12.)

[u] "Unde templum Vestæ non fuit augurio consecratum, ne illuc conveniret senatus: ubi erant virgines. Nam hæc fuerat regia Numæ Pompilii. Ad atrium autem Vestæ conveniebat (al. sane Vestæ conveniebatur), quod a templo remotum fuerat." (Servii in Æneid., lib. vii. c. 153.)

VIA NOVA.—There has been a great deal of discussion about *the* Via Nova in Rome, and it is one of the questions considered as still undecided; but may not the better translation be *a* Via Nova? and may there not have been *many* new ways or new streets in Rome? In fact, it is well known that there was another street called also by this name, near the Thermæ of Caracalla, where a deviation was made in the line of the old Via Appia in that part; and it is evident from the treatise on the Aqueducts by Frontinus, that he uses the name Via Nova for what is now called the Via Appia Nova; at two miles from Rome he mentions a *Castellum Aqua* of the Anio Vetus, as on the Via Nova; and this ancient reservoir of the first century or earlier, has been found (by some excavations made for the Archæologists in 1870) at exactly two miles from the Porta Maggiore and from the Porta Latina: it happens to be exactly the same distance from each of these gates, because the first Regio, in which the Porta Latina is situated, projects so much from the direct line of the wall, that this Castellum or reservoir makes exactly the point of a triangle, as may be seen by measuring it on the map. There must have been many other new streets in Rome at many different periods[x]. This Via Nova, near the Forum Romanum, is frequently mentioned by the classical writers, and it had long been doubtful which was the direct line of it; this seems now to be settled, as so many other long-disputed questions have been by the recent excavations. The remains of the Temple of Vesta brought to light in 1874, being in the Via Nova, this street must have gone close under the eastern side of the Palatine. It will be remembered that this was the temple erected between the two hills, when they were first united in one city, and enclosed in one wall, as we are told by Dionysius[x].

---

[x] The name might also be retained for a long period, like New College in Oxford, which still retains that name, though it was built in the fourteenth century. In recent times in Rome also, the Via Nuova, near the fountain of Trevi, retained the name for three centuries, from the time of Sixtus V., the founder of the modern Rome of the Popes, from 1574 until 1874, when the municipality thought proper to change the name to Via del Panetteria, or street of the bake-house, apparently on the principle of *lucus a non lucendo*, since there is no bake-house in the street.

[x] Dionysius, Rom. Ant., bk. ii. c. 66.

MONUMENTUM ANCYRANUM.

This document is without doubt the most important of Latin historical inscriptions, and is of great value for the topography of the city, and particularly of the Forum. It is a summary of the acts and achievements of Augustus, written by him a year and four months before his death. In his will, to which it was attached, he ordered that it should be incised on bronze plates, and set up in front of his mausoleum in the Campus Martius, on the bank of the Tiber^y. Copies of it were also sent to the cities which he had founded, amongst others to Ancyra, the metropolis of Galatia, where it was inscribed on marble instead of bronze, and by that means has been fortunately preserved. It was accompanied by a Greek translation, of which some fragments are found at Ancyra, and others of no great magnitude at Apollonia. The text and Greek version have been carefully edited by Th. Mommsen[z], and recently by Bergk[a]. The matter is divided into three parts: 1. the honours which he received on account of his services to the commonwealth; 2. the expenses which he incurred by various acts of popular liberality, including the erection and restoration of public buildings, to which the attention of the reader is specially directed; 3. a summary of his acts at home and abroad.

At Ancyra it was placed in the temple of *Divus Augustus*, in the Middle Ages turned into a Christian church; then into the Mosque of Hadj Beira in the fifteenth century: since this time it has been used by the Turks as a cemetery. Scholars had long been anxious to obtain a more accurate account of it, which has now been supplied. It was described by Tournefort in his *Voyage du Levant* (Leyden, 1717). His copy was edited, with the help of other materials, by Chishull, in 1728, but without the requisite accuracy. That of Paul Lucas, made about the same time, is of greater value. Several travellers have visited the monument during the present century, such as Texier, Kinneir, and Hamilton, but no new copy was published till that of Mordtmann, who was sent out for the purpose in 1859, by the Berlin Academy. This formed the basis of Zumpt and Franz's edition. It has now been superseded by that made in 1861, under the direction of Napoleon III., by George Perrot and Edmond Guillaume, which is extremely accurate. Reproductions of it were published in the *Bullettino dell' Instituto*, 1861, and *Correspondance de l'Académie*, 1862, from the last of which our reduction is taken[b].

---

[y] Suetonii Octavianus, c. 101; cp. Tac. ii Annales, i. 11.
[z] "Res gestæ DIVI AUGUSTI ex monumentis Ancyrano et Apollonensi, edidit Th. Mommsen, accedunt Latinæ tres." Berlin, 1865, 8vo.
[a] "Augusti rerum a se gestarum index cum Græca metaphrasi, ed. Th. Bergk." Gottingen, 1873, 8vo.
[b] See Plates XXVIII., XXIX.

THE Church of S. Martina[e] and S. Luca, although entirely rebuilt, is on an ancient site, on which there has been a church from a very early period. It was formerly called *S. Martina in tribus Foris*[d], from its vicinity to the three Forums, Romanum, of Augustus, and of Julius Cæsar. It is at the north-east corner of the Forum Romanum, close to the Arch of Septimius Severus, and on the direct way to the other two Forums.

The earliest mention of this church that has been noticed is, that Leo III. repaired the roof of it in the beginning of the ninth century, as recorded by Anastasius. This only proves that the church was then in existence, and probably not new, or it would not have needed repairs. It was rebuilt and consecrated as a parish church by Alexander IV. in 1255, and so continued until, in 1588, Sixtus V. gave it to the Society of Artists, who established themselves there, and gave it the name of S. Luke, the care of souls being divided among other neighbouring parish churches. About 1630 Cardinal Barberini, under his uncle, Urban VIII., wished to rebuild the church according to the bad taste of his age; accordingly the body of S. Martina, who had been martyred A.D. 230, was conveniently found, and the church was entirely rebuilt, the architect being P. Berettini da Cortona, who gave part of his own house to enlarge it, and at his death left his fortune of 100,000 scudi to the academy. The plan of the church is a Greek cross, with a large dome over the centre. The altar is of bronze gilt, with a fine bas-relief, representing S. Martina at the foot of the Virgin; her relics are in a sarcophagus in the crypt. Round the sanctuary are eight columns of *pavonazetto*, and four of *cipollino;* and

---

[e] Photos., No. 306.

[d] "Publica opera plurima exstruxit; in quibus vel præcipua, Forum cum æde Martis Ultoris, templum Apollinis in Palatio, ædem Tonantis Jovis in Capitolio. Fori exstruendi caussa fuit hominum et judiciorum multitudo, quæ videbatur, non sufficientibus duobus, etiam tertio indigere. Itaque festinantius, nec dum perfecta Martis æde, publicatum est cautumque, ut separatim in eo publico judicio, et sortitiones judicum fierent. Ædem Marti bello Philippensi, pro ultione paterna, suscepto, voverat. Sanxit ergo ut de bellis triumphisque hic consuleretur Senatus; provincias cum imperio petituri hinc deducerentur, quique victores redissent huc insignia triumphorum inferrent." (Suetonius in Augusto, c. 29.)

"Mars ædes: et satia scelerato sanguine ferrum;
Stetque favor causa pro meliore tuus.
Templa feres, et, me victore, vocaberis Ultor.
Voverat, et fuso lætus ab hoste redit.
Nec satis est meruisse semel cognomina Marti:
Persequitur Parthi signa retenta manu."

(Ovidii Fasti, lib. v. 575.)

in the apse a marble seat of the thirteenth century, with sculpture. This church contains the tomb of the learned Cardinal Baronius. The church contains several good paintings, and the tombs of celebrated painters; in the crypt is the tomb of the architect and second founder, P. da Cortona.

THE CHURCH OF S. HADRIAN or Adrian was founded by Honorius I., c. A.D. 626, and the outer walls are still of that period, of good brickwork[e], but quite plain. The interior has been altered and renewed several times. It was repaired by Hadrian I. A.D. 772, as recorded by Anastasius, who describes it, like its neighbour S. Martina, as *in tribus foris*, misprinted in one place, *in tribus fatis*. Pope Anastasius III. again repaired it in 913. In the middle ages there was a custom of washing the feet of a celebrated image of the Saviour at this church on certain occasions, when it was carried in procession. Near the door of the sacristy is an inscription of A.D. 1228, recording the finding of the bodies of S. Martha, S. Adrian, and the three Hebrew children thrown into the burning fiery furnace by order of King Nebuchadnezzar, Shadrach, Meshech, and Abednego (!), whose relics (!) are said to be deposited under an altar, which is ornamented with two columns of *verd-antique*.

CHURCH OF S. GEORGE AND S. SEBASTIAN, or S. GEORGIO IN VELABRO[f].

The first record of this church is, that it was in existence in the time of Pope Gregory I., who instituted a Cardinal deacon, c. A.D. 600. It was rebuilt by Pope Leo II., A.D. 683, in honour of S. Sebastian and S. George, the two military martyrs. Next, that the apse was rebuilt and adorned with a mosaic picture by Pope Zacharias, A.D. 742—752. But this early apse was decayed in the time of Gregory IV., A.D. 827, and entirely rebuilt by him.

The whole church was again rebuilt by Prior Stephen in the thirteenth century. The plan of the church is that of a basilica, with aisles and an apse: the sixteen columns are antique, including the capitals; some Ionic, others Corinthian; some of granite, others of marble; some fluted, others plain;—a very clear proof of their being brought from antique buildings, as is so often the case in Rome. These columns carry small round arches, which support the wall of the clerestory, the windows of which are modern. The roof

---

[e] Photos., No. 908.
[f] RIONE X. This church is not, properly speaking, in any Forum, but in the Velabrum; that site is, however, closely connected with the Forum Boarium, and this seems the most convenient place for a short account of the church. It is also called Ad Velum Aureum in an inscription, A.D. 1259.

of the church is quite plain, flat, and boarded, but not ancient; it was probably intended to have had a flat panelled ceiling as usual, the modern over-wrought ceilings being only a corruption of the mediæval flat ceilings. In front of the church is a fine PORTICO, quite of classical character, and made of antique columns, but really built by Prior Stephen in the middle of the thirteenth century, which he has taken care to record by an inscription on the entablature [g]. The iron railing is modern, but the old rings, for hanging the curtains or veils, remain in their places on the soffits of the stonework under the entablature. The Ionic capitals and bases are part of the work of the thirteenth century, the columns only being antique. The doorway is also quite of classical character, both the jambs and the lintel having classical mouldings. Doorways of this character are so common in Rome, that it may well be doubted whether they are not often imitations of classical models: that the antique columns should be preserved, and used again was quite natural, but that so many classical doorways should also be preserved, taken to pieces, and put together again so cleverly, that they seem made for the place they occupy, is hardly credible. In the present instance, however, the jambs and the lintel do not fit well together, and are antique.

At first sight it appears to the eyes of an English antiquary absolutely incredible that this purely classical portico can really be the work of the middle of the thirteenth century, yet no historical fact can well be established by more clear evidence [h]. The inscription is in the characters of the time: the Prior, afterwards Cardinal, is buried in the church, and the inscription on his tombstone records his benefactions to the church. The mouldings of the pediment are those used in Rome in the twelfth and thirteenth centuries. Those of the CAMPANILE adjoining are identical with them, and prove that also to be part of the work of Prior Stephen.

This campanile stands at the north end of the west front; the outer wall of it on the north side is built upon one side of the arch of Septimius Severus, close to the Arcus Quadrifrons or Janus, with its four arches. The south wall of the campanile forms in its lower part the side wall of the nave of the church so far as it extends;

[g] *On the front of the porch:—*
STEFANUS EX STELLA CUPIENS CAPTARE SUPERNA
ELOQUIO RARUS, VIRTUTUM LUMINE CLARUS
EXPENDENS AURUM STUDVIT RENOVARE PRONAUM
SUMPTIBUS EX PROPRIIS TIBI FECIT SANCTE GEORGI
CLERICUS HIC CUJUS PRIOR ECCLESIE FUIT HUJUS
HIC LOCUS AD VELUM PRÆNOMINE DICITUR AURI.

[h] It is actually engraved in some English works of good reputation as an example of the classical period. See Photos., Nos. 196, 390, 1092.

the east wall of the campanile forms the west end of the north aisle of the church: several fragments of ornamental work from the old church are built into this wall. It is a very fine campanile, and valuable for helping to date others by comparison, where the history is less clearly known. This has six storeys above the roof, with the usual open windows, with marble mediæval shafts, and each of the storeys separated by a cornice or corbel-table, as in all the other mediæval campaniles in Rome.

Fragments of the ornamentation of the old church are built into the walls of the present one. The altar[i], with the confessio under it and the baldachino over it, are good examples of the church furniture of the thirteenth century in Rome, with Cosmati-work. At the end of the south aisle are several Pagan inscriptions, brought from the Catacombs, and built into the wall. The inscription on the tombstone of Cardinal Capocci is on the north side of the apse[k]. The walls of the church are of brickwork, of the thirteenth century, built upon old foundations, which are visible in places.

The walls of the convent are of several periods, part of the ninth, of small stones, with layers of tiles; another portion of brickwork of the twelfth century, another of the thirteenth, and the rest more modern. Part of the mosaic pavement of the thirteenth century remains on the floor of the apse. The south doorway belongs to the work of the ninth century.

From an expression in the account given by Anastasius, it appears that it was the custom in this church to separate the sexes, and that the north side was the women's side. The same custom is maintained at S. Peter's. A similar custom is common in many old-fashioned churches, both in England and France, but it does not appear to have ever been a universal practice or a rule. The custom of placing nuns in galleries behind grilles is common in Rome, though all these grilles are modern; there is one in the cathedral of Rheims, at the end of the north transept, which is mediæval, nearly as old as the cathedral itself.

---

[i] See Photos., Nos. 1254 and 1255.
[k] IN NOMINE DOMINI, AMEN. DOMINUS PETRUS CAPOCCIUS HUJUS ECCLESIE SANCTI GEORGII CARDINALIS LEGAVIT HUIC ECCLESIE TERRAS SUAS EXTRA URBEM DICTE ECCLESIE QUE DICITUR AD VALLARANUM EO DICTE ERI ALIQUO TITULO ALIENARI NON POSSINT ET TENEANTUR CLERICI HUJUS ECCLESIE ANNUATIM DICTE CARDINALIS ANNIVERSARIUM SOLEMPNITER CELEBRARE ET CAPITULUM IPSIUS ECCLESIE JURAVIT OMNIA SUPRADICTA INVIOLABILITER OBSERVARE ET STATUIT DE CLERO NULLUM RECIPERE NISI PRIUS JURET SERVARE OMNIA SUPRADICTA ANNIVERSARIUM VERO PREDICTUM FIERI DEBET XIII. KL. JUNII QUOTIESQUE LEGERIT OBIIT PRO FACTUM EST HOC ANNO D.M.CCLIX. CONFIRMATUS DOMINI ALEXANDRI IV. PAPE ANNO V.

S. THEODORE[1].

The church of S. Theodore at Rome was erected by Pope Adrian I., c. A.D. 790, on the ruins of a round Temple[m]. It has a mosaic on the hemispherical vault or tribune, behind the altar, which is supposed to be original; at the top is the hand of the Almighty holding a crown over the head of Christ, who is seated on a globe and holds a long cross in His left hand. To the right of the figure of Christ is S. Paul, with the book in his hand, presenting a young man who carries a crown on a rich cushion; to the left is S. Peter presenting S. Theodore. This mosaic has been much restored in the fifteenth century, the parts that are original may be of the eighth.

The exterior of this circular church is as plain as possible, a mere mass of brickwork. The interior, with the exception of the apse, has been entirely rebuilt, and deprived of all interest, by Nicholas V. in 1450; his arms are on the vault and over the doorway; and again restored by Clement XI. in 1704. There appear to be no other grounds for saying it is built on the site of the temple of Vesta, than its circular form, on the old foundations. The chief ground for thinking that the conjecture may be true is, that the matrons of Rome and the neighbourhood continue to bring their children to be blessed every Thursday morning, just as they did to the heathen temple before the Christian era. The construction of the brickwork is not of ancient character, and it has large pointed windows of single lights, badly proportioned and clumsy, such as are usually of the fifteenth century in Rome. The old apse, with the mosaics, which has been preserved, is quite of different character from the rest, being built of rough stone. The clerestory and roof of the central space are modern; the vault has a stone covering under the roof, which seems to have been originally open to the weather; but, as in other instances, was probably not found water-tight. The interior is plain, and quite modern in appearance, with the exception of the apse with the mosaic.

---

[1] RIONE X. REGIO X. This church is, strictly speaking, on the Palatine; that is, within the boundary of it; but the entrance is from below, in the street that leads from the Forum Romanum to the Forum Boarium. It is only open at certain hours, and persons wishing to see it should bespeak the key of the Sacristan.

[m] This is generally considered to be that of Augustus, but Dr. Fabio Gori, in his book on the Palatine, endeavours to shew that the altar (*ara*) in this church was that for the sacrifices, "Diis manibus servilibus *ad sepulcrum Accæ Laurentinæ.*" According to the legend, Acca was the nurse of Romulus and Remus, and for that reason children are still brought to this altar to be blessed on certain occasions.

THE CHURCH OF S. MARIA IN ARA CŒLI (on the Capitol)[n].

This church is said to owe its origin and its name to the ALTAR erected by the Emperor Augustus to the Son of the Virgin, whom the Sibylla Tiburtina shewed him in the sky in a circle of light, and whom he adored, and who engaged to make him acknowledged by the Senate, and adored as God[o].

The plan of the church is a T cross, with aisles to the nave and side-chapels added, originally terminated by an apse, which was altered in the seventeenth century into a square chapel.

The date of the earliest part of the present construction is 1252, under Innocent IV. It has twenty-two antique columns brought from different places, of granite, *cipollino*, and white marble. The third column on the left has inscribed upon it, A CUBICULO AUGUSTORUM. The windows of the clerestory have pointed arches, and originally had tracery; they are almost all now blocked up or mutilated. In the west front are two small round windows, which have preserved their tracery; and another is built up in a side wall, but these are of the fourteenth century[p].

There is an inscription recording the building, in 1348, of the grand marble staircase which leads up to the west front of the church, rebuilt at that period[q]; the central doorway is later, belonging to the period of the Renaissance. The staircase is of one hundred and twenty-four steps, and was erected at the expense of the Senate and of the people, by Lorenzo Simeon Andreozzi. It was built of marble taken from the ancient temple of Quirinus (?), and was repaired by the same means in the sixteenth century. In the upper part of this west front are traces of a mosaic picture of the fourteenth century, but traces only: it has been quite destroyed.

The pavement is remarkably fine mosaic, said to be the finest in Rome; it is made of hard stone and marble, and is of the date of the church, 1252. In the richness of the work, and the variety of design, it is quite unrivalled, but it has been much mutilated in

---

[n] RIONE X. REGIO VIII.

[o] The legend of the Ara Cœli is, that the Senate wished to give to Augustus the name *Divine*. He refused this title, but went to the Temple of Jupiter Capitolinus and asked the Cumæan Sibyl whether there would come into the world a greater man than he. Whilst she prayed, a vision appeared to her of a circle around the sun, and in the middle a woman with a male child in her arms. *She shewed Augustus the vision, and a voice came from heaven saying, Hæc est Ara Cœli.*

[p] The cartoon (for the use of the workmen) of one of the round windows is etched upon a marble slab, now built into the ambo for the Epistle, on the south side of the altar, which has been altered in the fourteenth century.

[q] Photos., No. 583.

many parts; the most perfect portions are in the transept and the apse, which is distinctly marked out by it, the mosaic terminating in a round end, while the modern square chapel beyond has no mosaic. A very perfect portion also remains in two of the side chapels on the south side, but this part has been relaid, and somewhat mutilated in the process, the chapels being of the fifteenth century; the first and the fourth from the west end are the two chapels in which it is preserved. The south-west chapel is that of S. Bernardin, erected in 1464; it is very perfect, with a Gothic window, which retains its tracery, and has on the exterior a very good and rich cornice of trefoils with foliage round the window [r]. It is vaulted and painted by Pinturicchio, who has represented on the vault the four Evangelists; on the walls, right and left, the life of S. Bernardin of Siena; and at the end, S. Louis, Bishop of Toulouse, S. Bernardin, and S. Antony of Padua. There are some fragments of painted glass. The vaults of the aisles are of the same period, built at the expense of Cardinal O. Caraffa.

This church was long a very favourite burying-place, and the pavement, especially in the aisles, is full of mediæval tombstones, many of which have the effigies in low relief, according to the Italian fashion, generally much mutilated by being long trampled upon; these are chiefly of the fifteenth and sixteenth centuries. Some are also ornamented with mosaic ribbons and crosses. Besides these, there are a number of inscriptions only [s]; and some of these inscriptions are very curious, as shewing the mixture of Paganism with Christianity for which the Roman populace has always been celebrated. One of these, of 1438, contains distinct appeals to Venus and Jupiter, along with Paul [t]. In the nave is also the tomb of Cardinal Le Breton. The ceiling is very rich: it was erected in 1586 by the Senate, to commemorate the battle of Lepanto, in which a great victory had been obtained over the Turks, and the ceiling was gilt with the gold brought home on that occasion. This is recorded on a large inscription over the west door.

The SOUTH PORCH on the side towards the place on the Capitol, was opened in 1564, and has a vault within in the style of the thirteenth. On the exterior is a mosaic picture of the Virgin, supported by two angels, carrying candles, of the date A.D. 1564, and built

---

[r] Photos., Nos. 584, 591.   [s] These inscriptions are given by Forcella, extending from 1028 to 1867.
[t] HUNC VENERIS NUNQUAM TETIGERUNT MUNERA PAULUM.
PAULUM CUI MUSE MUNERA SACRA DABANT.
JUPITER HUNC PRIMUS SACRIS PREFECERAT :
ILLUM NUNC SUPERI GAUDENT ASTRA TENERE POLI.

in here by A. Mattei; it has the character of Byzantine work. In the SOUTH TRANSEPT, which is the chapel of the family of Savelli, are two fine tombs on the east and west sides; that on the east is the tomb of Luke Savelli, senator of Rome, deceased 1266, father of Pope Honorius IV., and of Pandulphus and his daughter, and of Andrew Savelli, deceased 1306. It is a very handsome tomb of mosaic of that period, placed upon an early Christian sarcophagus, richly sculptured, but which forms no part of the original tomb; it has suffered from subsequent alteration, when the canopy was cut off, and the present ugly classical pediment and pillars introduced in its place. On the west side is another very handsome tomb, that of Honorius IV., A.D. 1286, with a recumbent effigy, and rich mosaics. These tombs were executed by the artists Augustin and Agnolo, of Siena. The pavement of this chapel is also of the same period, with the rose of the Savelli introduced; it is very handsome, and well preserved.

In the NORTH TRANSEPT. At the end is the tomb of Cardinal D'Acquasparta, deceased 1303, which has a Gothic canopy, with a recumbent effigy under it. The ornaments and arms are in mosaic; these represent, in a very quaint manner, rain falling from heaven. Dante has sung the praises of this tomb in the twelfth chant of his *Paradiso*, but it is not so fine as some others of the work of the Cosmati in Rome. On the wall is a monumental slab of 1528, with an inscription " to the memory of Felix de Fredis, recording that the celebrated statue of the LAOCOON was found by him on the Esquiline.

In the centre of this transept the relics of S. Helena are deposited under an altar, in a porphyry urn, with a dome over it, supported on eight marble (*broccatello*) columns, under which is an inscription x. This altar was erected in 1605; under it is another altar-frontal of the twelfth or thirteenth century, a very rich piece of work, which has been engraved by Fontana; it is in the style of the twelfth, but in Rome that style was frequently continued in the thirteenth, and this altar may be of the date of the church. On it are carved the figures of Cæsar, of the Virgin Mother, and the Paschal Lamb, ornamented with enamels; and it has an inscription[y] relating to Octavius Cæsar.

The HIGH ALTAR was erected in 1723, in the bad taste of that age, but at the back a fine mosaic frontal of the thirteenth century has been preserved. The CHOIR behind the altar was rebuilt in 1691, and painted with the legend of the Sibyl of Tivoli. The mosaic pavement of the old apse is preserved, in strange contrast with the modern one of the part added (as before mentioned).

The AMBONES are very fine, but have been made up afresh and enlarged in the fourteenth century, chiefly with the materials and the beautiful mosaic ribbons of the thirteenth, but with additions to make them higher, and with some additional mosaic patterns also. The one for the Gospel, to the north, has the paschal candlestick used for the corner of the parapet of the staircase at the back; in front it has an eagle carrying a lizard in its claws. The one for the Epistle, on the south side, is more evidently made up of old materials; on the inside are fragments of ancient carving of the eighth or ninth century, and on the step at the base is the cartoon of a round window of the fourteenth, before mentioned, the window itself being in the west front of the church. This ambo is inscribed in the old work[z], HVIVS OPERIS MAGISTER FUIT LAURENCIUS . CUM . IACOBO . FILIO . SUO: being two of the family of the Cosmati.

There is said to have been a convent here from a very early period, some authors say as early as the time of Constantine. The abbot of the Capitol is mentioned in councils held in 985 and 1015; it was then a Benedictine abbey, but in 1250 the remaining monks of that order were distributed by Innocent IV. among other monasteries, in order to give the site to the Franciscans.

The present CONVENT was built, or rebuilt, at the same time as the church, in the thirteenth century, and the inner cloister, of two storeys, is of that period[a]. The arches are low and round, with the exception of two, which are pointed; they are carried on short columns, which appear to be antique, with Ionic capitals, which are of the thirteenth century; the upper part has been repaired in the

---

[y] + LUMINIS HANC ALMAM MATRIS QUI SCANDIS AD AULAM
CUNCTARUM PRIMA QUE FUIT ORBE SITA
+ NOSCAS QUOD CESAR TUNC STRUXIT OCTAVIANUS
HANC ARA CELI SACRA PROLES CUM PATET EI.

[z] MAGISTER . LAURENTI . SYMEONI . ANDREOTII . ANDREE . KAROLI . FABRICATOR . DE . ROMA . DE . REGIONE . COLVMPNE . FUNDAVIT . PERSECUTUS . EST . ET . CONSUMAVIT .
UT . PRINCIPALIS . MAGISTER . HOC . OPVS . SCALARUM . INCEPTUM . ANNO . DOMINI . M. CCC. XL. VIII. DIE . XXV. OCTOBRIS.

[a] Photos., No. 1080.

sixteenth. In the outer cloister the arches are larger, round-headed, and square-edged, not moulded, carried on octagonal pillars, with capitals of rude foliage, very short, and bases which have the foot-ornament at the angles, after the same fashion, though not so good, as those at S. Cross, near Winchester, in the twelfth century[b]. This outer cloister has been rebuilt in the fourteenth; it corresponds exactly with that of S. Francesca Romana, which is dated by an inscription. Here also, over the doorway, between the two cloisters, is built in, the frontal of an altar or a *confessio*, pierced with three very pretty Gothic panels, an angel kneeling at each end, and an inscription with the date 1372. The cloisters were painted with the legend of the Virgin, in 1634, but these paintings are much decayed.

In both these cloisters the peculiar ugly Roman buttress is used, consisting of a straight slope, without any break or set-off. This buttress is universally copied in the cloisters of the friaries, commonly miscalled abbeys, in Ireland. As this was the seat of the head of the Grey Friars, it was quite natural that they should copy the architecture along with the rules and practices of the order. The popular notion in Ireland is that this architecture came to them from Spain, but it is far more probable that both the Spanish and the Irish copied from Rome; and as Rome was always at least a century behind England and France in each change of the mediæval styles, so we find the same in Ireland. The architecture of the friary churches and convents of the fifteenth century in Ireland, as in Rome, is often a bad imitation of that of England in the twelfth or thirteenth, as in this cloister of the fourteenth century at Ara Cœli. It was only in the Renaissance, or revival of the Pagan style, that Rome was in advance of the Western nations.

Both convent and church were built, or rebuilt, by Innocent IV., A.D. 1250, for the reformed Franciscans, and the head of the order has always resided here. The palace of the Popes on the Capitol was a part of the great Venetian palace, of which the greater part is in the valley to the north, near the Corso, and is connected with the portion of the palace on the hill by a passage carried through the backs of the houses, and on arches across the streets. It now forms part of this friary; it was built by Paul II. in 1468, and was given to the friars by Clement VIII. about 1600, when he removed to the Belvedere at the Vatican, which he had built. This ancient palace now contains the library of Clement XII. attached to the convent, and to which the entrance is from the cloister. These

[b] Photos., No. 432.

friars were popularly known in England by the name of the Grey Friars, from their costume [e].

The buildings of this friary are now occupied as a barrack for the municipal guards; the municipality having followed the example of the Pontifical government in this respect, who occupied many of the old monasteries, including the buildings of the Inquisition, as barracks for their foreign army, to keep the Roman people in subjection to the pope-king. The officers of the municipal guards are very obliging to strangers, and allow the building to be seen without difficulty. The passage from the upper palace to the lower palace still exists, as built in the fifteenth century, and carried on small bridges or arches across the streets, as has been mentioned. The lower palace is now occupied as the residence of the Austrian ambassador, and is therefore private, but here also the Austrians are generally obliging to strangers, and the building can be seen without difficulty. The original smaller court near the Capitol is very fine; the larger one beyond is still unfinished, and not so good. This lower palace is known as the Venetian palace, the passage from one to the other has not at present been opened, but probably will be.

---

[e] For further information, see *Padre Casimiro da Roma Memorie Storiche della Chiesa del Convento di S. Maria in Ara Cæli di Roma*. 4to., Rome, 1736, with plates.

Cappelle Reali nella Chiesa di S. Maria in Ara Cæli, in 10 tavole incise in Roma.

Discorso Storico intorno la Prodigiosa Effigie di Gesù Bambino che si venera nella Chiesa di S. M. in Ara Cæli dal P. Antonio da Cipressa, &c.

Decrisione della Chiesa ed' altri Edificii di Roma dal secolo xi. fino in giorni nostri, raccolta e publicata da Vincenzo Forcella. Roma, 1870-75.

FORUM ROMANUM.

PLATE I.

THE FORUM ROMANUM IN 1650,
At the Time of the Jubilee.

Description of Plate I.

THE FORUM ROMANUM IN 1650,
At the time of the Jubilee.

This plate is a reproduction on a smaller scale of a scarce print of that period, and the object is to shew to how great an extent the soil of the Forum was raised at that period. It will be observed that the central arch, on the left of the view in the foreground, is the great triumphal building of Septimius Severus, filled up to half its height, and the side arches almost to the top. The three columns of the Temple of Saturn (?) have only one-third of their height above ground. The column of Phocas, and the celebrated three columns of the Dioscuri, have no bases visible. Of the Basilica Julia not a vestige can be seen. The Palatine is a spruce garden, with no ruins at all visible. The pontifical procession for the Jubilee gives life and interest to the scene, and the figures serve for a scale.

How was it possible for the best scholars of that period (and it was a learned period) to do more than guess at the site of any of the buildings in the Forum? We can fully understand by this view the cause of the many disputed and doubtful points of the historical topography of the City of Rome. This view appears to be taken from the top of the Capitoline tower, and shews the very picturesque character of old Rome at all periods. The distant hills make an admirable background from almost every point of view. We understand by this why Michael Angelo left the south side of his great building for the Offices of the Municipality so extremely plain. During the excavations made in 1832 on this spot, human bodies were found interred, with quick-lime poured over them. They were supposed to have been buried here at the time of the great plague, a further proof of the neglected state of this part of Rome at that time.

THE FORUM ROMANUM IN 1650 — AT THE JUBILEE.

FORUM ROMANUM.

PLATE II.

GENERAL VIEW OF THE FORUM.

Temple of Castor and Pollux.
The Basilica Julia, &c.

Forum Romanum.

Description of Plate II.

GENERAL VIEW OF THE FORUM.

Temple of Castor and Pollux [a] (or the Dioscuri).
The Basilica Julia, &c., in 1874.

This view is taken from the Palatine Hill. The temple with the celebrated THREE COLUMNS, which stands in the front of this picture on the left hand, is the one the name of which has been a matter of dispute and discussion for the last three centuries, and which has been called by many different names at different periods, and is now settled beyond all dispute for the future. It is seen that the basement of it extends far enough to admit of seven more columns at the same distance apart (as shewn in Plate XIV.), and the width admits of five (Plate XV.). Behind the temple is the raised platform of the Basilica Julia, with steps up to it from the street in the centre of the Forum, and with brick bases built upon it by Signor Rosa in 1873. At the farther end of this are remains of the stone (travertine) arches of the original Basilica of Julius Cæsar, before it was rebuilt by Augustus—and brick arches, some of the fourth century, others modern imitations. This great building was much damaged by another fire in the fourth century, and rebuilt according to the fashion of that period.

Beyond this is seen the modern road on a high bank of earth, made across the Forum with an arch under it. To the right is the fine triumphal arch of Septimius Severus, and in front the great mass of the Capitolium; two of the small square windows of the Ærarium are seen, and on a higher level the one arch of the Tabularium that has been re-opened since the whole arcade was walled up by Michael Angelo. Over this are the three storeys of the Municipal Offices of his time, left quite plain, because they were then entirely concealed by houses. To the left of the picture, in the background, are the houses over Monte Caprino, under which is the Tarpeian rock, but not visible. The tall tower of the Municipium is a conspicuous object from many parts of Rome, and the view from it is the most commanding in the City.

[a] Photos., Nos. 911, 912.

FORUM ROMANUM – TEMPLE OF THE DIOSCURI, BASILICA JULIA ETC. IN 1874

FORUM ROMANUM.

PLATE III.

TEMPLE OF CONCORD, TABULARIUM, AND ÆRARIUM.

PAVEMENT OF THE TIME OF THE REPUBLIC.

FORUM ROMANUM.

DESCRIPTION OF PLATE III.

TEMPLE OF CONCORD, TABULARIUM, AND ÆRARIUM.

IN the front part of the view is seen a piece of flat pavement probably of the time of Sylla, on the slope of the Clivus Capitolinus. This paved street is seen passing on the left-hand side of a low wall, of the time of the Kings, which was the middle wall between two gateways of the Porta Saturnii [b]; this was a double gate, the entrance into the Capitoline fortress from the Forum. To the right is seen the raised platform of the Temple of Concord, which was several times rebuilt, and has remains of different periods. The entrance of a passage is seen going through the basement under the platform; this passage has old walls faced with *Opus Reticulatum* of the time of the Republic. It is stopped abruptly at the further end by a wall of the time of Augustus, erected when the temple was rebuilt; this thick wall of the early Empire touches the wall of the Ærarium, in which two of the small square windows are seen. Over this is the one arch of the arcade, or *porticus* of the Tabularium, the only one that has been opened since Michael Angelo walled them up to carry the stone wall of the offices of the Municipality, which had always been of wood before his time, and had been burnt again just before. They had been burnt previously in the time of Sylla, as recorded by Tacitus and others [c]. He also filled up with concrete the passage inside the building, in continuation of this on the outside. His object was to make solid foundations for the lofty stone wall he had to build above, over the Tabularium. It has been pointed out that it would have been impossible for so numerous a body as the Roman Senate to have assembled for debates in so small a space as the cella of this temple, although it was sometimes called the Senate-house, because the entrance of the large hall behind it was through this temple. Several passages in support of this view are cited in the Appendix to Construction, p. 48, and a still stronger one occurs in the life of the Emperor Pertinax, by Julius Capitolinus (c. 4), "The Emperor came at night to the *Curia* or Senate-house and found it closed, and while his attendants sought for the door-keeper, *he seated himself in the Temple of Concord.*" This clearly shews that the temple was not the Senate-house, but was closely connected with it.

[b] Varro, De Ling. Lat., l. v. c. 7, p. 48.

[c] See Part III., Appendix to Construction on the Capitolium or Municipium, &c., p. 45. Photograph No. 3156 shews the *podium*; see also No. 3145 the veneering with marble, 3146 the subterranean passage.

FORUM ROMANUM

FORUM ROMANUM.

PLATE IV.

TEMPLE OF CONCORD.—SENATE-HOUSE.

A. PLAN OF THE HALL OF MEETING,
A LITTLE ABOVE THE LEVEL OF THE TABULARIUM, BEHIND THE EAST END OF IT.

B. PLAN OF THE SUBSTRUCTURE,
ABOVE THE LEVEL OF THE ÆRARIUM.

Forum Romanum.

Description of Plate IV.
TEMPLE OF CONCORD.—THE SENATE-HOUSE.
In the Capitolium—called also Senaculum and Curia.
A. Plan at the level of the Hall of Meeting.
B. Plan of the Substructure.

It has been pointed out in this work, that although the Temple of Concord was called the Senate-house, and the decrees of the Senate were given out on the top of the steps of that temple, there was not room for the Senate to assemble in that building, and a large number of marble statues are also recorded to have been placed there. It is thus almost evident that the temple was only the entrance to the real place of assembly in the great building at the back of it, but as the communication has been entirely cut off, this arrangement has not been generally understood. The large hall itself has been destroyed, only the walls of the substructure (B) remaining now as evidence; these evidently were under a great hall, and are cross walls to support the floor of it. At the end next the Ærarium are stone steps, leading originally from a doorway under the *podium* or basement of the temple, at the end of the passage which remains, but the doorway has long been closed [d].

The great hall was behind the eastern end of the Tabularium (A), but with no original communication from one to the other. There is an opening (now made into a doorway) from the Tabularium into the vestibule of the senate-house, but at a different level, and wooden steps have been made up to it on both sides; it seems rather to have been only an opening for air to the vestibule. The old steps now ascend from the Ærarium; another flight of steps goes up to the higher level of this great hall; these evidently turned to the left, or north, and so went to the back door of the hall, at the south-east corner; but the whole building was shortened by Michael Angelo at this end, though the original wall is left at the lower level [e], and a passage is cut off between that and the building, and is left open. The size of the great hall itself is made clear by the plan of it. There seems to have been another entrance or passage on the level of the floor of the temple, at the corner where the mediæval tower now stands. Part of this passage is visible in the inside, but has been filled up with concrete by Michael Angelo, in order to make a more solid foundation for the new upper building, at the same time that he filled up the arches of the *porticus*, or arcade of the Tabularium.

[d] Photos., Nos. 3146, 3147.
[e] Photos., No. 122, and Plate III. of the Capitolium in vol. i.

THE SENATE HOUSE
IN THE CAPITOLIUM, CALLED SENACULUM AND CURIA.

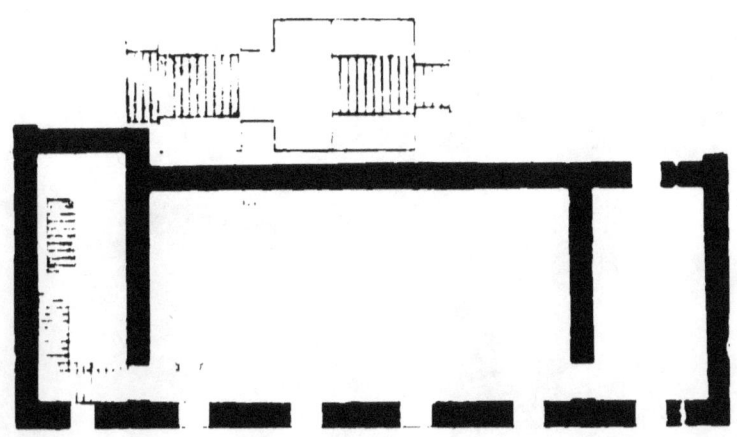

FORUM ROMANUM

PLATE V.

TEMPLE OF CONCORD.—SENATE-HOUSE.

Sections.

Description of Plate V.

TEMPLE OF CONCORD.—THE SENATE-HOUSE.

Senaculum, or Curia, in the Capitolium.—Sections.

These Sections correspond with the Plans in Plate IV., and the two together are a demonstration that this was the real place of meeting of the Roman Senate for debate, and that the Temple of Concord was the entrance to it. The fact mentioned in the text on the authority of the contemporary life, that the Emperor Pertinax, when he wanted to go into the *Curia*, or Senate-house, at night, and had to wait for the key, sat down in the Temple of Concord until it was brought, is a clear proof of this. The hall itself was destroyed by Michael Angelo, having been much damaged by the fire in his time, but the substructure and the vestibule, with the stairs to the hall remain, as is shewn in the plan and section.

A. shews the length of the hall, with the substructure and the vestibule, and the connection with the Tabularium; but the entrance to it was at a lower level, and under the Tabularium, passing by the entrance to the Ærarium, or Public Treasury, to which this was the only entrance. By this excellent practical arrangement the officers of the Senate had the complete control of the money in the Treasury; the clerks of the Treasury had to pass up another staircase, with no side doors in it, and then through the Senate-house, before they could obtain the money. The Roman army being paid in copper, or bronze money, an enormous space was required for it, which was provided in the Ærarium, over which a complete check was put in this manner. Some experience in architectural construction and in archæology was necessary to trace this out; but when once this has been done, it is easily seen, and no account of the Temple of Concord is complete without it.

B. shews the vestibule with the steps, and the connection with the Tabularium. This has been partially shewn in the section of the Capitolium as a whole, but this part required to be made out more in detail to be fully understood.

THE SENATE HOUSE, CURIA OR SENACULUM IN THE CAPITOLIUM
SECTIONS.

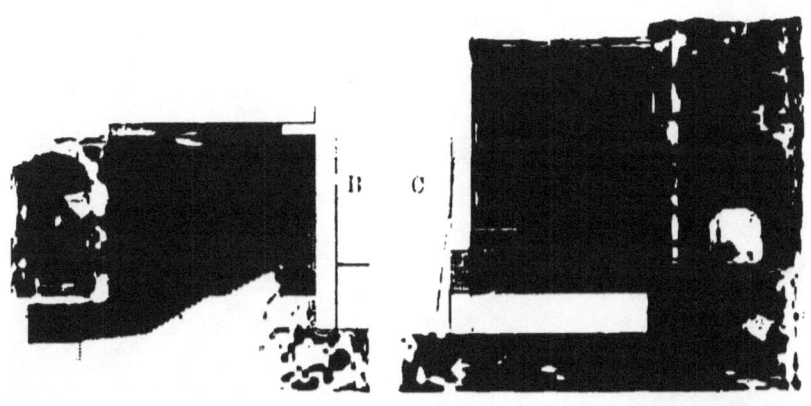

A. LONGITUDINAL WITH THE SUBSTRUCTURE
THE VESTIBULE AND ONE BAY OF THE TABULARIUM
B. AND C. THE VESTIBULE WITH THE STEPS
LONGITUDINAL AND TRANSVERSE

FORUM ROMANUM.

PLATE VI.

THE TEMPLE OF SATURN IN 1810.

DESCRIPTION OF PLATE VI.

THE TEMPLE OF SATURN IN 1810.

THIS view is a reproduction of an engraving from a work published under the authority of the French Government[h] at that time, to shew the state of the Forum just before they began their excavations in this part, which were afterwards followed up by the Duchess of Devonshire, with her usual public spirit. We see that the three remaining columns of this temple were buried even more deeply at that time than they had been in 1650. It is evident that this part of Rome had been entirely neglected and despised for a long period. The name of this temple, as of many others in Rome, has been a matter of doubt, and discussion, and dispute for centuries, and has been changed many times. In 1810 it was called the Temple of *Jupiter Tonans*, and it is known that there was a bell in a temple at the entrance to the Capitolium. But the present road up to it is modern; the old Clivus Capitolinus, or sloping and zigzag road up the hill, passed under the modern road, the pavement of it remains visible ten or twelve feet below the modern road, and points on towards Monte Caprino. It is quite possible that the entrance of the sacred enclosure round the temple, on the top of the Tarpeian rock (using that name in the sense of the place of public execution, visible from the Forum Romanum), was just at the angle where the zigzag road turned to go to the Capitolium.

In the Itinerary for the use of the pilgrims in the twelfth century, called *Mirabilia Romæ*, or *Descriptio Plenaria totius Urbis*, the miraculous bell is said to have been held by the statue of PERSIDA, in the Temple of Jove *and* Moneta, on the Capitolium, and the bell is said to have sounded when any province was in rebellion. According to the tradition of the twelfth century then, it appears that the Temple of Jupiter Tonans and of Moneta were the same[i]. By the same authority the church of Ara Cœli is called *S. Maria in Capitolio*. The pilgrims, therefore, evidently did not consider *that* as the site of the *Templum Jovis et Moneta*.

---

[h] "Etudes Statistiques sur Rome, par le Comte de Tournon," 2e. edition, 8vo., Paris, 1810, 3 volumes, avec atlas.

[i] "In cujus reversione tintinnabulum statuæ Persidæ quæ erat in Capitolio sonuit, in templo Jovis et Monetæ (Unius cujusque regni totius orbis erat statua in Capitolio cum tintinnabulo ad collum, statim ut sonabat tintinnabulum, cognoscebant illud regnum esse rebelle." (Descriptio Urbis, s. xii. *apud* Urlich's Codex, p. 99.)

THE FORUM ROMANUM IN 1810

N.E. CORNER AND PART OF TABULARIUM
BEFORE THE EXCAVATIONS WERE COMMENCED

FORUM ROMANUM.

PLATE VII.

TEMPLE OF SATURN IN 1874.

DESCRIPTION OF PLATE VII.

TEMPLE OF SATURN IN 1874[k].

This temple is of very early origin[l], and has been rebuilt more than once; to which of the two temples close together in this part of the Forum the name applies, has long been a matter for discussion and dispute; of late years, that with three columns at one angle has been more usually called the Temple of Vespasian. These two temples are only separated by the paved road of the Clivus Capitolinus; but Varro says[m] that it stood at the entrance to the Capitolium, and there is a doorway into the Capitolium remaining, partly concealed by the rebuilding of the *podium*, but originally under it, before the rebuilding took place, as shewn in Plate VIII.; it was one of the three buildings that were considered to belong to the city of the Sabines before the arrival of the Romans, and must therefore have been within the walls of the early fortress of the hill of Saturn, the other two buildings being the Gate of Saturn, and the Capitolium behind it. The pavement of this Clivus is made like many of the old streets of Rome in the foss of the early fortress. This temple must therefore be within that line, and the other temple must be that of Vespasian. The latter could not have been in existence in the time of the celebrated inscription of Augustus, of which a copy was preserved at Ancyra. This is a fine example of the Corinthian order, with three fluted columns, and although it has been restored, as appears from part of the inscription that remains upon it, *r*ESTI-TUER*unt*, it is probable, almost evident, that the old materials were used again; the character of the work is of the first century. A portion of the cornice is preserved in the Museum of Architecture belonging to the Municipality, made in the Tabularium.

[k] Photo., No. 897.
[l] It was dedicated in A.U.C. 259, B.C. 494, Livii Hist., ii. 21; rebuilt, A.U.C. 738, B.C. 15, Suetonius, Octavianus, 29; again rebuilt, A.D. 267.
[m] Varro de Ling. Lat., lib. v. c. 7.

FORUM ROMANUM

TEMPLE OF SATURN

FORUM ROMANUM.

PLATE VIII.
TEMPLE OF SATURN.
The Podium.

Description of Plate VIII.

TEMPLE OF SATURN.

TEMPLE OF SATURN (the *podium* or basement), and DOORWAY OF THE ÆRARIUM (the head of which is seen over the *podium*).

This temple was rebuilt by Septimius Severus, and the present remains, as far as they are visible, are of his time; another entrance was then made to the Ærarium, and the old doorway was closed. The large stones of the wall of the Ærarium are seen in the background, with small holes in them, where the floors of mediæval houses have been inserted. The pavement is of the time of the Empire. That this temple was that of Saturn (and not that of Vespasian, as is commonly said), is proved by the mention in cotemporary authors that the Ærarium or public treasury was turned into the Temple of Saturn[n]. It appears evident that when the old temple stood there, with an entrance to the Ærarium through the doorway of the basement, the treasury might be considered as the cell of the temple, which consisted only of the portico without a cell. This door opened at the foot of the steep flight of stone steps believed to be mentioned by Cicero as the steps of the Ærarium, and the mounting of which is jocularly compared by him to "climbing the Alps." In the same manner the Temple of Concord, which is close to this, was called the Senate-house, and there was a doorway to the Senate-house in the basement of it, as shewn in the view of the temple.

This is the temple with three columns remaining, and the one nearest the Ærarium, against the wall of which this *podium* or basement is built[o].

[n] See the authorities cited in vol. i. p. 44, of Appendix to Construction.
[o] See also the Photograph, No. 929, shewing the three columns, and Plates XIX. and XX. of the Supplement.

FORUM ROMANUM

FORUM ROMANUM.

PLATE IX.

PORTICO OF THE DEI CONSENTES,
AND
SCHOOL OF XANTHUS.

Description of Plate IX.

PORTICO OF THE DEI CONSENTES, AND SCHOOL OF XANTHUS [p].

THESE were excavated in 1832-35. They occupy the north-west corner of the Forum, and stand under the western end of the front of the Capitolium, with the wall of the Ærarium and Tabularium behind them on the right, and the present sloping road up to the Capitolium and Municipium to the left. They had previously been excavated in 1547, as recorded by Lucius Faunus, and were then stripped of the marble casing of the brick walls of the lower building, with the bronze tablets and inscriptions. These inscriptions distinctly identify it with the SCHOLA XANTHI in Regio VIII. of the Regionary Catalogue. The marble steps descending to it are original, so that it was always on this low level.

The colonnade over this is that of the Dei Consentes, whose images in gilt bronze were placed between the columns. Behind these, on the higher level, are shops, the remains of three of which are seen through the columns. Others remain under the modern road, they were cased with marble. The paved space in front was called the Area of the Dei Consentes.

The bases of these columns were in their places, and the lower part of one column. The other columns, the quasi-Corinthian capitals, which are a step in the history of architecture intermediate between the proper Classical type and the mediæval, and the cornice, were found lying about in fragments, and were cleverly put together and restored in the time of Nibby and Canina.

The inscription also records that the images were restored by Vettius Agorius Prætextatus, who was Prefect of Rome A.D. 367, and is mentioned by contemporary writers as one of the most vigorous supporters of paganism under Julian; and this work was probably begun at that time, though not finished until a few years afterwards.

The names of the Dei Consentes are given by Ennius, (preserved by Apuleius, *de deo sacratis*).

IVNO . VESTA . MINERVA . CERES . DIANA . VENVS . MARS .
MERCVRIVS . JOVI . NEPTVNVS . VVLCANVS . APOLLO.

[p] Photos., Nos. 913, 914, 1076, 2325.

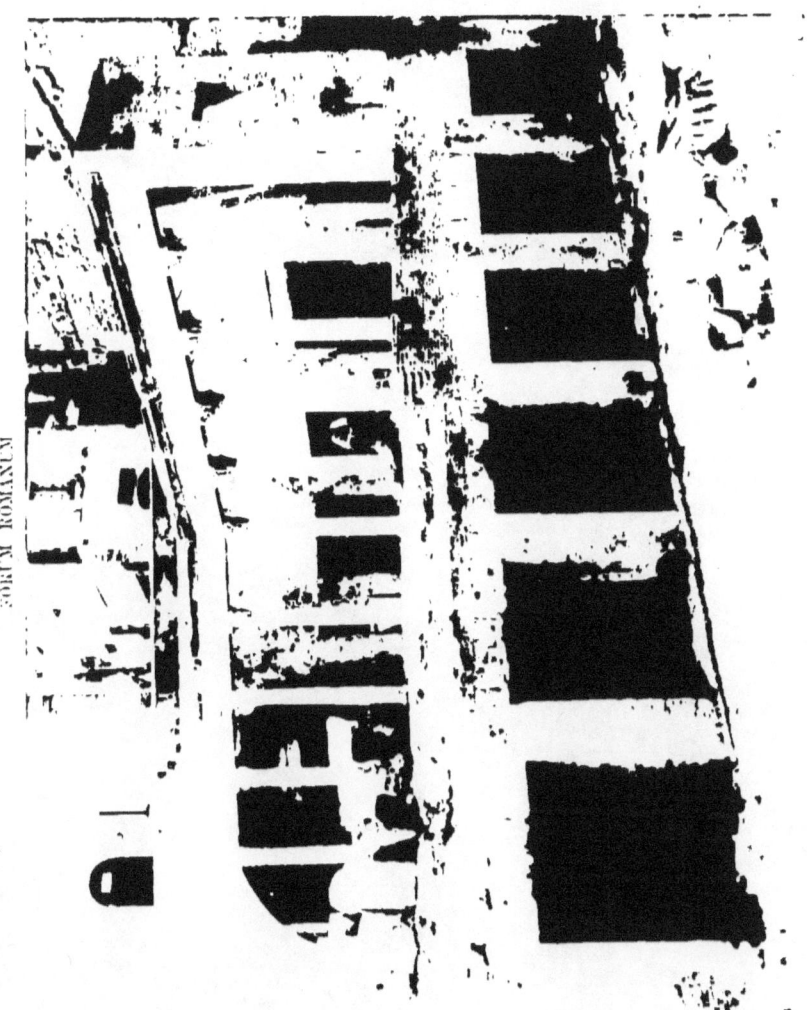

FORUM ROMANUM

PORTICO OF THE DEI CONSENTES AND SCHOOL OF XANTHUS

FORUM ROMANUM.

PLATE X.

TEMPLE OF VESPASIAN (?) IN 1874.

Description of Plate X.

TEMPLE OF VESPASIAN (?) IN 1874.[q]

The basement of this temple has now been thoroughly excavated, and there are no traces of any vaults for money for a Public Treasury. The Ærarium must have consisted of large vaults, to hold the copper and bronze money with which the Roman army was paid. We read of Julius Cæsar finding money of the time of Servius Tullius in the Ærarium. There is not, and never could have been, any such place in or under this temple, whereas the adjoining temple, between this and the wall of the Capitolium, has remains of a doorway that has been under the *podium* of it, leading direct into that great public building, which without doubt contained the treasury. The temple has been rebuilt by Septimius Severus, but of the old materials, with columns of the Ionic order.

In the old Catalogue of the Emperors published by Eccard, and in the *Curiosum Urbis*, Reg. VIII., a temple of Vespasian *and* Titus is mentioned, but as they were joint Emperors for a time, and we have no remains of another temple here, it is probable that only one temple is intended, the one built by Domitian. A temple built in their time or in their honour, might be called by either name or by both. In the *Notitia de Regionibus*, Reg. VIII., the temples of Saturn and Vespasian are mentioned together, but that is only because they are close together.

[q] Photos., No. 897, 929.

FORUM ROMANUM – TEMPLE OF VESPASIAN? ETC. IN 1874

FORUM ROMANUM.

PLATE XI.

MILLIARIUM ET ROSTRA.

FORUM ROMANUM.

DESCRIPTION OF PLATE XI.

MILLIARIUM ET ROSTRA[r].

THE small remains of these are shewn in this plate as they appeared in 1874, on the left, or western side of the great triumphal arch of Septimius Severus. The upper one represents the site of the celebrated Milliarium Aureum, or gilt mile-stone, in the exact centre of old Rome, and therefore also called Umbilicum Urbis. The round base of brick here shewn is believed to be the exact site. It was the intention of Augustus, when he erected this mile-stone (B.C. 28), to have had all the mile-stones on the carriage roads measured from this point[s], but this excellent design was never carried out. Some of the roads continued to be measured from the gates in the inner wall of Servius Tullius, others from the gates in the outer wall or *agger*, originally of the Tarquins, on which the great Wall of Aurelian was built. This is evident from the inscriptions relating to the aqueducts over the Porta Maggiore, and from the work of Frontinus on that subject, in which the distances are also given from that gate[t].

The lower plate represents the remains of the Rostra Antiqua. There were three Rostra in the Forum Romanum[u]. One was that of Julius Cæsar at the south end, this is near the north end, the third was near where the marble walls or screen stand. This plate represents the remains of the one on the site from which Cicero usually spoke, as is evident from several of his Orations. In his ninth Philippic he mentions a proposal to place a bronze statue to S. Sulpicius, because it would be conspicuous from the Forum, being on rather higher ground than the general level, as this is[x]. The remains visible in this Plate are of the time of Septimius Severus, when most of the buildings in this part of the Forum were rebuilt. The Rostra are represented in the sculpture of the Forum on the Arch of Constantine (see Plate XVI.).

[r] Photos., Nos. 915, 916, 917.
[s] Taciti Hist., lib. i. c. 27, he calls it under the Temple of Saturn; Suetonii Otho, c. 6; Plinii Nat. Hist., lib. iii. c. 9. The latter mentions the measuring of the distances from the Milliarium Aureum to each of the thirty-seven gates of Rome.
[t] Frontinus de Aqueductibus, c. 13, 14, and the Chapter on the Aqueducts in this work.
[u] Plinii Nat. Hist., lib. xxxiv. c. 14.
[x] Ciceronis Orat. Philippica, ix. 7.

FORUM ROMANUM. MILLIARIUM ET ROSTRA.

FORUM ROMANUM.

PLATE XII.

ARCH OF SEPTIMIUS SEVERUS, &c., IN 1874.

Description of Plate XII.

ARCH OF SEPTIMIUS SEVERUS[r], &c., IN 1874.

This great triumphal arch was erected A.D. 203. The sculptures are so much mutilated that it is difficult to make out the subjects, but they have often been published. They relate to the wars of the Emperor in the East, his two campaigns against the Parthians and others in Arabia, &c. The two lower panels, which are better seen, represent the goddess Rome receiving the homage of the eastern nations. In the inscription the name of his brother, GETA, has been erased, with his titles, and the place supplied by the words OPTIMIS FORTISSIMISQUE PRINCIPIBUS. The photo-engraving shews this patch in the inscription very clearly. As the ground rises rapidly at this point, which is the beginning of the Clivus Capitolinus, there are steps up in the two side arches, and there were others in the central one also, so that the procession originally went up on foot from the Forum; but this was altered at an early period, to allow the chariots to go up. In the Middle Ages the church of SS. Sergius and Bacchus was built up against this arch, and the bell-tower upon it, as in the other arch of that emperor at S. Giorgio in Velabro, where the Campanile still stands partly upon the arch. The coins of this Emperor shew that there was originally a Quadriga, or chariot with four horses, on the top of the arch, and the want of this gives it too flat an appearance. In the background of the picture are seen, on the right, the mediæval tower at the south-east corner of the Capitolium, and the sloping path up to the Piazza del Campidoglio, made by Michael Angelo, when he rebuilt the upper part of this great building. To the left is the temple of eight columns, which has been shewn to be that of Vespasian, but it is commonly called of Saturn. The carriage-road up to the same Piazza, passing by the door of the Municipium and Tabularium, conceals a considerable part of the Forum, and ought to be removed. The old Clivus Capitolinus passes under it, ten or twelve feet lower down, and some of the shops of the Forum are buried under it. The arch was restored by Pius VII. in 1803.

[r] Photos., Nos. 772 and 1209.

FORUM ROMANUM – ARCH OF SEPTIMIUS SEVERUS ETC. IN 1874

FORUM ROMANUM.

PLATE XIII.

COLUMN OF PHOCAS, ARCH OF SEPTIMIUS SEVERUS, &c.

Description of Plate XIII.

COLUMN OF PHOCAS, &c.

This was 'the nameless column' of the time of Byron; the inscription giving the name was found on the base when it was excavated in 1813, after his time. It stands near the north end of the Forum. This photograph was taken in 1873, when the marble walls in the Comitium had just been found in fragments, which were being put together under the shed shewn in the right-hand corner in the excavations. To the left stands the column of the Emperor Phocas, of A.D. 608, resting upon a basement on the top of a great flight of steps, built of old materials, of large blocks of stone or marble, taken from buildings that had been destroyed. The column itself appears to have been taken from the Temple of Saturn, of which three other columns are left in their places at one angle of that temple, shewn in Plate VII. The capital and the column are so identical with those of the temple, that there can scarcely be a doubt that one is taken from the other. Behind this is the Arch of Septimius Severus, the well-known landmark for all the visitors to Rome; to the right is the modern church of S. Luke, and part of the buildings of the Academy of S. Luke. In the right-hand corner of the plate is the church of S. Hadrian, the brick wall of the front of which is said to be of the eighth century [z], but the pediment and cornice are later. This view gives a good idea of the manner in which the excavations of the Italian Government are carried on, and the great depth of earth that they have to clear away.

[z] See also Photograph of the Column, No. 2288; of the Arch, No. 1209.

FORUM ROMANUM.

PLATE XIV.
ONE OF THE MARBLE WALLS IN THE COMITIUM.

Forum Romanum.

Description of Plate XIV.

ONE SIDE OF ONE OF THE WALLS (OR SCREENS) IN THE COMITIUM, in fragments, as it was found in 1872, before it was put together.

A PROCESSION of persons carrying books or tablets is distinctly visible; they are supposed to represent the tablets of the taxes which Hadrian had cancelled, and they are bringing them up and throwing them into a heap to be burnt: the sculpture thus representing an historical event of importance, mentioned by Spartianus in his life of Hadrian (c. 7). In the background are seen the porticoes of two temples, with an arch between them, which there is reason to believe is also a view of the Forum. Some consider that the sculptures on these two marble walls in the Comitium must be considered as a continuation of the same subject, and this most probably is the great donation to the Roman people by the Emperor Hadrian. He cancelled the public debt of the Roman citizens. Others argue that the two subjects are distinct, one relating to the great donation of Hadrian, the other to the munificence of Trajan, who was the first to found an Orphanage in Rome. Some deny that these walls are in the Comitium, the exact site of which has not been ascertained. Each of these subjects is represented on the coins of those Emperors.

In his panegyric of Trajan, Pliny the Younger mentions that it was his habit to speak to the people from the rostra as a mark of his humility, contrasting then with the pride of other princes [a]. But the sculpture is certainly of the time of Hadrian, who may in this instance have only recorded the acts of Trajan, or he may have carried them out after his death.

Spartianus says that these tablets or bonds (*syngraphis*) were burnt in the Forum of Trajan, but in the time of Hadrian, as the debt was cancelled by that Emperor.

The figures in the procession are so much mutilated that there is necessarily a good deal of conjecture in the interpretation of them, which naturally leads also to difference of opinion [b].

In this view the original stone wall of foundation, of an earlier period, is seen under the marble wall [c].

---

[a] "Jam toties procedere in rostra inascensumque illum superbiæ principum locum terere... hoc pro concione, pro rostris pro jurejurando," &c. . . . (Plinii Sec. Paneg. Trajani dictus, c. lxv.)

[b] A more detailed and minute account of them will be found in the *Bullettino dell' Instituto Archeologico*, by Dr. Henzen, and in the *Annali* of the same Society for 1872, by D. Brixio.

[c] See also the Photographs, Nos. 2962, 3170.

FORUM ROMANUM   MURUS COMITII

FORUM ROMANUM.

PLATE XV.
THE TWO MARBLE WALLS IN THE COMITIUM.

Description of Plate XV.

THE TWO MARBLE SCREENS IN THE COMITIUM[d].

In this view the two marble walls are seen as actually replaced on the old stone bases of the time of the Republic, but with new marble bases placed upon them by Signor Rosa to elevate the sculptures. It is seen that these two walls are now again parallel to one another at a short distance apart, about ten feet, as is seen by the six-foot rule placed at the angle of the left-hand wall as a scale. On this wall the three animals prepared for sacrifice are seen, and it will be observed that they are placed on the inner side, and the procession on the outside. The procession of persons carrying tablets, and throwing them into a heap to be burnt, is seen on the other wall, but in sharp perspective, and a better view is seen in the other plate. It is supposed by some good scholars that one object of this wall was to protect the voters going up to vote for Consuls from the pressure of the mob in the Forum, and this, being the most public place, was selected for the purpose of commemorating the great event or events here represented. The actual voting-place is supposed to have been a little further to the east (under what is now a modern road on the higher level), and that the Emperor Hadrian, or the officer who recorded the votes, sat in state, as represented on the other wall.

"Hadrian remitted innumerable sums which were due from private debtors to the privy purse of the Emperor, in the city and in Italy, and even in other provinces: he collected the bonds of the sums remitted in the Forum of Trajan (?), and for greater security he enclosed them in oak boards and burnt them all, and he forbad any of the money that had been condemned to be received into the public treasury." (Spartianus in Hadriano, c. 7, ap. Script. Hist. Aug.)

The census at Rome took place every five years, it was called a Lustrum. On these occasions there was always an expiatory sacrifice called the *Suovetaurilia*—Bull, Ram, and Boar—by which the city was supposed to have been purified. The Comitium was therefore a very natural place for these representations of them.

[d] Photos., Nos. 2959, 2960, 2961, 2962, 3160.

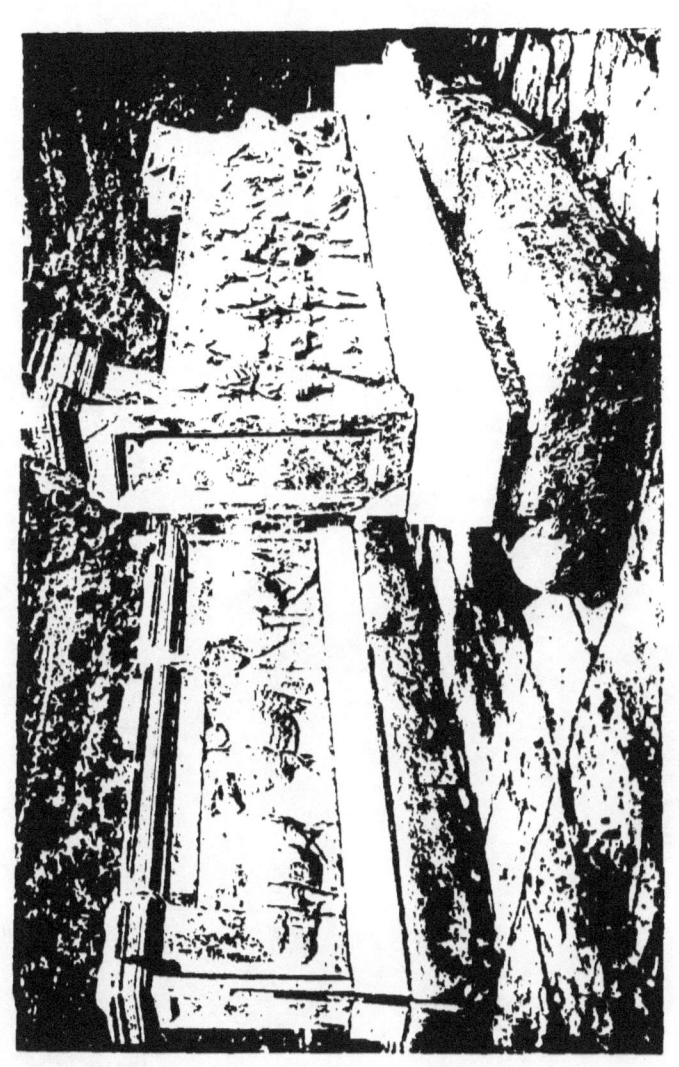

FORUM ROMANUM.

PLATE XVI.

MARBLE WALL IN THE COMITIUM.
Sculpture from the Arch of Constantine.

FORUM ROMANUM.

DESCRIPTION OF PLATE XVI.

ONE SIDE OF ONE OF THE MARBLE WALLS OR SCREENS OF THE COMITIUM.

This sculpture shews the Magistrate (?) or the Emperor (?) seated on his curule chair surrounded by the officers of the court, and the procession of persons with an orator at their head, standing on a rostrum and addressing the Emperor; in the background the entablature and cornice of a basilica, or market-hall, is represented. This is believed to be a view of the Forum Romanum itself at that period; it is of the time of Hadrian, and the figure seated on a throne is probably that Emperor. According to another theory the two figures on the raised *podium*, or basement, are sculptures; the male figure seated, the Emperor Trajan; the female figure standing, Italia, with a baby in her arms in long clothes, to commemorate the foundation of an Orphanage by that Emperor.

The figure under the fig-tree at the end of the wall is either Silvanus, or Marsyas, with his wine-bag. The same fig-tree and idol is represented on both the walls. Some good authorities say that this is Silvanus, because Marsyas is never represented with a wine-bag in any of the sculptures or bassi-relievi of that god. On the other hand, Seneca (De Beneficiis, vi. 32) mentions a figure of Marsyas in the Forum. This is also mentioned by Servius (in Virgil, Æneid, iv. 50, and iii. 20). Each of these subjects is also represented on the coins of those Emperors. A base of a large column of the time of Constantine, with the same three animals, called the *suovetaurilia*, carved upon it, was found in the Forum, and was placed at the door of the Farnese Gardens, now called the Palaces of the Cæsars [e].

SCULPTURE FROM THE ARCH OF CONSTANTINE.

This long flat panel is of the time of Constantine, and represents the Forum Romanum of that time[f]; in the centre are the two rostra, with the idols or statues upon them, and the *transenna*, or low screen of pierced marble, in front. Behind these are the tall columns, with images of the gods on the top of them. The arcade or *porticus*, at the back, appears to be the Tabularium, or it may perhaps be the Basilica Julia.

[e] See Photo., No. 2291.   [f] No. 3168.

FORUM ROMANUM — TEMPORIS HADRIANI DE MURO COMITII

FORUM ROMANUM.

PLATE XVII.
BASILICA JULIA.

Forum Romanum.

Description of Plate XVII.
BASILICA JULIA.

In this view is seen, to the left, part of the original basilica of the time of Julius Cæsar, built of the large blocks of travertine usual at that period, as is seen in the Arch of Dolabella, which is dated by an inscription upon it of the names of the Consuls corresponding to A.D. 10. The walls of the original part run from west to east, as is here seen, whilst the brick walls to the right in the view run from north to south. This agrees with the words of Augustus in the "Monumentum Ancyranum," in which he says, "that when he completed this Basilica after it had been damaged by a fire, he enlarged it so much, that what had been the length became the breadth." It originally ran from east to west, and was altered into the opposite direction from north to south. The brick walls seen to the right of the view were built by Canina about 1840, as a restoration of the work of the fourth century, when it had been rebuilt after another fire. The arches at the end, seen in the middle of the picture, are of that period.

The Curia Hostilia had been on the same site, and were rebuilt A.U.C. 710—725, when it was consecrated and called after Julius Cæsar[g]. The Basilica Julia is also mentioned by Suetonius among the works of Augustus[h]; and in his life of Caligula, as the place where the Emperor distributing money to the common people[i], threw it down from the gallery. Pliny the Younger, in one of his letters to his friend Rufus[k], mentions it as a law-court, which was at the time he wrote (the end of the first century) the usual meaning of the word Basilica. In another of his letters, addressed to Romanus[l], he calls it the Tribunal, and mentions *the upper part of it* as a place from which men and women could see well, but not hear well; this shews that there were galleries round it. The Curia Julia was probably another name for the same building. Two inscriptions were found during the excavations; one recording the rebuilding, A.D. 283, under the Emperor Maximianus, after a fire, under Carinus and Nemesianus[m]; another recording the repairs of the building and placing statues in it, A.D. 377, by the Prefect Q. V. Probianus. Two fragments of the marble plan were placed here by Canina on his map, one of which has the name JVLIA upon it, the other the letter B, but this latter is on a different scale, and the two do not fit.

[g] Dion. Cass., Hist., lib. xlvii. c. 19.
[h] Suetonius, Octavianus, c. 29.
[i] Ibid., Caligula, c. 37.
[k] Plinii Epistolæ, lib. v. ep. 21.
[l] Ibid., lib. vi. ep. 33.
[m] Gruter, inscr. clxxi. 7.

FORUM ROMANUM.

PLATE XVIII.

BASILICA JULIA.

TEMPLE OF CASTOR AND POLLUX, &c.

FORUM ROMANUM.

DESCRIPTION OF PLATE XVIII.

BASILICA JULIA.

ON the right in the front part of this view is the southern part of the great BASILICA JULIA, with the original steps down from the platform of it to the paved street down the middle of the Forum, whatever its name may have been; some say it was a continuation of the Via Sacra, others call it the Via Nova. A mediæval drain is seen passing across the street. On the platform of the Basilica are the modern brick bases built by Signor Rosa in imitation of the old ones which he believes stood there, and carried the arcade round the sides of the platform. A little further to the north, but not seen in the view, he has also erected one of the piers of the arcade up to the springing of the two arches, and part of the pier rising above that springing shews that this arcade was of two storeys, as in other basilicas.

At the further end of the platform we see the celebrated three columns of the Temple of Castor and Pollux. Between this and the extreme right of the view is seen the modern church of S. Maria Liberatrice. Through the columns is seen the modern residence of the Superintendant of Archæology, at the entrance to the Palaces of the Cæsars: to the left of the Arch of Titus, near the centre of the view, over the grove of trees, is the campanile of S. Francesca Romana, believed to be almost on the site of the great Colossus of Nero, and of about the same height. To the left of this, a portion of the great Basilica or market-hall of Constantine is seen, and below it on the lower level the church of SS. Cosmas and Damian, made out of three temples; the one in front, the *tholus* or domical vault of which is seen, with a belfry and round cupola upon it, was the temple of Romulus, the son of Maxentius; this has been demonstrated by Signor de Rossi in his *Bulletino di Archeologia Christiana*[n]. The other two must have been the temples of Roma and Venus. And close to the left of the picture is the Temple of Antoninus and Faustina[o].

[a] De Rossi, Bulletino, vol. v. p. 64. Roma, 1867.
[o] See also Photographs of the construction of the Basilica, the wall of travertine, No. 3163 and 2731; also a general view from the Palatine, No. 3229.

FORUM ROMANUM.

PLATE XIX.

CLOACA MAXIMA.

Podium or Base of an Equestrian Statue.

FORUM ROMANUM.

DESCRIPTION OF PLATE XIX.

CLOACA MAXIMA, (B.C. 615; Livii Hist., i. 38).

THIS part is under the south end of the Basilica Julia, and on the site of part of the Curtian Lake, to drain which this great cloaca was made. The brick arch in the foreground is of the time of the early Empire, that behind it is one arch of the original vault, built of the large blocks of tufa of the time of the Kings, and it is evidently part of the original construction. The same early construction occurs in the subterranean passage connected with the Prison of the Kings, and both are attributed to the same period by Livy[p], (B.C. 638—532). The exact line of this great drain was not previously known; it is now evident that the Curtian lake was formed by the meeting of three streams from natural springs,—one from the Palatine, near the Arch of Titus; a second from the Quirinal, behind the church of S. Adrianus; and the third from the Capitol, under that part of the old prison called the "Prison of S. Peter:" they were all drained by this great ancient drain, of which there were several branches. The main line, discovered in 1874, passing under the Forum Romanum, goes on towards the Forum Boarium, passing near the church of S. Giorgio in Velabro. Another branch, coming from the Thermæ of Agrippa, falls into it near that point, and passed under the Arcus Quadrifrons, or Arch of Janus. Another very distinct branch has been found in 1875, between the Colosseum and the Cœlian Hill, at a great depth.

PODIUM OR BASE OF AN EQUESTRIAN STATUE.

This is near the centre of the Forum, on the eastern side; the podium is of brick, of the time of Constantine, and the very thick marble casing of it, made of *giallo antico*, a valuable marble, is seen in the foreground to the right—it was probably the basement of the horse of Constantine, although it is usually called that of Domitian. On each side is one of the wine shops(?) of the third century, usually called bases for the tall columns down the centre of the Forum, with statues upon them, but they are hollow, and have doorways[q].

[p] Livii Hist., i. 33 and 56; Varro, de Ling. Lat., v. c. 32, p. 157. See also Photograph, No. 3164.   [q] See Photograph, No. 3169.

FORUM ROMANUM. CLOACA MAXIMA

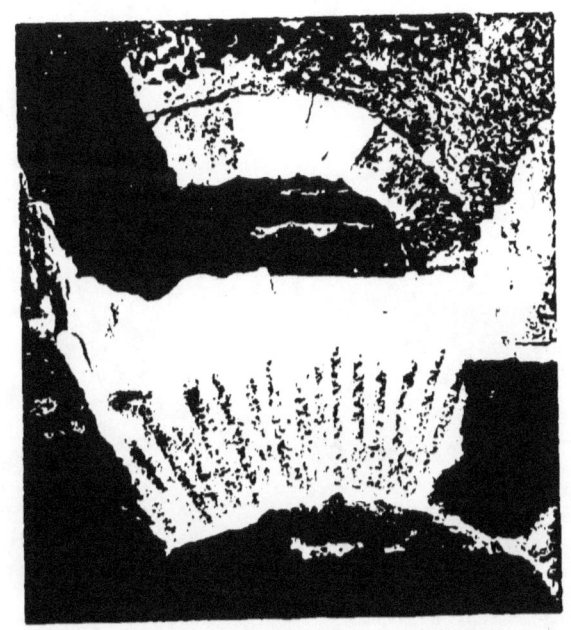

FORUM ROMANUM.

PLATE XX.

ROSTRUM AND TEMPLE OF JULIUS CÆSAR.

Forum Romanum.

Description of Plate XX.

ROSTRUM AND TEMPLE OF JULIUS CÆSAR.

This is situated at the extreme south-east corner of that Forum, and near to the Temple of Antoninus and Faustina, which is in the Via Sacra, and not in the Forum. In this view is seen to the left part of the curved wall of the Rostrum, built of travertine of the character of the period of Julius Cæsar himself. It is evident that the speaker stood on the flat side of the rostrum, not on the curve; the latter almost touches the temple behind it, whereas in front is a paved platform for a large number of people to stand and listen to the speaker. The fragments of sculpture seen in the picture were merely built up temporarily, to preserve them whilst the work of excavation was going on around them. To the right of the view are seen the ruins of some of the palaces of the Cæsars, on the Palatine Hill. The Temple of Vesta is close under them, but is not seen in the view. The depth of earth excavated is seen very distinctly, and shews the great work going on in this part of Rome in 1874.

FORUM ROMANUM.

PLATE XXI.

TEMPLE OF CASTOR AND POLLUX, &c.

Description of Plate XXI.

NORTH-EAST CORNER OF THE PALATINE, AND THE TEMPLE OF CASTOR AND POLLUX.

A. Remains of the Palace of Caligula.

B. Modern church of S. Maria Liberatrice, on the site of the Regia, afterwards the residence of the Pontifex Maximus, and then of the Vestal Virgins. When the modern church was built in the seventeenth century, several inscriptions were found, with the names of the Vestal Virgins which had been on the bases of statues, clearly shewing that this had long been their residence, close to their temple, the remains of which were excavated in 1874.

TEMPLE OF CASTOR AND POLLUX.

C. The Temple of Castor and Pollux, or of the Dioscuri, with the celebrated Three Columns, the name of which was so long disputed; they are now proved to have belonged to this temple, the *podium* or basement of which is of the time of the Kings; the columns are of the time of Tiberius, when it was rebuilt *from the foundations*, but these were not disturbed, and are now brought to light for the first time [r].

[r] See also Photographs of the *podium* of the Temple, No. 3157; and the Three Columns, Nos. 911, 2289.

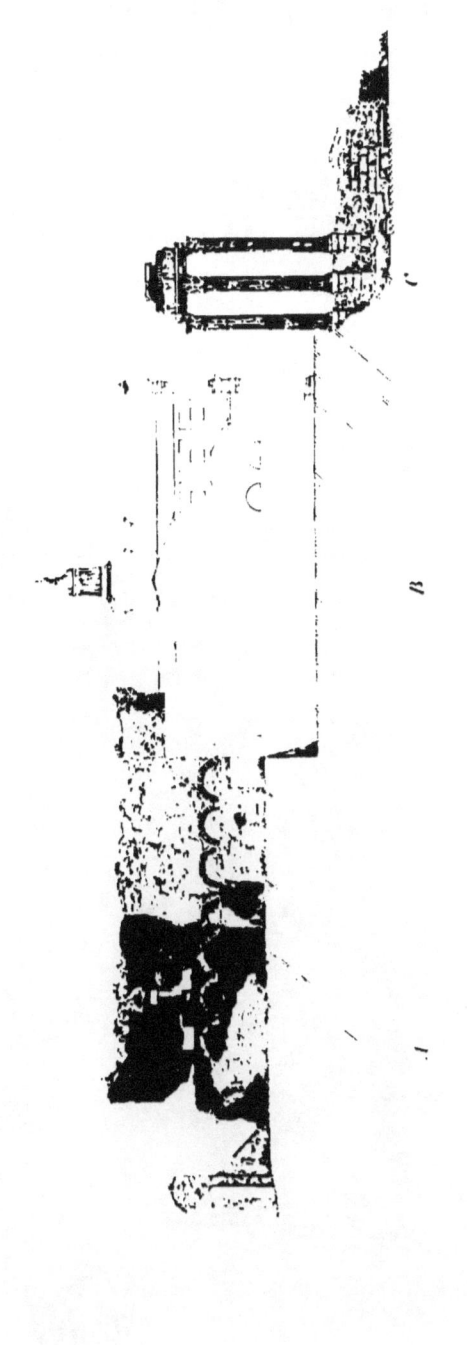

FORUM ROMANUM.

PLATE XXII.

TEMPLE OF CASTOR AND POLLUX, &c.

Description of Plate XXII.

PROBABLE RESTORATION OF THE TEMPLE OF CASTOR AND POLLUX, &c.

A. TEMPLE, north side.

The celebrated three columns, *in situ*, are shewn by the darker tint. The others are restored from the basement, the cornice, and the fragments that have been found. At the west end of it is a doorway connecting it with the Palace of Caligula, and to which it served as the vestibule, as Suetonius states (c. 22).

B. Part of the Palace of Caligula, joining on to the temple at present concealed by modern houses.

C. Pier of the Bridge of Caligula, with the springing of the arches that went across at the west end of the Forum.

D. Part of the Bridge and of the Palace; they cannot be separated. Part of the Bridge joins the west end of the Palace, and the Temple may be said to join the east end of it. The part of the Palace on the cliff of the Palatine, shewn above the level of the bridge in the picture, may be part of the Palace of Caligula on the hill, and to the west of that of Hadrian at the corner.

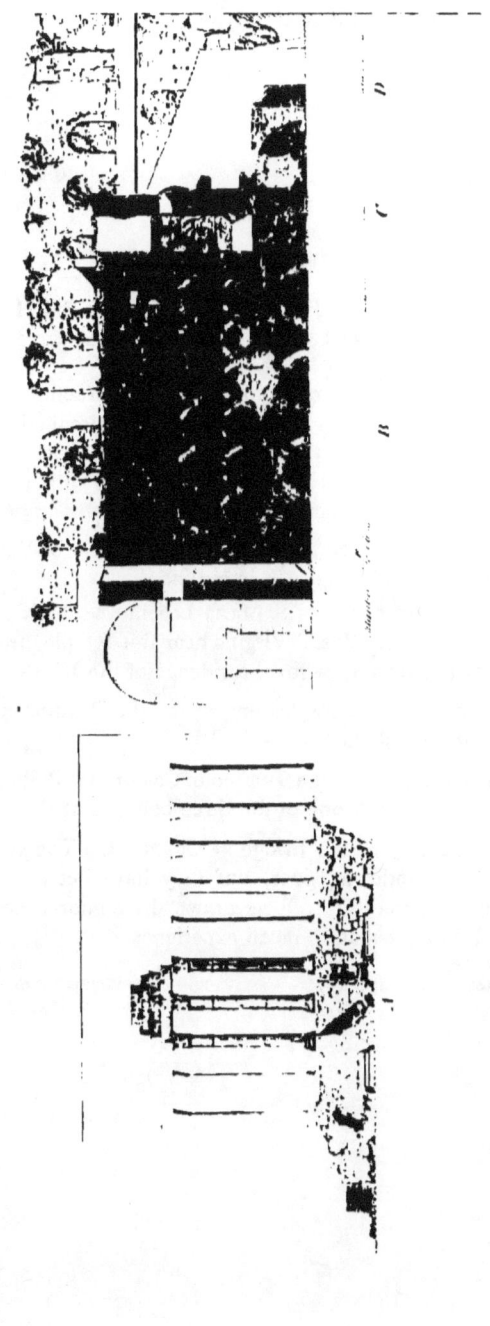

Description of Plate XXIII.

PROBABLE RESTORATION OF THE TEMPLE OF CASTOR AND POLLUX, &c.

A. PART of the Palace of Hadrian, the construction is identical with that of his Villa at Tivoli. It is usually miscalled the Palace of Caligula, but that is on the lower ground, level with the Temple of Castor and Pollux; or if *part* of it was on the hill, as is not improbable, it was behind that of Hadrian [s].

B. The *podium* or basement of the round temple of Vesta [t], excavated in 1874; behind it is seen in outline,

C. The modern church of S. Maria Liberatrice, built on the site of the residence of the Vestal Virgins near this temple, and this was on the site of the REGIA, or royal residence of the Kings.

D. Some remains of steps leading up to the Palatine are shewn, but the remains are slight.

E. The front portico of the Temple of Castor and Pollux, restored from the basement, with one of the three columns at the angle [u].

F. A continuation of the Bridge of Caligula [x]. The remains are much concealed under a house, but they have been carefully examined and measured, as well as drawn, by Signor Cicconetti, an architectural draughtsman of much experience.

[s] Photos., Nos. 2972, 2973.   [t] Photos., No. 3230.
[u] Photos., No. 3157.   [x] Photos., No. 1757.

2 FORUM ROMANUM – PALATINE N E CORNER TEMPLE OF CASTOR ETC

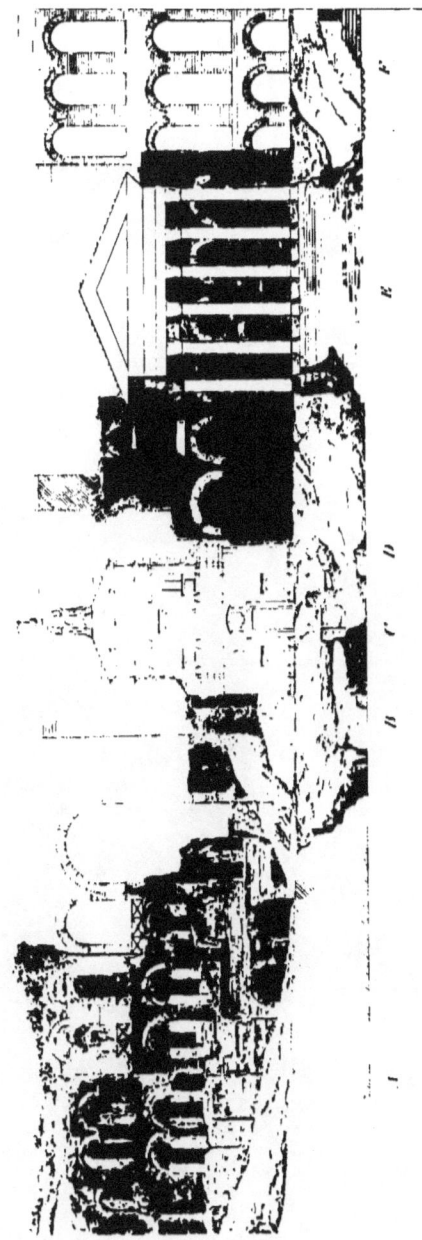

FORUM ROMANUM.

PLATE XXIV.

NORTH-EAST CORNER OF THE PALATINE,
PALACE AND BRIDGE OF CALIGULA.

Forum Romanum.

Description of Plate XXIV.

PROBABLE RESTORATION OF THE PALACE AND BRIDGE OF CALIGULA, LOOKING WEST.

A. NORTH-EAST corner of the Palatine, with part of the Palace of the time of Hadrian.

B and C. Part of the Palace and Bridge of Caligula.

D—D. Probable restoration of the bridge. This points in a direct line to the place of public execution on the Tarpeian Rock, and the remains of the Temple of Jupiter Capitolinus on the top of that rock [y].

In the photo-engraving from the drawing by Signor Cicconetti, the part that is shewn by darker tints is traced from photographs, the light parts are restorations made to follow on the lines, as an architect would see that they must have gone. The ruins are now concealed by modern buildings, which has caused them to be overlooked. The construction is of the time of Cajus, commonly called Caligula, and the site is identified by having ascertained that this temple with the three fine columns, so long a matter of discussion, is the Temple of Castor and Pollux. Suetonius states that Caligula used this temple as a vestibule to his palace, which must be the one that is here visible, and is close to it.

[y] See also Photograph, No. 1757, for a general view of this Palace; and 1451 for the springing of the arches of the bridge; and 1447 for two of the piers of the bridge; and 1532 for the aqueduct bridge of Ponte Lupo, for comparison; and 1756 for the construction of the brick wall.

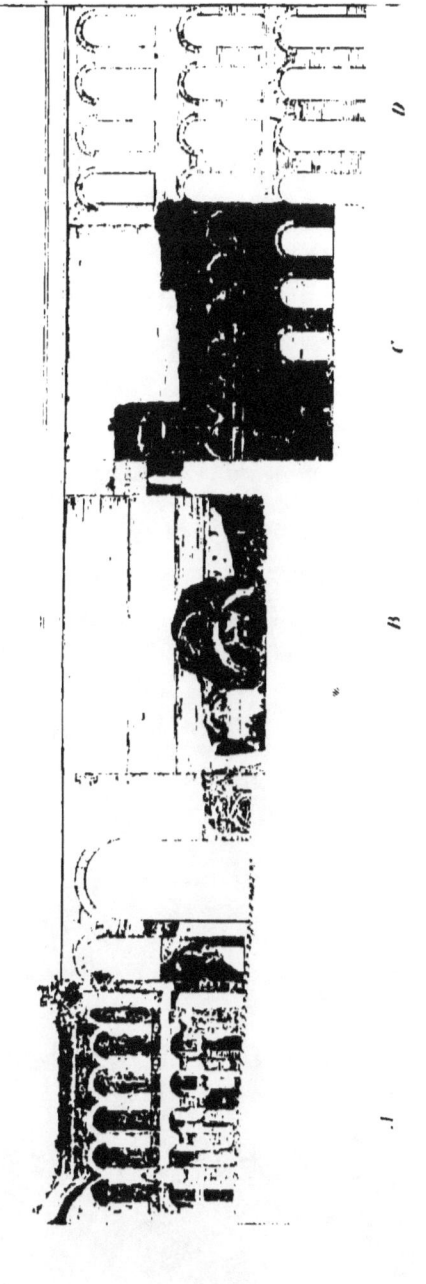

FORUM ROMANUM.

PLATE XXV.

COINS OR MEDALS,
With Representations of Buildings and Sculptures in the Forum.

Description of Plate XXV.

FOUR MEDALS RELATING TO THE FORUM.

1. The Temple of Concord.

This is a large bronze medal of Tiberius, A.D. 11. On the obverse is the head of that Emperor, with the legend; on the reverse is this temple, with portico of the Corinthian order, flanked wings, and standing on a lofty *stylobate*, or basement; in the centre is the figure of Concord, seated, and a warrior on either side. The central figure is in front of the doorway.

Of this the sill remains *in situ*, with the sockets for the pivots, which were used instead of hinges.

2. The Basilica Æmilia, from a Medal of M. Lepidus, A.D. 14.

The legend is,

AIMILIA S. C. REF. M LEPIDUS.

It is one of the coins or medals of the family, or Gens Æmilia.

3. *Obverse:*—HADRIANVS AVGVSTVS.

Reverse:—COS. III. S. C. The Emperor standing on a rostrum, addressing the citizens, who hold up their hands in acclamation. In the background is the portico of a temple.

(It is probably the rostrum and Temple of Julius Cæsar.)

4. *Obverse:* — IMP.[erator] CAESAR TRAIANVS HADRIANVS AVG-[vstus] P.M. P[ontifex] M[aximus] T.P. T[ribunus] P[lebis] PATR[iæ] P[ater] COS. III. [consul third time].

Reverse: — RELIQVIAE VETERA H. S. NOVIES MILL[ia] ABOLITA. Figure of a lictor, with his hatchet and a torch, setting fire to a heap of deeds of paper or parchment. These two medals or coins are therefore both of the same year, A.D. 119, when the Emperor Hadrian was consul for the third time, and relate to the same event, the cancelling of the public debts, which he celebrated on his birthday, January 24, of that year; the one represents the burning of the deeds, the other the Emperor informing the people of what had been done, and this shews us the occasion.

FOUR MEDALS RELATING TO THE FORUM.

FORUM ROMANUM.

PLATE XXVI.

COINS OR MEDALS,
WITH REPRESENTATIONS OF BUILDINGS AND SCULPTURES IN THE FORUM.

Forum Romanum.

Description of Plate XXVI.

1. OCTOSTYLE TEMPLE OF VENUS, on a coin of Hadrian,—legend,
VENERI . FELICI . S. C.

This portico was probably on the south side of the temple, on the west side of that of Roma, of which a doorway of the time of Hadrian remains; if so, it must have been destroyed when the great basilica of Maxentius and Constantine was built. Or it may have been on the northern side, where the monastery now is, and destroyed when the travertine was sold to the Jesuits in the sixteenth century, as materials for this great church.

2. DECASTYLE TEMPLE OF ROME, with the legend—
ROMAE . AETERNAE . S.C.

On a coin of Hadrian, with the head of the Emperor on the obverse. On the reverse is this temple dedicated to Rome.

The group of figures on the top of the pediment are supposed by Professor Donaldson to be Rome, and Venus, and Cupid. They may be so, but there were two temples under one roof.

3. TOMB OF MAXIMIANUS, on a coin of Maxentius, with the legend—
AETERNA . MEMORIA . NOSTR.

This has been mistaken for the circular Temple of Romulus, son of Maxentius, built in the Via Sacra, against the back of the Temple of Roma, which had its front towards the Forum Pacis. The Church of SS. Cosmas and Damian was made out of these three temples.

4. MARS VLT[or].

Obverse:—Head of Cæsar Augustus, with that legend.
Reverse:—Hexastyle circular Temple of Mars Ultor.

Between the columns on each side are the Roman military standards. In the central one, the Imperial Eagle, with extended wings, rests on the Brutum Fulmen.

5. TETRASTYLE CIRCULAR TEMPLE OF AUGUSTUS.

Obverse:—Head of Augustus, with the legend—
DIVVS . AVGVSTVS . PATER . S.C.

Reverse:—The circular temple.

There is reason to believe that this was on the site now occupied by the Church of S. Theodore, and that the house in which Augustus was born was on the same site.

6. HECASTYLE TEMPLE OF ANTONINUS AND FAUSTINA, in the Via Sacra, with the legend—
AETERNITAS . S.C.

On the obverse is the head of the Empress Faustina. The reverse is this temple.—The variations from the existing building are so great as to make it evident that these medals were made from the designs before the buildings were erected.

COINS OR MEDALS OF BUILDINGS IN THE FORUM.

FORUM ROMANUM.

PLATE XXVII.

COINS OR MEDALS,
WITH REPRESENTATIONS OF BUILDINGS AND SCULPTURES IN THE FORUM.

FORUM ROMANUM.

DESCRIPTION OF PLATE XXVII.

COINS OR MEDALS.

1. TEMPLE OF JUPITER FERETRIUS.

On the obverse is a head, supposed to be the portrait of M. C. Marcellus, the conqueror of Sicily. This medal was struck by his descendant, Cornelius P. Sertulus Marcellinus, B.C. 18, with the Cicilian symbol, the triquetra, or triple leg, with the name MARCELLINVS. It is singular that the triple leg is the heraldic badge of the Isle of Man, between England and Ireland, and it may be said Scotland also; perhaps the triple leg is an allusion to this circumstance, that the tribe of Marcellinus may have occupied an island similarly situated.

On the reverse is represented Marcus Claudius Marcellus dedicating the *spolia opima*, a term by which those trophies were specially known, that the general had taken from the body of a general of the enemy, whom he had himself slain.

2. TEMPLE OF JANUS.

On the obverse, the head of Nero, with the words—

IMP . NERO . CAESAR . AVG . PONT . MAX .
TR . POT . P . P

On the reverse is a representation of a temple of Janus, with the legend—

PACE . PER . TERRA . MARIQ . PARTA .
JANVM . CLVSIT

Peace having been proclaimed by land and sea, he shut the Janus; and the sigles s . c.

3. TEMPLE OF JUPITER CAPITOLINUS.

On the obverse, the head of the emperor, with the legend—

IMP . CAES . VESPASIANVS . AVG . P . M .
TR . P . P . P . COS . VII.

IMPerator CAEsar VESPASIANVS AVGustus, Pontifex Maximus, Tribunitiâ Potestate, Pater Patriæ, cons. VII.

On the reverse is the hecastyle Corinthian temple of Jupiter Capitolinus, raised upon three steps, with the sigles s . c. in the exergue.

COINS OR MEDALS OF BUILDINGS IN THE FORUM

4. Temple of Trajan.

On the obverse, the head of Trajan, with the inscription—

IMP . CAES . NERVAE . TRAIANO . AVG .
GER . DAC . P . M . TR . P . COS . V . P . P .

On the reverse is the legend—

S . P . Q . R . OPTIMO . PRINCIPI

with s . c in the exergue, which surrounds a perspective representation of an octastyle Corinthian temple, apparently in the centre of an open area, with a distyle portico on either side, and in front the representation of an altar.

5. Temple of Jupiter Ultor, or the Avenger.

On the obverse is the head of the emperor, with the legend—

IMP . C . M . AVR . SEV . ALEXANDER . AVG .

On the reverse is the epigraph, in continuation, apparently, of the one just quoted on the obverse—

IOVI . VLTORI . P . M . TR . P . III . COS . II . P . P .

There is a large-sized hecastyle temple raised on three steps.

6. Temple of Vesta.

On the obverse, the head of Vespasian, with the legend—

IMP . CAES . VES . AVG . CENS
IMPerator CAESar VESpasianus AVGustus CENsor.

The reverse has the word VESTA, and a representation of one of the temples of the goddess.

FORUM ROMANUM.

PLATES XXVIII., XXIX.
INSCRIPTION OF AUGUSTUS, NOW AT ANCYRA,
CALLED THE
MONUMENTUM ANCYRANUM.

Rerum gestarum diví Augusti, quibus orbem terra[rum] imperio populi Rom(aui) subiecit, et inpensarum, quas in rem publicam populumque Ro[ma]num fecit, incisarum in duabus aheneis pilis, quae su[n]t Romae positae, exemplar sub[i]ectum.

Annos undeviginti natus exercitum privato consilio et privata impensa comparavi, per quem rem publicam [do]minatione factionis oppressam in libertatem vindic[avi. *Propter quae sen*]atus decretis honori[*fi*]cis in ordinem su*m*m [*me adlegit C. Pansa et A. Hirti*]o consulibu[*s, c*]on[*sula*rem locum [*mihi tribuens. Eodemque tempore imp*]erium mihi dedit. Res publica, n[*e quid accideret, a senatu mihi*] pro praetore simul cum consulibus [*t*]r[*adita est tuenda. Populus*] autem eodem anno me consulem, cum [*consul uterque bello ceci*]disset, et trium virum rei publicae constituend[*ae in quinquennium creavit.*

Qui parentem meum [*occideru*]n[*t, co*]s in exilium expuli iudiciis legitimis ultus eorum [*scelus et p*]ostea bellum inferentis rei publicae vici [*acie bis.*

A]rma terra e[*t*] mar[*i civilia exter*]naque toto in orbe terrarum s[*ustinui* victorque omnibu[*s superstitib*]us civibus peperci. § Exte[*rnas* gentes, quibus tuto [*parcere pot*]ui, [*co*]nservare quam excidere m[*alui. . . . . .* Millia civium Roma[*norum in*] sacramento meo fuerunt circiter . . . . . . ta . § Ex quibus dedu[*xi in coloni*]as aut remisi in municipia sua stipen[*dis emeri*tis millia aliquanto [*plus qu*]am trecenta et iis omnibus agros a [*me emptos* aut pecuniam pro pr[*aediis a*] me dedi. § Naves cepi sescen[*tas practer e*]as, si quae minore[*s quam trir*]emes fuerunt. §

Bis o]vans triumpha[*vi, tris egi cur*]ulis triumphos et appella[*tus sum viciens se*]mel imperator. [*Cum deinde plu*]ris triumphos mihi sen[*atus decrevisset, iis su*]persedi [*et tantummodo laur*]us deposui, § in Capi[*tolio votis, quae quoque bello nuncu*[*param, reddi*]tis. § Ob res a[*ut a me aut per legatos* meos auspicis meis terra ma[*riqu*]e prospere gestas qu[*inquagiens ? et quin*quiens decrevit senatus supp[*lica*]ndum esse dis immo[*rtalibus. Dies, pe*]r quo[*s*] ex senatus consulto [*s*]upplicatum est, fuere DC[*CCLXXXV. In trium*phis] ducti sunt ante cu[*rrum me*]um reges aut re[*g*]um lib[*eri VIIII. Consul fuer*]am ter deciens, [*cum scripsi*] haec, [*annumque trigesimum septimum tribu*[*niciae potestatis* [*agebam.*

Dictatura]m et absent[*i et praesenti mihi datam a senatu populoque M. Marce*]l[*lo et*] L. Ar[*runtio consulibus non accepi. Non recusavi in summa frumenti p*]enuri[*a curam annonae, qua non neglegenter facta meis sumptibu*]s [*met*]u et pe[*ri*]c[*ulo praesenti populi*]m univ[*ersum paucis diebus liberavi. Tum*] con[*sulatum mihi datum et a*]nnuum [*et perpetuum non accepi.*

Consulibus M. Vinucio et Q. Lucretio et postea P.] et Cn. L[*entulis et tertium Paullo Fabio Maximo et Q. Tuberone senatu populo*]qu[*e Romano consentientibus*] . . . .

Trium virum fui rei publicae constituendae annis continuis decem ; princeps senatus usque ad eum diem, quo die scr]i[*psi haec, per annos quadraginta ; pontifex, augur, quindecim viru*]m [*sac*]ri[*s faciundis, septem virum epulonum, frater arvalis, sodalis Ti*]t[*ius, fetialis.*

INSCRIPTION OF AUGUSTUS, NOW AT ANCTRA

Monumentum Ancyranum.

Patriciorum numerum auxi consul quintum iussu populi et senatus. § Senatum ter legi. et In consulatu sexto censum populi conlega M. Agrippa egi. § Lustrum post annum alterum et quadragensimum feci. § Quo lustro civium Romanorum censa sunt capita quadragiens centum millia et sexaginta tria millia. [*Iteru*]m consulari cum imperio lustrum solus feci C. Censorin[*o et C.*] Asinio cos. § Quo lustro censa sunt civium Romanoru[*m capita*] quadragiens centum millia et ducenta triginta tria m[*illia*. *Tertiu*]m consulari cum imperio lustrum conlega Tib. Cae[*sare filio meo feci*] § Sex. Pompeio et Sex. Appuleio cos. Quo lustro ce[*nsa sunt civium Ro*]manorum capitum quadragiens centum mill[*ia et nongenta tr*]iginta et septem millia. § Legibus novi[*s latis et reduxi multa e*]xempla maiorum exolescentia iam ex nost[*ra civitate et ipse proposui*] multarum rer[*um exe*]mpla imitanda pos[*teris*.

Pro valetudine mea quinto quoque anno per cons]ules et sacerdotes [*ut vota susciperentur, senatus decrevit. Ex quibus*] votis s[*aep*]e fecerunt vivo me ludos . . . . *modo sacerdotu*]m quattuor amplissima collegia modo consules . . . . *Privati*]m etiam et municipa[*ti*]m universi cives sacrificaverunt continuo] apud omnia pulvinaria pro valetudine mea].

Nomen meum senatus consulto incl]usum est in saliare carmen et sacrosanctus ut essem . . . . *et ut qu*]o[*ad*] viverem, tribunicia potestas mihi esset, lege sanctum est. Pontif*]ex maximus n[*e fi*[erem in vivi [*l*]o[*cum, r*]ecusavi, populo illud sacer]dotium deferente mihi, quod pater meus antea habuerat. Cepi id] sacerdotium aliquod post annos eo mortuo qui id per civiles dissens]io[*nes*] occupaverat, cuncta ex Italia ad comitia mea tanta multit]udine, quanta Romae nun[*quam antea fuisse traditur, cocunte P.*] Sulpicio C. Valgio consulibus.

Aram Fortunae reduci iuxta? ae]des Honoris et Virtutis ad portam [*Capenam* . . . . *pro reditu meo se*]natus consacravit, in qua ponti[*fices virginesque Vestales au*]niversarium sacrificium facere iussit, quo die consulibus Q. Luc]r[*e*]tio et [*M. Vinucio*] in urbem ex Syria redieram, diemque ex nomine nostro Augustalia appell]avit. *Senatus consulto eodem tempor*]e pars [*praetorum et trib*]uno[*ru*]m una cum consule Q. Lucretio] et princip[*i*]b[*us viris obvi*]am mihi m[*issi sunt in Campaniam, qui h*]onos [*ad h*]oc [*tempus*] nemini praeter [*me decretus est. Cum e*]x [*Hisp*]ania Ga[*l*[*liaque, rebus in his pr*]ovincis prospe[*re gestis, Romam redibam T*]ib. N[*ero*]ne P. Qui[*ntilio consulibus*], aram Pacis Augu]st[*ae senatus pro*] redi[*t*]u meo co[*nsacrari censuit*] ad campum Martium, in qua ara ma]gistratus et s[*a*]c[*erdotes virginesque V*estales anniversarium sacrific*]ium facer[*e iussit.

Ianum] Quiri[*num, quem cla*]usum esse [*maiores nostri voluerunt, cum p*]er totum i[*mperium po*]puli Roma[*ni esset terra*]s[*tris*] nav[*atisque*] pax, cum p[*rius quam*] nasceret[*e*]r, [*ab urbe condita*] bis omnino clausum fu]isse prodatur m[*emori*]ae, ter me pri[*ncipe senatus cla*]udendum esse c[*en*]sui[*t*].

Fil]io[*s*] meos, quos iuv[*enes mi*]hi eripuit fo[*rtuna, Ga*]ium et Lucium Caesares honoris mei caussa senatus populusque Romanus annum quintum et decimum agentis consulis designavit, ut [e]um magistratum inirent post quinquennium. Et ex eo die, quo deducti sunt in forum, ut interessent consiliis publicis, decrevit senatus. § Equites autem Romani universi principem iuuentutis utr[u]mqu[e eo]rum parm[is e]t hastis argenteis donatum appellaverunt.

Plebei Romanae viritim HS trecenos numeravi ex testamento patris mei, et nomine meo HS quadringenos ex bellorum manibiis consul quintum dedi, iterum autem in consulatu decimo ex [p]atrimonio meo HS quadringenos congiari viritim pernumer[a]vi, § et consul undecimum duodecim frumentationes frumento pr[i]vatim coempto emensus sum, § et tribunicia potestate duodecimum quadringenos nummos tertium viritim dedi. Quae mea congiaria p[e]rvenerunt ad homi]num millia nunquam minus quinquagin[t]a et ducenta. § Tribu[nic]iae potestatis duodevicensimum consul XII trecentis et vigint[i] millibus plebis urbanae sexagenos denarios viritim dedi. § In colon[i]s militum meorum consul quintum ex manibiis viritim millia nummum singula dedi; acceperunt id triumphale congiarium in colonis hominum circiter centum et viginti millia. § Consul tertium decimum sexagenos denarios plebei, quae tum frumentum publicum accipieba[t], dedi; ea millia hominum paulo plura quam ducenta fuerunt.

Pecunia[m pro] agris, quos in consulatu meo quarto et postea consulibus M. Cr[asso e]t Cn. Lentulo Augure adsignavi militibus, solvi municipis. Ea s]u[mma sest]ertium circiter sexsiens milliens fuit, quam [pro] colla[t]icis praed]is n]umeravi, et ci[r]citer bis milli̇ens et sescentiens, quod pro agris provin[c]ialibus solvi. § Id primus et solus omnium, qui [d]eduxerunt colonias militum in Italia aut in provincis ad memor[i]am aetatis meae feci. Et postea Ti. Nerone et Cn. Pisone consulibus, item[q]ue C. Antistio et D. Laelio cos., et C. Calvisio et L. Pasieno consulibus, et [L. Lentulo et] M. Messalla consulibus, § et L. Caninio et Q. Fabricio co[nsu]li[bus veteran]os emeritis stipendis in sua municip[ia remis]i, praem[ia aere n]umerato persolvi, quam in rem seste[rtium . . . . m]illi[ens . . . .] impendi.

Quater pecunia mea iuvi aerarium, ita ut sestertium millien[s] et quingenties ad eos qui praerant aerario detulerim. Et M. Lep[ido et L. Ar[r]untio cos. i[n a]erarium militare, quod ex consilio [meo co[nstitu]tum est, ex [quo] praemia darentur militibus, qui vi[ce]n[a plurave] sti[pendia] emeruissent, HS milliens et septing[e]nti[ens Ti. Caesaris nomi]n[e et m]eo detuli.

. . . . anno qu]o Cn. et P. Lentuli c[ons]ules fuerunt, cum def[i]cerent . . . ., centum millibus h[omi]num [ex meis] opibus [emp]to fru- m[ento] . . . . . . um . . ia . . . st . . . . [dedi].

INSCRIPTION OF AUGUSTUS, NOW AT ANCYRA – 2

Monumentum Ancyranum.

Curiam et continens ei Chalcidicum, templumque Apollinis in Palatio cum porticibus, aedem divi Iuli, Lupercal, porticum ad circum Flaminium, quam sum appellari passus ex nomine eius qui priorem eodem in solo fecerat Octaviam, pulvinar ad circum maximum, aedes in Capitolio Iovis feretri et Iovis tonantis, § aedem Quirini, aedes Minervae et Iunonis Reginae et Iovis Libertatis in Aventino, aedem Larum in summa sacra via, § aedem deum Penatium in Velia, aedem Iuventatis, § aedem Matris Magnae in Palatio feci.
Capitolium et Pompeium theatrum utrumque opus impensa grandi refeci sine ulla inscriptione nominis mei. § Rivos aquarum compluribus locis vetustate labentes refeci. et aquam quae Marcia appellatur duplicavi fonte novo in rivum eius inmisso. § Forum Iulium et basilicam, quae fuit inter aedem Castoris et aedem Saturni, coepta profligataque opera a patre meo, perfeci § et eandem basilicam consump[*tam*] incendio ampliato eius solo sub titulo nominis filiorum m[*eorum i*]ncohavi et, si vivus non perfecissem, perfici ab heredib[*us meis iussi*]. Duo et octoginta templa deum in urbe consul sext[*um ex decreto*] senatus refeci, nullo praetermisso quod [*eo*] temp[*ore refici oporteret*]. Co[*nsul*] septimum viam Flamini[*am ex*] ma[*nibiis*] Ari[*mino tenus et in ea pontes* o[*mnes*] praeter Mul[*v*]ium et Minu[*c*]ium [*refeci*].
In privato solo Martis Ultoris templum [*f*]orumque Augustum [*ex manibiis feci.* § Theatrum ad aede[*m*] Apollinis in solo magna ex parte a p[*r*]i[*v*]atis empto feci, quod sub nomine M. Marcell[*i*] generi mei esset. § Don[*a ex* manibiis in Capitolio et in aede divi Iuli et in aede Apollinis et in aede Vestae et in templo Martis Ultoris consacravi, § quae mihi constiterunt HS. circiter milliens. § Auri coronari pondo triginta et quinque millia municipiis et colonis Italiae conferentibus ad triumphos meos quintum consul remisi et postea, quotienscumque imperator a[*ppe*]llatus sum, aurum coronarium non accepi decernentibus municipii[*s* et colon[*iis st*]u[*dio eodem*] adque antea decreverant.
Te[*r*] *munus* gladiatorium dedi meo nomine et quinqu[*i*]ens filiorum m[*eo*rum aut nepotum nomine ; quibus muneribus [*plu*[*g*]]naverunt homi- nu[*m*] ci[*rc*]iter decem millia. § Bis [*at*]hletarum undique accitorum spec[*taculum po*]pulo pr[*aebui meo*] nomine et tertium nepot[*is*] me[*i*] nomine. § Lu[*do*]s feci me[*o nomine*] quater, aliorum autem m[*agis- trat*]u[*u*]m ter et vice[*ns*. § Pro] conlegio XV virorum magi[*s*][*er con- *]l[*gg*]ii co[*n*]leg[*a*]] M. Agrippa [*ludos saeculare*]s C. Furnio C. Silano cos. [*feci. C*]on[*sul XIII*] ludos M[*arti Ultori feci, quos post i*]d tempus deinc[*eps* . . . . *consules fecerunt.* Venationes b]est[*ia*- rum Africanarum meo nomine aut filiorum meorum et nepotum in ci[*r- co aut i*]n *foro* aut in amphitheatris populo d]edi sexiens et viciens, quibus confecta sunt bestiarum circiter tria [*mill*]ia et quingentae. §
Navalis proeli spectaculum populo [*dedi tr*]ans Tiberim, in quo loco nunc nemus est Caesarum, cava[*to solo in*] longitudinem mille et octingentos pedes, in latitudine[*m mille et*] ducent[*os*]. In quo triginta rostratae naves triremes [*et birem*]es, pluris autem minores inter se confluxerunt. [*In quibus c*]lassibus pugnaverunt praeter remiges millia ho[*minum tr*]ia circiter. §
In templis omnium civitatium p[*rovinciae*] Asiae victor ornamenta reposui, quae spoliatis tem[*plis hostis*] cum quo bellum gesseram privatim possederat. § Statuae [*meae*] pedestres et equestres et in quadrigeis argenteae steterunt in urbe XXC circiter, quas ipse sustuli exque ea pecunia dona aurea in aede Apollinis meo nomine et illorum, qui mihi statuarum honorem habuerunt, posui. §

PLAN 01

PLAN OF THE FORUM ROMANUM AND VIA SACRA.

A. Mons Capitolinus.   B. Tarpeian Rock.
C. Mons Palatinus.   D. Forum Romanum.

1. Capitolium: the Ærarium, with the steps to the Senaculum on the right, leading up to a large hall behind the Tabularium, which is over the Ærarium, and has the Municipium over it. (See the eight Plates at the end of vol. i.)

2. Temple of Concord: the Podium (with a passage under it, which led originally to the steps of the Senaculum); in front are seen the sockets of the pivots of the great doors, on the top of a triple flight of steps. (See Pl. III., IV., V., and Photos., Nos. 3145, 46, 50.)

3. Temple of Saturn: the Podium, with three columns remaining at the corner. Behind it is the head of a doorway, at the foot of a steep flight of steps, which passes under and behind the Ærarium and Tabularium, and goes straight up to the third floor, without any doorway into it. (See Pl. VIII., IX., X., and Photos., No. 3148.)

4. Porticus of the Dei Consentes, with three shops behind it. These shops are continued under the modern road to the left. (See Pl. XI., and Photos., Nos. 914, 2325.)

5. Temple of Vespasian: the Podium and seven columns. (See Pl. XII., and Photos., Nos. 897, 929.)

6. Site of the Porta Saturnii, called also the Postern Gate of the Fortress of Saturn. (See Pl. III., and Photos., No. 3147.)

It was a double gate, and the foundation of the wall between the two gates remains. The pavement on the left is of the time of the Republic, that on the right is of the time of the Early Empire. This gate is on the Clivus Capitolinus, and originally was also on the boundary-line between the fortified Hill of Saturn and the Forum Romanum. The ground is on a higher level within the line of the old wall.

7. Remains of one of the Rostra. (See Pl. XIII., and Photos., No. 916.)

8. Remains of the Milliarium Aureum, or gilt mile-stone, called also Umbilica Urbis. (See Pl. XIII., and Photos., No. 917.)

9. Arch of Septimius Severus. (See Pl. XIV., and Photos., No. 1209.)

PLAN O

THE FORUM ROMANUM AND VIA SACRA, IN JANUARY, 1876.

10. Vestibule of the great Prison. (See Pl. XXII., XXIII., and Photos., Nos. 721, 1152.)

This is called the Prison of S. Peter, with the church of S. Giuseppe (Joseph), or of the Crucifixion, over it. A stream of water running from it is shewn, meeting other streams from the Quirinal and the Palatine, all now underground.

11. Basilica Julia: the northern and original part built of Travertine stone, the walls going from west to east. (See Pl. XXXIV., and Photos., No. 3165.

12. Basilica Julia: the southern part added by Augustus; rebuilt after a fire in the third century, with the modern brick bases. (See Pl. XXXV., and Photos., No. 2289.)

13. Paved street and steps up to the raised platform of the Basilica Julia.

And on the other side a row of shops (?) down the middle of the Forum, called by some bases of great columns, but they are hollow, and are built of brick.

14. Vicus Tuscus.

15. Cloaca Maxima: the part left open where it passes under the south end of the Basilica Julia, and across the Forum. (See Pl. XXXVI., and Photos., No. 3164.)

16. Column of Phocas. (See Pl. XXIX., and Photos., No. 2959.)

17. Marble Screen, walls in the Comitium. (See Pl. XXXI., XXXII., XXXIII., and Photos., Nos. 2961, 2962, 3160.)

18. Base of an equestrian statue of Domitian (?) or Constantine(?). (See Photos., No. 1658, 3169.)

19. Site of the Regia and the house of the Vestal Virgins. (See Photos., No. 3195*.)

20. Palace of Caligula. (See Pl. XIV., and Photos., No. 3170.)

21. Bridge of Caligula. (See Photo., No. 1757.)

22. Temple of Castor and Pollux, or the Dioscuri. (See Pl. XV., and Photos., No. 3157.

23. Rostrum of Julius Cæsar. (See Pl. XXXVI., and Photos., No. 3159.)

24. Temple of Julius Cæsar. (See Pl. XXXVII., and Photos., No. 1686.)

25. Pavement and steps of street to Palatine.

26. Fountain of Juturna (?). (See Photos., No. 3158.)

27. Temple of Vesta. (See Photos., No. 3149—3158.)

28. Arch of Fabianus (?.

29. Temple of Romulus, the son of Maxentius, now part of the church of SS. Cosmas and Damian. (See Photos., No. 268.)

30. Portico of the Temple of Antoninus and Faustina. (See Photos., Nos. 298, 824, 839, 1220.)

31. Temple of Roma, now part of the church of SS. Cosmas and Damian. (See Photos., No. 1135.)

32. Wall against which the Marble Plan of Rome was placed. (See Photos., No. 783.)

33. Excavations made in 1867, in search of fragments of the Marble Plan. (See Photos., No. 782.)

34. Basilica of Constantine. (See Photos., Nos. 204, 205, 784.)

35 to 39. PALACES OF THE CÆSARS. (See Part I., Pl. IX. and X., and Photos., 2224 to 2256, and 2295 to 2303.)

35. Palace of Trajan (?). (See Part III., Pl. VIII., and Supplement, Pl. XVI.)

36. Part of that of Caligula (?). (See Photos., No. 1757.)

37. Passage of Caligula (?), leading to his Bridge. (See Photos., No. 2255.)

38, 39. Palaces of Trajan (?) and Hadrian (?). (See Pl. XIV., and Photos., Nos. 2251, 2252.)

a a a. Modern houses.

b. Monastery and church of S. Giuseppe, over the Prison of S. Peter (?). The probable site of the Græcostasis is between this and the Temple of Concord, where the sloping path of Michael Angelo now is. (See Photos., Nos. 580, 848, 849, 1152, 1790.)

c. Church of S. Martina, with the Academy of S. Luke and Gallery of the Fine Arts. (See Photos., No. 306.)

d. Church of S. Hadrian. (See Photos., No. 998.)

e. Cella of the Temple of Antoninus and Faustina, now the church of S. Lorenzo in Miranda. The walls are built of large blocks of tufa taken from the second wall of Rome, which passed near this; the marble casing has been removed. (See Photos., No. 298.)

f. Church of SS. Cosmas and Damian, made out of three temples. (See Photos., Nos. 268, 418, 1135.)

g. Church of S. Maria Liberatrice, on the site of the Regia, afterwards the house of the Pontifex Maximus, and subsequently of the Vestal Virgins. (See Pl. XXI. and XXIII.)

h. Farnesi Gardens. (See Photos., Nos. 103, 104.)

i i i. Streams of water.

THE VIA SACRA IN ROME.

BY

JOHN HENRY PARKER, C.B.
Hon. M.A. Oxon., F.S.A. Lond.;
Keeper of the Ashmolean Museum of History and Antiquities
in the University of Oxford, etc.

✦

OXFORD:
JAMES PARKER AND CO.
LONDON:
JOHN MURRAY, ALBEMARLE-STREET.
1876.

PREFACE.—VIA SACRA.

At this stage of my work on the Archæology of Rome it seems expedient to give some further account of its origin, its object, and the causes of the long delay in bringing it out. It originated in the desire of regular employment for my time in Rome, having been sent to spend my winters there by my physicians after a severe attack of rheumatic fever. I well knew how many books had been written on the history of the city of Rome, which is a necessary part of the history of the world and of the civilization of the human race, but that no one had applied the principles of the modern science of archæology to this subject. I thought it would be an easy matter for me to do this, and put the information I thus obtained into a popular shape for the general reader. I purchased all the most recent and best books on the history of the city of Rome, in English, French, and Italian, and friends translated for me from the German as much as appeared necessary for my purpose, which was to ascertain THE TRUE HISTORY OF THE CITY OF ROME. None of these works satisfied me. The writers have in no instance studied architectural history on the principle of comparison with well-dated examples, or made that the basis of their work, which appears to me to be essential.

As a younger man, for twenty years of my life my favourite study had been the comparative progress of architecture in England and France, by a careful examination of the construction and the details of *dated examples*. In England I had the assistance of Professor Willis and the leading members of the Royal Archæological Institute, in the foundation of which I had assisted materially, by taking all the outlay and risk of the publications on myself for the first five years; in France I had the help of M. De Caumont* and the French Archæological Society, of which I have been a member for these thirty years—I was therefore well accustomed to the work, and the method of examination of the existing remains, and could readily apply the same principles and practice to Rome. I was also able to compare the remains there with similar buildings in other countries, and Roman buildings are often more perfect in the provinces

---

* At an International Congress of Archæologists, held at Antwerp under his direction, the medal (the only one that was given) was presented to me by him, for my services in Rome.

than in Rome. But as the chief interest of Roman architecture belongs to a period of which we have few or no remains in England or the north of France, I had a fresh lesson to learn in Rome, and required the help of the local antiquaries, which I readily obtained. On my first visit to Rome I had been introduced to the Baron Visconti, and his nephew, the Cavaliere C. L. Visconti, from whom I have received much kind assistance; and his former pupil, Signor Lanciani, now one of the best archæologists in Rome, and Secretary of the Archæological Commission of the Municipality, has also given me similar assistance. I found that both Visconti and Lanciani adhered to what they call the "Roman traditions," with which I could not agree, as I soon saw that they were only the conjectures of learned men during the last three centuries, and were of no real authority whatever. After the first two or three seasons I became acquainted with Dr. Fabio Gori, and employed him to assist me in that part of my work which relates to the Aqueducts, which he had studied and understood better than most people, from the circumstance of his being a native of Subiaco, the place from the neighbourhood of which all the chief aqueducts come to Rome. Dr. Henzen, the head of the German Archæological Institute, also allows me to consult him frequently, on the subject of Inscriptions chiefly, and has rendered me much service. I also have the use of the excellent library of that Institute, and have frequently attended their meetings, but I cannot *always* agree with any of my friends; it seems to me that some are right on one point and others on another point, and that the only safe plan is to compare the exact words of the Classical authors (*without note or comment*) with the existing remains, of which the dates are soon seen by comparison with other similar buildings, by experienced eyes. This is the principle on which my work is carried out, to obtain the best information that I can get either from books or from living authorities, and then form my own conclusions from them after consideration. I have thus explained the *origin* of my work.

The *object* is to explain in a popular manner the *true* history of the city of Rome; the received history, as taught in all our schools, is founded almost entirely on *conjecture*, because many of the most interesting and important buildings were buried, and had been so for centuries, until the recent excavations were made. Soon after I began my work I saw the necessity of making many excavations, and I spent a large sum upon them (and upon the drawings and photographs necessary to explain them), having obtained permission from Cardinal Antonelli, on behalf of the Pontifical Government. His holiness Pius IX. himself took an interest in the matter, allowed me to present him with a volume of my photographs, and to have a private interview to explain them; he then called me a benefactor of Rome, and gave me his silver medal in remembrance of my visit.

Under the Italian Government, H.R.H. Prince Humbert has also honoured me with a private interview to explain my views and objects, and after that interview recommended Signor Rosa to attend to any suggestions of mine, as I was evidently an archæologist of much experience; and this led to the great and important excavations in the Colosseum. Signor Bonghi, as Minister of Public Instruction; and Signor Fiorelli, the head of the Department of Archæology in the Italian Government, have been most kind to me, and encouraged me to go on with my work, of making English and American people understand the remains of the buildings of ancient Rome.

I make no pretension to know more than other people, but I have often been told that I have the art of explaining antiquities in a very natural manner, easy to be understood and remembered. The late Earl Stanhope frequently said publicly, both to the Society of Antiquaries of London and to the Kent Archæological Society, that "if other people could teach Archæology as Mr. Parker does, it would be far more popular than it is; the subject itself is most interesting, but it is usually taught in such a dry technical manner that most people are soon disgusted with it, and find that they have not time to learn it *in that manner;* but if it can be learned in so agreeable a manner as we learn it on our excursions, taking a pleasant walk or drive, and having the architectural history of each building explained to us when we come to it, and have time to see it, we should all be glad to take such lessons in Archæology."

My great object is to explain antiquities by the eye rather than by the ear, for this reason I have had a very large number of photographs taken, which, next to seeing the objects themselves, are the best means and way of understanding them. Whenever I can do so, I shew the objects themselves, and explain them on the spot. This has been my practice for many years with the various archæological societies to which I belong; I learnt the lesson first in my youth, from the late M. De Caumont, of Caen, one of the leaders of the French Society, who set the example of making archæological excursions, and going to different parts of France for that purpose, and afterwards urging his friends and pupils to establish local societies for the study of Archæology in each place that they had visited. I had been introduced to M. De Caumont by a mutual friend, Dr. Buckland, the geologist, at a meeting of the Norman

Society at Caen, in the year 1834. The late Mr. Albert Way and myself had attended these meetings of the French Society, or *Congresses* as they are called, and we endeavoured to introduce them into England in the annual excursions of the Royal Archæological Institute; but M. De Caumont had often three or four such excursions in a year, and in Rome the British and American Archæological Society, for some years, has had them once or twice a week during the season, when the weather permits. This has enabled me to learn the opinions of all parties, and compare them, and correct any errors into which I may have fallen, for archæologists are not more infallible than other people; I have now followed this plan for some years, and believe that few have had more opportunity of arriving at the truth. It is certainly a case in which "the multitude of counsellors ought to give wisdom," or at least the best information.

I have long seen that the best drawings cannot always be depended on for the history of architecture. Some of the best architectural draughtsmen of my time have made drawings for me, such, for instance, as the lamented Orlando Jewitt, and Mackenzie before him; others have given them to me from love of the subject, such as Mr. W. Twopeny, Mr. E. Blore, Mr. R. C. Hussey, and Professor Willis; but on comparing these drawings on the spot, I have found errors in many of them, and sometimes such errors as would mislead in studying the history of the building. Drawings are usually made in the study, from hasty sketches made on the spot, and perhaps not finished for years after the sketch was taken, when the person who made it has often forgotten part of what he intended to shew; more often the drawing is made for the engravers by an artist who has never seen the object, and has only a rough and incorrect sketch to go by. For this reason photographs are indispensable for the explaining the history of the building. No artist ever thinks of shewing the thickness of the mortar between the joints of the stones, or the thickness of the bricks; yet on these two points the date of a building often hangs, at the most important turning-points in the history of architecture.

The violent prejudices there would be to contend with in establishing THE TRUTH soon became evident; no one is willing to believe that what he was taught as true history in youth, and has since taught to others, is almost entirely based upon conjectures, yet this is undoubtedly the case with the history of the city of Rome; it could not be otherwise, when most of the important historical objects were buried, and had been so for centuries.

For this reason also I have adopted photo-engravings[b], which are reproductions of nature by the action of light only, not touched by the human hand, instead of woodcuts, which have to be drawn upon the wood, and depend entirely on the accuracy of the artist who makes the drawing.

Unfortunately the best scholars are just the most difficult persons to be made to see the blunders into which they have been led by what are called the "Roman traditions," or the "received interpretation of the text," which are in fact nothing but the conjectures of learned men during the last three centuries, as has been shewn. The Forum Romanum and the Via Sacra are the chief battle-fields of the archæologists, and especially the Summa Sacra Via, with the ruins upon it. Scholars are often annoyed at being told that the two apses there, back to back, are *not* the Temple of Venus and Rome, and yet this is *demonstrated* in the present volume; the facts are undeniable. That name is quite modern, it is only the conjecture of the great scholars of the last century. Palladio, at the end of the sixteenth century, gives an engraving of one of these apses as the "Temple of the Sun and Moon," which is more near the truth, for they are on the *site* of that temple; but no temple ever had an apse to it, and the construction of these two is identical with the apse *added* in the time of Constantine to the great building of Maxentius, on the site of the Temple of Peace, and probably at first intended to be a rebuilding of that temple on a grander scale, but altered into a basilica in the time of Constantine. In one sense a basilica may be called a market-hall; there was evidently one to each market-place or forum, and as three markets were held on the Summa Sacra Via, three basilicas would be required for them. It is shewn by the records of Dio Cassius and others, that Apollodorus told Hadrian "*he ought to have built* his temple of Roma on this spot," but it is equally plain *that he did not*. This is one of the most conspicuous and important buildings in Rome, and may be taken as a fair example of the rest.

Scholars who have never been in Rome frequently confuse the Via Sacra of the Empire with the Via Sacra or Sancta[c] of the

---

[b] It is not probable that a tenth part of my historical photographs can ever be engraved by any process, but they are records of what has been visible in my time, very much of which is now buried again or entirely destroyed. Any schoolmaster or college tutor, who wishes to explain a particular subject, can get the photographs to illustrate and explain it for a shilling each, at Charing-cross.

[c] The Via Sacra, or Sancta, of the Popes, was the processional path for visiting the relics of the martyrs, starting from the Lateran Palace, where the Pope then resided, and returning to it after going the round on horseback; it may be called the "Pilgrims' road."

Popes, but they are quite distinct things. The Via Sacra was a short street full of temples, divided into three parts; the first part went from the Forum to the foot of the Clivus Sacer, which led up to the Summa Sacra Via. The church of SS. Cosmas and Damian, made out of three temples, one of which is that of Romulus, the son of Maxentius, is at the foot of the *clivus*, and at the southeast end of the old Via Sacra, strictly so called. This road on the high level, made by filling up the old foss-way, was probably then a new road, as the lower part of the church of S. Clement was filled up with earth to that level shortly before that time, after the raid of the Normans under Robert Guiscard. The Via Alesandrina, which is a continuation of the same line to the Forum of Trajan, was probably made by Alexander II., A.D. 1061—73. The expression used both in going and returning by this road, when passing near the Colosseum, is *juxta Colosseum*, which correctly states the fact. The church of S. Francesca Romana is on the Summa Sacra Via; this church was previously called S. Maria Nova, because another S. Maria, then called *antiqua*, was close to it, between that site and the cliff of the Palatine Hill, and that part was excavated in 1874 only (see Plates XXXIX., XL.). The Pontifical Registers give us the date for both parts of it: these were issued by Anastasius, the Librarian, in the ninth century, who was authorized by the Pontifical Government of his time to publish the Registers of the Bishops of Rome from the earliest period, and although for the time of Constantine he has interpolated or forged a long string of very doubtful history[d], yet in other parts there was no reason for his doing so.

The line of it is described in the *Ordo Romanus* under Innocent II., A.D. 1130—1143. (*Codex Urlichs*, pp. 79—85.) The procession in going out from the Lateran passed by the church of S. Clement on the left, and near the Colosseum, then going through the Forum of Trajan and the Piazza di S. Apostoli ... to the bridge and castle of Hadrian, ascended to the Vatican and S. Peter's church; then, in returning to the (Lateran) palace, ascends from near the Temple of Romulus (now SS. Cosmas and Damian) up the pavement on which Simon Magus fell, that is—according to the Church traditions—the Clivus Sacer, where the steps in front of S. Francesca Romana now stand, then going under the Arch of Titus and Vespasian, which is called after the seven-branched candlestick carved upon it, descending to the Meta Sudans before the triumphal arch of Constantine, and turning to the left before the amphitheatre by the Sacra Via, and near the Colosseum, returning to the Lateran,—that is, it ascended again to the high level, passing the Colosseum or amphitheatre, which is one and the same enormous building; the procession passed first along the front of it, and then along the north side, but the writer avoids the repetition of the same word.

[d] All those who are acquainted with mediæval manuscripts know that an immense number of title-deeds for property were forged by the monks, and even an entire Chronicle by the name of Ingulphus. This interpolation of Anastasius gives title-deeds to the property of the great ecclesiastical corporations of Rome, the Vatican, the Late-

It was an ancient Christian custom for the bishop of each diocese to keep a register, in which each succeeding bishop recorded what had been done by his predecessor. In England, in the diocese of Lincoln, the bishops' registers have been preserved from the twelfth century to the present time. Twenty years since I endeavoured to persuade the late Mr. Dimock to publish these, with archæological notes, explaining what remained of each church of the period recorded (which no one could have done better), but the necessary funds were not forthcoming. A similar edition of Anastasius would give the history of architecture from the third century to the ninth, over a great part of Europe; and the Lives of the Cardinals, by Ciaconius, would give a continuation of such a history down to the sixteenth. Scholars are too apt to set down the work of Anastasius as altogether worthless, which is not really the case; it is valuable for certain purposes, and for a certain period, to which the ruins remaining of S. Maria Antiqua belong. The *clivus*, or sloping road, which ascends from the triumphal arch of Constantine to that of Titus, must be the Clivus Triumphalis; the arches are all built over the line of march of the army for the triumphal processions. The *clivus* so called by the Roman authorities, at the north-east corner of the Palatine, must be the Clivus Palatinus. Under the south-east end of the platform of the Summa Sacra Via are remains of substructures of the time of the Kings or of the Republic, and not of the time of Hadrian, where Apollodorus told him he *ought to have* made a place for the machinery of the Colosseum, which it is quite evident he has not done. There are a few of the old stones of tufa, of the second wall of Rome, remaining there *in situ*, and marks of many others in the plaster on the face of the rubble wall, as is often the case in Rome; the mortar has become harder than the stone, and often more durable.

To explain some of the causes of the long *delay* in bringing out my work, reference must be made to the habitual procrastination of the Italian character, and the general ignorance of the people, and the local prejudices that are the consequence of their ignorance. Cardinal Antonelli had warned me, in the first instance, that I should find the subordinate members of the Government extremely jealous of me, and always ready to impede my researches in every way that they could, both directly and indirectly, *more especially the latter*.

ran, and others, attributing them all to Constantine, when he declared THE PLAN OF THE CHURCH, but the Latin of these interpolations is of the ninth century, not of the fourth.

This I have found to be *most true*, and the change of government has made no change in this respect; among the subordinates the same stupid local prejudices exist as before. Rome is jealous of Naples and Florence, and these cities return the compliment; and all are equally jealous of the English, and unwilling to have their antiquities explored and explained. Nevertheless, by patience and perseverance much has been done, and much more may be done if the necessary funds are forthcoming.

Before these excavations were begun, the Cardinal had told me that it seemed so extraordinary, at first sight, to allow an Englishman to do what the Romans themselves were not permitted to do without special permission,—to make deep excavations; there was some fear of an *emeute* (Rome being then in a very feverish state of excitement), therefore I had better have it done in my absence in the first instance. This was done. I gave the commission to the Cavaliere Guidi to make the excavations for me in the name of Dr. Fabio Gori, who superintended them, and sent me a weekly report of what was done and what was found. We there found one of the short *aggeres* of Servius Tullius, the one from the Cœlian to the Aventine, by digging seven pits in a line, each about twenty feet deep, and always finding the *agger* faced by a great wall of tufa, and with the aqueducts upon it, passing over the Porta Capena, and through the western tower of that ancient gate, the lower part of which remains, with a modern tower built upon it, which now forms part of the gardener's house in the garden of the monks of S. Gregory; this house is made out of an ancient *castellum aquæ*, or reservoir of the aqueducts. These excavations proved an important point in the history of the city of Rome,—that the short *aggeres* of Servius Tullius were carried as high up in the valleys as possible, in order to use the old fortifications on the hills to protect the approaches to his gates, and that he did *not* build a continuous wall round Rome across the mouths of the valleys, as has long been assumed from taking a passage in Dionysius *too literally*, a common cause of the popular blunders in the history of the city.

These excavations made a considerable sensation in Rome, and Napoleon III. heard of them from my friend M. Viollet-le-Duc, and directed that in future his excavations in the Farnese gardens, on the Palatine Hill, should be carried on for historical objects also, and not merely to search for statues for the Paris museum, the purpose for which they had been begun. The Emperor had bought the Farnese gardens for that object, but in this he had been entirely deceived, as it was well known to Roman antiquaries that when the Farnese gardens were made the whole of that ground had been thoroughly searched for statues, and the greater part of the Farnese collection now at Naples was found there. Soon after this the Italians took possession of Rome as the capital of united Italy, and they have carried on the excavations for historical objects only, on the Palatine, in the Forum, the Via Sacra, and the Colosseum. Simultaneously with these the Municipality have made numerous excavations on the Quirinal, the Viminal, and the Esquiline, and in the Exquiliæ, the large space eastward of those hills, or *colles*, between the inner and outer wall of ancient Rome, from the Porta Maggiore to the Pretorian Camp. Between the engineers of the railway and the authorities of the Municipality nearly the whole of the great *agger* of Servius Tullius has been carried away. This was not in the least necessary, and only proves the carelessness of the engineers and architects then employed. There was abundance of room for the new city outside of the great *agger*, on the level ground, between that and the outer wall, which varies in width from half-a-mile to a mile, and is at least two miles long. This great *agger* should have been left as a public promenade, as at Vienna, and many other fortified cities, or used as a boulevard, as at Paris. In making the drains for the NEW CITY (which are at a great depth, and very fine drains), they have cut through buildings of the time of the Empire in all directions, and have uncovered the old pavement of the streets in many places, of which fortunately a record is preserved by their Archæological Commission.

Ever since the year 1868, Professor Cicconetti, one of the best draughtsmen in Rome, has had in hand for me a set of plans of the fourteen Regiones of Rome, with the view of making an atlas to accompany this work[c]. In these plans we endeavour to indicate and to explain many points not usually understood,—the different levels of the hills, and the valleys, and the foss-ways, the lines of the aqueducts, and of all the streams of water, whether now above ground, or underground only. Many streams of water are now underground, in the great drains, that were formerly visible and natural boundary-lines, especially those now running in the Cloaca Maxima, which was at the time of the foundation of Rome the natural boundary between the Palatine Hill and the Hill of Saturn ; one of these passes under the Arch of Janus, or *Arcus Quadrifrons*.

---

[c] Professor Jordan, of Berlin, has forestalled me in one part of this work, that relating to the fragments of the Marble Plan of Rome, as has been pointed out in a note, p. 72.

There can be little doubt that there was originally a drawbridge over this stream at that point.

We indicate also the principal ancient reservoirs of water,—the buildings of the time of the Kings, the Republic, the Empire, and the Middle Ages, are distinguished by different tints,—the fragments of the Marble Plan of Rome, as far as they can be placed with any certainty, but not following Canina blindly, nor using the *conjectural* boundaries of the Regiones of Nardini or of Canina, making use of the learned works written about the time the greater part of the fragments was found (these works are collected in the fourth volume of the great *Thesaurus* of Grævius), but neither always following them blindly; these authors evidently supposed the plan to have been a pavement, which it was not, and therefore they did not perceive that it was on three different scales, according to the distance from the eye of the different parts of the high wall on which it was placed (see Plate XLII.).

We have also traced out the lines from the *Milliarium Aureum* to the thirty-seven gates, as described by Pliny. Of these gates, twenty-five were in the outer wall, or wall of *enceinte*, which is a necessary part of any fortification. In Rome it was begun by the Tarquins as part of the great earthworks of the Kings, and the aqueducts were carried upon this *vallum, agger,* or bank [f], before the Wall of Aurelian was built upon it. Several of the existing gates in the outer wall are as old as the time of Pliny. The other twelve gates are in the line of Servius Tullius, the boundary of THE CITY proper until the time of Aurelian, on the eastern side of Rome. Pliny tells us not to count these *twelve inner gates* twice over, although in measuring from the centre of Rome to the outer gates it was necessary to pass through each of these twice. This simple explanation of the thirty-seven gates of Rome was first published in the present work. It is now acknowledged by the best-informed Roman antiquaries on the spot, who have every opportunity to go and verify it, that this is the true and the only possible explanation of the passage which has been declared to be inexplicable by all the editors of the works of Pliny, from the time they were first printed to the present day, because no one had thought of examining the ground. We have also traced the lines of the Itinerant Pilgrims in search of the relics of the martyrs in the Middle Ages, and also the line of the *Ordo Romanus*, of the twelfth century. All this required a good deal of careful investi-

---

[f] This is the high bank mentioned by Frontinus, in his treatise on the Aqueducts. See my Chapter on that subject.

gation and research, and examination of the ground, and necessarily took time; the delay has been much increased by the impediments studiously thrown in our way by the jealousy of the half-educated Romans. The great excavations carried on during the last five years in preparing the ground for the new city on the high ground, also gave rise to many questions, and gave new ideas on many points. These excavations are even now, in 1876, not completed, though so nearly that I may go on now with confidence, and hope in another season to complete this work.

The lower class of officials, both of the Government and of the Municipality, impede the British archæologists as much as they can, not seeing the truth that they are the best friends the modern Romans can have. The greater part of them are persons of good education, who have also travelled a good deal, and those who have seen the most ought to be the best archæologists; and to understand many of the great buildings of the Romans it is necessary to have travelled a good deal. Some of the members of the British and American Archæological Society of Rome are Indian officers, who have spent several years in India, and have seen the magnificent buildings of the East and of Egypt, from some of which the Romans learned, and where they also have left many of their own buildings. We have also had as members of the Society for a time masters of the public schools, and Professors from the Universities of England, of the United States, and of Canada. We thus have the opportunity of comparing notes from all quarters in a friendly manner, and by having long been placed in a leading position in the proceedings of this and similar societies, I have had more opportunities of obtaining accurate information than most people have had. The results are, I hope, visible in my work.

CONTENTS.—VIA SACRA.

	PAGE	PLATE
TEMPLE OF ANTONINUS AND FAUSTINA . . .	65	XXXVI.
———— Built A.D. 165, and consecrated as the Church of S. Lorenzo in Miranda in 1430	ib.	
———— The Monolithic Columns stand on a flight of steps* .	66	XLIV.
———— It is represented on a Coin of Antoninus . .	ib.	
Line of the Via Sacra, Clivus Sacer, and Summa Sacra Via, or *Caput* (see the Plan)	ib.	
House of Ancus Martius and Ædes, or Sacellum Larium, situated on the Summa Sacra Via	67	XXXII.
———— Called also Sacellum Streniæ	ib.	
Three Markets held on the Summa Sacra Via . . .	ib.	
Procession of the Augurs	68	
TEMPLE OF ROME, or Templum Urbis	69	XXX.
———— On the site of SS. Cosmas and Damian . .	ib.	
———— South doorway, excavated in 1868 . .	ib.	XXXI.
———— built by Hadrian	70	
———— Speech of Apollodorus on the occasion . .	ib.	
———— Panvinius places it on this site . . .	ib.	XXXII.
———— This Church is made out of three temples . .	ib.	
MARBLE PLAN OF ROME	71	XLII.
———— All the fragments of this were found on the same spot, under the east wall of the Church or Sacristy behind it .	ib.	
———— Excavations made here in 1867 by Tocco . .	ib.	XLIII.
———— The work of Professor Jordan on the Marble Plan .	72	
The Temple of Roma is represented on a Coin of Hadrian, A.D. 128	ib.	
Prudentius calls these two Temples the "Twins" . .	73	
The circular Temple is that of Romulus, son of Maxentius .	ib.	
Parts of the Columns of the Portico remain . . .	74	
This Temple dedicated to Constantine by the Senate .	75	
———— Was made into the Church of SS. Cosmas and Damian, A.D. 527, by Felix IV.	76	
———— The round Church forms a vestibule to the others .	77	
———— The other two were under one roof . . .	ib.	
———— The apse, with the Mosaic Picture, is an insertion .	78	
———— The church restored and endowed by Pope Hadrian I., A.D. 772	79	
———— in 1139, Innocent II. mentions it as *juxta templum Romuli*, or, as some MSS. say, *Romæ* . . .	80	
Church of SS. Peter and Paul, made A.D. 760, in the Basilica of Constantine	ib.	
———— Legend of Simon Magus	ib.	

* See the Appendix to this Chapter.

	PAGE	PLATE
TEMPLUM PACIS AND BASILICA OF CONSTANTINE .	82—86	XXXIII.
———— Originally built by Vespasian . . .	83	
Basilica of Constantine, called also Basilica Nova . .	*ib.*	XXXIV.
Antiquaries not agreed as to the site of the Templum Pacis .	*ib.*	
Marble Columns removed in the fifteenth century . .	84	
———— One in 1620 placed in front of S. Maria Maggiore .	*ib.*	
———— Seven others form the triumphal car of the Farnese in their palace	85	XXXV.
The spoils of Jerusalem were placed in this Temple . .	*ib.*	
The Apse is an addition to the building . . .	*ib.*	

PORTICUS LIVIÆ.

A fragment of the Marble Plan of Rome has this name upon it, and shews the Plan	86	XXXVI.
The only place in Rome that fits that Plan is the platform on the Summa Sacra Via	*ib.*	
It is mentioned by Strabo	87	
The base shewn on the Plan is for the great Colossus .	*ib.*	
This platform is that on which Apollodorus said that Hadrian *ought to have* placed the Templum Urbis, but he has *not* done so	*ib.*	
The building with two Apses back to back was not a Temple .	88	XXXVII.
The three Markets held on the Summa Sacra Via required three Basilicæ	*ib.*	
The substructures opposite to the Colosseum are of rough rubble walling, and not of the time of Hadrian . . .	*ib.*	XXXVII.
A small Aqueduct to supply the Fountains was made upon them .	*ib.*	
This substructure to lengthen the platform of the Summa Sacra Via is of the time of Vedius Pollio, a libertine and drunkard, who bequeathed his property to Augustus . . .	89	
———— his house destroyed by Augustus, and the Porticus Liviæ built on the site of it	*ib.*	
Division of the Regiones uncertain	90	
The old Fortifications are often the Boundaries . . .	*ib.*	
The Porticus Liviæ became the Temple of Apollo, or the Sun, when the Colossus of Nero in the character of Apollo was placed in it	*ib.*	XXXVIII.
The porticus was a double Colonnade	91	
The foundation of it was excavated in 1830 and 1874 . .	*ib.*	
Other excavations made in 1874, between the platform and the Palatine	*ib.*	
Three objects found by these excavations: 1. Guard Chambers; 2. The Lavacrum of Heliogabalus; 3. The Church of S. Maria Antiqua, founded in 800, enlarged in 855 .	92	XXXIX. XL.
Sculpture from the Tomb of the Aterii, of the first century, represents the Summa Sacra Via, &c. . . .	93	
The *Colossum altum* is the Colossus of Nero, in the character of Apollo, or the Sun	*ib.*	
This was first placed in the vestibule of the Golden House of Nero	94	

	PAGE	PLATE
It was moved by Hadrian to make room for the Templum Urbis Romæ	94	
The elephants dragged it up the CLIVUS SACER to the platform on the SUMMA SACRA VIA	95	
The site where it had stood originally is now part of the Church of SS. Cosmas and Damian	ib.	
The Marble Plan of Rome was fixed against the east wall	ib.	
The *podium* in front of the Colosseum is not large enough for the great Colossus, but was used for a smaller one of Gordianus	96	
This great bronze COLOSSUS was destroyed by Pope Silvester in the time of Constantine, as an idol of the Sun .	ib.	
The smaller Colossus is represented on a Coin of Gordianus, and the brickwork of the *podium*, or basement, is of his time .	ib.	
THE TEMPLE OF THE SUN rebuilt by Heliogabalus on this site	97	
The description of it in the *Mirabilia Urbis* agrees with the site, and that in the *Graphia Urbis* also	ib.	
CHURCH OF S. FRANCESCA ROMANA	99	
———— formerly called S. Maria Nuova . . .	ib.	
———— is not the same as that of SS. Peter and Paul, nor S. M. Antiqua, remains of which last were excavated in 1873	100	XXXV.
— ——— S. Francesca Romana rebuilt A.D. 860 . .	ib.	
———— Tombs and Sculpture contained in it . . .	ib.	
———— The Campanile is of the thirteenth century . .	ib.	
———— The Cloister was built in 1370 . . .	101	
Temple of Jupiter Stator (?), site of (?)	ib.	
ARCH OF TITUS	102	XLI.
AQUEDUCTS IN THIS REGIO	113	
OTHER CHURCHES IN THIS REGIO	ib.	
Church of SS. Quiricus and Giulitta	ib.	
———— SS. Dominicus and Sixtus	114	
———— S. Maria de Monti	115	
and Convent of S. Francesco di Paola . .	ib.	

APPENDIX.

Temple of Antoninus and Faustina . .	116

REGIONARY CATALOGUE OF REGIO IV.

Templum Pacis.

	PAGE
Templum Pacis, *Continet*	
Porticum Absidatam	104
Aream Vulcani	ib.
Aureum Bucinum	106
Apollinem Sandaliarium	ib.
Templum Telluris	ib.
Horrea Chartaria	108
Tigillum Sororium	ib.
Colossum altum pedes cii. s. (102½) habet in capite radia vii., singula pedum xxii. s. (22½)	93
Metam Sudantem	108
Templum Romæ [et Veneris *] [b]	69
Ædem Jobis [Jovis * Statoris]	101
Viam Sacram	65
*Basilicam Constantinianam	82
Templum Faustinæ	65
Basilica Pauli Æmilii [novam et Pauli]	109
Forum Transitorium	ib.
Siburram (Suburam)	110
Carinæ	111
Balneum Dafnidis	112
Vici viii. (8). [Vicus Sceleratus]	ib.
Ædes viii. (8).	ib.

Vico-Magistri xlviii. (48).
Curatores ii.
Insulæ iidcclvii. (2757).
Domus lxxxviii. (88).
Horrea xviii. (18).
Balnea lxv. [lxxv.] (65 *Curiosum*, 75 *Notitia*).
Lacus lxxi. [lxxviii.] (71 *Curiosum*, 78 *Notitia*).
Pistrina xx.
Continet Pedes [M] xiii. [tredecim.] (1013 *Curiosum*, 13000 *Notitia* [c]).

---

* Those marked thus * are in the *Notitia* only, not in the *Curiosum Urbis*.

[b] Perhaps Romæ et Romuli.

[c] 15,600 according to one MS., Cod. Vat., cent. xv.

THE VIA SACRA.

At the south-east corner of the Forum Romanum, where it joins to this street, stands the celebrated Temple of Antoninus and Faustina[a], which is not in the Forum, but in the Via Sacra. It is the most perfect that remains in Rome, and stands just opposite to the Temple of Vesta. The splendid monolithic columns, with the beautiful sculpture on the frieze, of griffins, &c.[b], are so well known as scarcely to need any further account of them. These columns were buried to half their height, and houses built up against them and between them, in the Middle Ages; the marks of the roofs of those houses are still visible on the columns. These remained until the sixteenth century, when they were removed by Palladio, who had more respect for antiquities than most of his contemporaries. He excavated these columns down to their bases[c].

There are seven columns in front and three on the flanks. The *cella* is constructed of large masses of tufa, and was ornamented with pilasters, but of these only the small capitals and the frieze remain; the rest of the wall has been cased at a barbarous period. Considerable excavations here were made in the time of Palladio, who gives an account of them in his work on architecture[d]; but those now left open were made by the French about 1812.

The temple was built about A.D. 165, and consecrated as a church in 1430 by Martin V., whose portrait and arms were placed in the church at the restoration of it in 1602. The frieze, of white marble, is one of the most beautiful examples of sculpture of that kind in Rome. The eight columns of the portico are of the green marble called *cipollino*, the entablature of square blocks of travertine. Among the ornaments on the frieze are candelabra guarded by griffins. It was originally begun by Antoninus Pius, to the memory of his wife Faustina, but being unfinished at his own death, it was called after both their names[e].

The approach to this temple is said by Palladio (who saw them in the excavation) to have been by a grand flight of steps, twenty-one in number, from the street below, though these were long deeply buried by the filling-up of the Via Sacra, until they were excavated again in 1876 by the Italian Government. The crypt is formed by the introduction of the modern floor in the original lofty temple; when it was converted into a church, this floor was placed at the level of the ground, after the filling-up of the foss-way. The bases of the columns of the portico stand upon the top of the flight of steps, this shews the depth of the original foss-way, as those bases are now ten feet below the level of the ground. The excavations made in 1874, on the opposite side of the Via Sacra, shew the same low level of the ground in that street.

This temple is represented on a coin of Antoninus [f]. Mr. Donaldson observes upon it :—"The cornice is of the simplest composition, but noble and imposing; the frieze is enriched on the flanks with a magnificent series of griffins and candelabra, superb in design and exquisite in execution. The shaft of each column consists of a monolithic block of cipollino marble, 38 ft. 9 in. high by 4 ft. 10 in.[g]"

The Via Sacra continued from this Temple of Antoninus and Faustina at the south-east corner of the Forum Romanum to the foot of the Clivus Sacer, in front of the round temple, now part of the church of SS. Cosmas and Damian [h]. The Clivus Sacer was a steep incline from that point to the upper level on which stands the Arch of Titus, and the present church of S. Francesca Romana. This large level platform is partly natural rock at its northern end, but as the level space was not large enough for the great *porticus* or colonnade, it was extended on rude vaulted substructures at the southern end towards the Colosseum. This great platform is on the SUMMA SACRA VIA, or *Caput Sacræ Viæ*.

From passages in various classical authors we learn that the palace of King Ancus Martius [i], and the temple of the tutelar gods,

---

[f] Donaldson, Coins, 4; Photos., No. 487 c, and Plate XXVI.

[g] Canina says 43 ft. 3 in., Roman feet, including the base, and 4 ft. 6 in. diameter.

[h] In the life of Felix IV., in Anastasius, it is stated that this church was erected in the Via Sacra. In the directions for the Church Processions in the Middle Ages, given in the Ordo Romanus, the rise and fall of the ground is clearly indicated :—

"Subintrat aream Nervæ inter templum ejusdem deæ [Palladis] et templum Jani, *ascendit* ante Asylum per silicem ubi cecidit Simon Magnus juxta templum Romuli, pergit sub arcu triumphali Titi et Vespasiani que vocatur septem Lucernarum, *descendit* ad Metam Sudantem ante triumphalem arcum Constantini reclinans manu leva ante amphitheatrum et per *sanctam viam* juxta Colosseum revertitur ad Lateranum." (Ordo Romanus, apud Mabillon, Museum Italicum, tom. ii. p. 143; Urlichs-Codex, p. 80.)

The *sancta via* of the Middle Ages was evidently the prescribed path for visiting the relics of the martyrs, starting from the Lateran palace and returning round the Colosseum back to the Lateran. It was distinct from the Via Sacra of the classical period.

[i] "Ancus Martius in summa sacra via ubi ædes Larium est." (Solinus, l. 23.)

were situated on the Summa Sacra Via, probably on the same site. An *ædes larium*, or temple of the tutelar gods, is mentioned by Solinus [k] in connection with this house of Ancus Martius. The Sacellum Larium, mentioned by Tacitus [l], seems to agree with the same situation. A *sacellum* is evidently not the same as a temple, though akin to it, probably a way-side altar. It is also mentioned by Cicero, and an altar of Orbona with it, both of which he saw consecrated, so that they must have been erected or rebuilt in his time [m]; they are also mentioned in a similar way by Pliny [n], Symmachus [o], and others.

The Sacellum Streniæ was on the Summa Via Sacra, according to Varro [p] and Festus [q], who speak of going from the King's house, or the Regia, at the north end of the Via Sacra, under the Palatine, and considered as on that hill, to the Sacellum Streniæ, which was near the south end of the Via Sacra, not at the Capitol, which was beyond the north end of it, but near the Carinæ.

Several markets were held on the upper Via Sacra, especially it appears for the use of country people bringing the produce of their gardens to market. Varro [r] mentions apples and honey as sold at the foot of the golden image, which probably was a gilt statue of Cupid that stood there in his time, B.C. 200. Ovid also mentions the western market [s] for the people in the suburbs, and on the Via Sacra. This was afterwards called the Forum Cupedinis [t], which is believed to have been on the high ground near the Arch of Titus, in the upper Via Sacra, a part of which was also called at one period *Corneta*, from a grove of cornel-trees (?), or perhaps from that fruit being sold there, as mentioned by Varro [u]. This

---

[k] Solinus, c. 2.

[l] "Inde certis spatiis interjecti lapides, per ima montis Palatini ad aram Consi, mox ad curias veteres, tum ad sacellum Larium." (Taciti Annales, xii. 24.)

[m] "Febris enim Fanum in Palatio, et Orbonæ ad Ædem Larum . . . consecratam vidimus." (Cicero de Natura Deorum, iii. c. 24.)

[n] "Ideoque etiam publice Febris Fanum in Palatio dicatum est, Orbonæ ad ædem Larium ara, et Malæ Fortunæ in Exquiliis." (Plinii Nat. Hist., ii. 5.) Orbona was the special goddess of parents who had lost their children.

[o] "Symmachus, lib. x. epist. 20 et 28.

[p] ". . . Quam rem etiam carius in sacra via quam sed venit." (Varro, De Re Rustica, i. 2.)

[q] ". . . Etiam a Regis domo ad Sacellum Streniæ." (Festus.)

[r] Varro, De Re Rustica, c. 2, and 16.

[s] "Rure suburbano poteris tibi dicere missa,
   Ille tibi in sacra sint licet empta via."
   (Ovidii De Arte Amandi, lib. ii. 263.)

[t] "Et modo pavonis caudæ flabella superbæ
    Et manibus dura frigus habere pila
    Et capit inatum talos me poscere eburnos
    Quæque nitent Sacra vilia dona Via."
    (Propertius iii. 17. 11.)

[u] "Ad Corneta Forum Cupedinis a Cupidio quod multi Forum Cupedinis a cupiditate . . . . Hæc omnia posteaquam contracta in unum locum

market-place is also mentioned by Terence in the *Eunuchus*ᵗ. Varro and Festusʷ treat the Macellum and the Forum Cupedinis as identical.

There was from the earliest period of the history of Rome a grand procession of the Augurs on New Year's day along the Via Sacra, carrying branches of verbena from the small temple and sacred grove on the Summa Sacra Viaˣ, to the Regia or palace of the King on the Palatine. This custom is as ancient as the time of Tatius, as mentioned by Symmachusʸ, and was continued in the time of the Empire, as recorded by Tacitusᶻ in his Annals, by Ciceroᵃ, and Lucianᵇ. The name of *strenia* was applied to New Year's gifts, which were considered as of good omen.

---

quæ ad victum pertinebant, et ædificatus locus, appellatum Macellum ut quidam scribunt quod ibi fuerit ortus. . . . Ut inter Sacram Viam et Macellum editum Cornetas a Corneis, quæ abscisæ, loco relinquerent nomen." (Varro, De Ling. Lat., lib. v. c. 32.)

ʷ " Ad Macellum ubi advenimus, Concurrunt læti mihi obviam Cupedinarii omnes," &c.
(Terentii Eunuchus.)

ʷ " Cupes et Cupedia antiqui lautiores cibos nominabant, inde et Macellum et Forum Cupedinis Romæ, Cupedia autem a cupiditate sunt dicta." (Festus, de Verbis Veteribus.)

ˣ "Itaque ne eatenus quidem ut vulgus opinatur sacra appellanda est, a regia ad domum regis sacrificuli, sed etiam a regis domo ad sacellum Streniæ et rursus a regia usque in arcem." (Festus.)

ʸ "Ab exortu pene Urbis Martiæ streniarum usus adolevit, auctoritate regis Tatii, qui verbenas felicis arboris ex luco Streniæ anni novi auspicia primus accepit." (Symmachi Epistolæ, x. 35.)

ᶻ Taciti Annales, xii. 23.
ᵃ Cicero, de Legibus, ii. 8.
ᵇ Lucian, pseudal. 8.

TEMPLE OF ROME.

THIS is considered by modern authors to be the building with two apses, back to back [c], in the garden of the monastery of S. Francesca Romana, on the great oblong platform near the Arch of Titus, in the *intermontium*, or valley between the Palatine proper and that part of it which was called the Velia (in one corner of which the great Basilica of Constantine is built). But it seems that this is a mistake, and that the Temple of the Sun was on this site, and that the Church of SS. Cosmas and Damian is on the site of the Temple of Roma, the east wall of which faced to the Forum Pacis (now built over),—there is every probability that the great Plan of Rome would be attached to the wall of the Temple of Rome. It was protected by a portico, also of the third century, fragments of which were found with the slabs. This wall, faced with brick [d], forms the east side of the *cella*, the south wall of which also remains, and is faced with squared stones of the character of the first or second century. The north wall has been destroyed or rebuilt, when it was turned into a monastery.

The Temple of Rome was originally covered with bronze plates, and these remained upon it until A.D. 625, when Honorius I. obtained a grant of them from the Emperor Heracleus, on his visit to Rome in that year, for the church of S. Peter in the Vatican, then rebuilding [e]. The marble columns of this fine portico were probably carried off at the same period, and for the same purpose; the portico must have faced the east towards the street now called the Via del Tempio della Pace. The lofty brick wall before mentioned is carried down to a considerable depth, probably to the level of the ancient foss-way, from which the flight of steps ascended to the floor of the temple, below the present level of the ground.

In the south wall, a stone doorway of the time of the early Empire, and very probably of the time of Hadrian, was shewn by some excavations made in 1868 [f]. It is in the narrow courtyard between the church and the Basilica of Constantine, and the pavement of an old street was found about ten feet below the present level. There was probably another pavement at a lower level, as the proportions of

[c] See Plate XXXIII.
[d] Photos., No. 850.
[e] "Hic [Honorius I. coopernit ec- clesiam omnem [S. Petri, ex tabulis] æneis quas levavit de templo quod appellatur Romæ ex consensu piissimi Heraclei Imperatoris." (Anastasius, S.)
[f] Photos., Nos. 782, 783.

the doorway were too wide to have been the original design. The following account of the building of this temple is given by Dion Cassius:—

".... These he [Hadrian] spared; but Apollodorus the architect, the same who constructed the works of Trajan at Rome,—the Forum, the Odeum, and the Gymnasium,—he first banished, and afterwards put to death, on the pretence that he had been guilty of some excess. But the truth was, that when Trajan was conferring with him about his works, he said to Hadrian, who was interrupting them by some observation or other, 'Go thou home and draw pumpkins, for of these matters thou understandest nothing.' Now it happened that at that time Hadrian prided himself upon some drawing of the kind.

"When, therefore, he became emperor, he bore in mind the offence, and could not tolerate Apollodorus' freedom of speech. For [on another occasion] when Hadrian sent him a plan of the temple of Venus and Rome, for the purpose of shewing that without his aid a great work could be executed, and asked whether the design was a good one; Apollodorus replied, that with regard to the temple, *it should have been* on an elevated site, and excavated underneath; that owing to its more lofty position, it *might have been* a conspicuous object from the Via Sacra, and [at the same time] receive the stage machinery into the excavated space, so that it could be suddenly put together, and secretly introduced into the theatre (or amphitheatre); and with respect to the statues, they had been made too large in proportion to the height of the building. For if the goddesses, said he, should wish to stand up and walk out, they would not be able to do so.

"At his writing in this bold, straightforward style to him, Hadrian was extremely indignant, and greatly grieved that he had fallen into an error which admitted of no remedy [g]."

Cardinal Maii found in the Vatican Library a manuscript in the handwriting of Panvinius, well known to him, but written in a very small hand, and which he had considerable difficulty in deciphering and transcribing. This was the Preface to his great work on the Antiquities of Rome, which had not previously been published, and he states that this church was made out of three temples.

"The first is round, and is that of Romulus, son of Maxentius.

"The second is nearly square, and is more ancient—(with the apse added in A.D. 527).

"The third is the most ancient of all, and is also nearly square, with a façade on the east side [h], and had a portico (under which the Marble Plan of Rome was placed). The travertine was removed from the north side to build the church of S. Ignatius [i], in the chief establishment of the Jesuits."

[g] Dionis. Cassii, Hist. Rom., lix. 4, and Summary by Ziphilinus.
[h] "Postrema pars Quadrata est, sed oblonga ex saxisque Quadratis." (Margiano Topogr. Urbis Romæ, lib. iii. c. 6.)
[i] Martinelli, Roma Ricercata, giorni vi.

Marble Plan of Rome.

"In the time of the Emperor Severus, as is evident from an inscription, a plan of the whole city was incised in marble, which was affixed to the wall of the *porticus* of the temple of the city of Rome for a long period, until it was broken into fragments and thrown down by the force of the fire which destroyed the city and the empire. Which marble was three years since in almost minute fragments, and some larger slabs in the ground adjoining to the church of SS. Cosmas and Damian, which was the Templum Urbis, according to the authority of writers. I also can bear witness that they were found deep in the rubbish with which they had fallen, by some excavators searching for what they could find for profit [k]."

Flaminius Vacca writes to the same effect :—

"I remember to have seen excavations made *behind* the church of SS. Cosmas and Damian, and to be found there the Plan of Rome incised on marble, which Plan served as an incrustation on the wall [l]."

Gamucci testifies to the same fact, in his "Guide to the Antiquities of Rome:"—

"There were found in our time by means of John Antonio Dosi, of S. Gemignano, ... behind the temple (of Roma), a facing on which was the drawing of the city of Rome [m]."

Du Peyrac [n], ten years later, bears witness of the same fact, that the Marble Plan was found *behind* the Church of Romulus and Remus, now called after the Saints Cosmas and Damian, in the time of Pius IV.

Whether the destruction of it was caused by fire, as supposed by

---

[k] "Severi imperatoris principatu, ut ex marmorea inscriptione liquet, lapidiis tabulis accuratam totius Urbis ichnographiam inciderunt, QVAE POSTICO TEMPLI URBIS ROMAE LONGO TEMPORE AFFIXA, cum imperii et Urbis interitu ignis vi conscissa corruit. Cujus infinita pæne marmorea frustula et aliquot tabulas triennio ante in campo qui Basilicæ SS. Cosmæ et Damiani adjacet, quam Urbis templum fuisse præter scriptorem auctoritatem es etiam testimonio confirmari potest, ruderibus alte egestis casu aliquot fossores terræ viscera lucri causa perscrutantes invenere." Panvinius, in the Preface to his projected work, *Romana Antiquita*, ap. M ii Spicil. Rom., t. vii. p. 654 ; Codd. Vat., No. 6780. De Rossi republished this in his *Bullettino di Archæologia Christiana* for 1867, p. 63.

[l] Fea, Miscellanea, t. i. n. 1.

[m] "Mi ricordo aver veduto cavare *dentro* alla chiesa dei SS. Cosma e Damiano e vi fu trovato la pianta di Roma propilato in marmo e della pianta servire per incrostatura del muro." F. Vacca, ap. Fea Miscellanea, vol. i. No. 1.

"S'e ritrovato nei tempi nostri per mezzo di M. Giovan Antonico Dori da san himignano .... *dentro* al templo [di Roma] una faccata, nelle quale era il disegno della citta di Roma." Le Antichità della Città di Roma, 1565, Gamucci, p. 33.

[n] "Dietro al detto tempio [di Romoli e Remo] fu trovato cavandosi ivi al tempo di Pio IIII. diverse Castre di Marmo sopra le quali ere perfilato la pianta di Roma ; te dotto santi Cosmi e Damiano." Du Peyrac, Romano Antichetà, 1875. [*Dietro*, 'behind,' is the right word ; but *dentro*, 'within,' is used in the same sense by many writers.

Panvinius, is more doubtful; there are no marks of fire on the slabs or fragments, and it seems more probable that the fall was caused by an earthquake. The marble pavement under the portico was also found about twenty feet below the present level of the soil, and there was lying upon it a great mass of the Basilica of Constantine, which had fallen down from an angle of the upper storey, and had turned over in its fall; it contains the upper part of a newel, or corkscrew staircase, of which the lower part remains in its place. This must have been thrown down by an earthquake, and the vibration caused by the fall of such a mass through the roof of the portico on to the pavement, would naturally cause such an agitation of the marble plates as to break the bronze hooks, and cause it all to fall to the pavement broken to pieces, and this is exactly borne out by all the fragments that have been found.

It is recorded that the Temple of Rome was much damaged by a fire in A.D. 307, in the time of Maxentius, and it was then partly rebuilt. The great height of the wall, and a set-off that is visible a few feet below the level of the ground, makes it appear that there had been a subterranean chamber under what was the yard of the monastery, and is now let to a stone-mason; but the marble pavement found about twenty feet below the present level of the ground, does not agree with this. This high wall would be supported by the portico in front of it; it has been pierced with modern windows for the convenience of the monks, when it was turned into a monastery, probably in the time of Urban VIII., A.D. 1638, when the church was last rebuilt[o]. The *cella* had stone walls at the north and south ends without windows, and the brick wall at the east end was also originally without windows, which are not required in a *cella*.

The MARBLE PLAN OF ROME, which hung up against the east wall of the temple, under the original portico (facing towards the great Forum of Peace, the largest market-place in Rome in the second and third centuries), was of the time of Septimius Severus and Caracalla, A.D. 192—217, and the wall of the Temple of Hadrian is faced with brick of that time to receive it. It was excavated

---

[o] De Rossi considers that the large chamber behind the altar, originally the *cella* of the Temple of Rome, was then made into the *matroneum*, or place for women. He supports this opinion by a passage from the life of Sixtus III. in the *Liber Pontificalis*, from which it appears that the aisle behind the altar in the church of S. Maria Maggiore, as rebuilt in the fifth century, was used for the same purpose. That aisle has been destroyed, but a similar one remains at the Lateran; this applies to the subterranean church, and has no reference to these windows, which are quite modern, though they may replace earlier and smaller ones. (Bulletino Cristiano, 1867, p. 72.)

in 1867, at the expense of a Roman archæologist named Tocco. All the fragments of the Marble Plan of Rome that have been discovered, both in the seventeenth century [p] and also in 1867, were found buried between that mass of building and the wall to which the map was attached [q]. The vibration of the marble plates, caused by the fall of such a mass of building in front of them, seems to have broken the metal hooks by which they had been attached to the wall. Remains of the hooks so broken off are still visible in the wall [r], and the fragments of the Marble Plan found there in 1867 are shewn in the photographs [s]. The larger number of these fragments were found on the same spot in the seventeenth century, and placed on the wall of the staircase of the Capitoline Museum.

This great Plan was evidently intended to display the magnificence of Rome, and not at all to serve as a guide for strangers. The upper part of it, being more distant from the eye, was made on a larger scale; there was also an intermediate part, on a scale between the other two; and as all the fragments were mixed together and buried alike where they fell, and half of them have probably been burnt into lime, any attempt to restore a complete plan of Rome of the third century from these fragments is hopeless. The German Archæological Institute in Rome have tried to do so for years with persevering industry and zeal, but have abandoned the case as hopeless [t].

[p] See the contemporary witnesses cited in the previous page, 71.

[q] Excavations were begun in April, 1875, at the back of this church, in a small garden which had belonged to the monks of SS. Cosmas and Damian. I had rented this garden of them for three years, from 1869 to 1872, for the purpose of making excavations there in search of more fragments of the Marble Plan of Rome; my plan was to have made a tunnel from a deep pit in this garden to the part under the back door of the monastery, where Signor Tocco was not permitted to excavate, and where some fragments of the marble plan might be found; but the monks, after first giving permission to dig there, afterwards retracted it. The Italian Government took possession of this monastery and its gardens in 1875, and began excavations there, but they have not been continued.

[s] These are shewn in the photograph, No. 783. This photograph, published in 1868, No. 850 in Mr. Parker's Catalogue of Photographs, is from a drawing of Signor Lanciani, made at the time of the excavations, and since re-published in the *Bullelino del Municipio* for 1874; and by Professor Jordan in his work entitled *Formæ Urbis Romæ Regionum* XIII., edidit Henricus Jordan. Berlin, 1875, folio.

[s] See Nos. 782, 816.

[t] What has been done by Professor Jordan in Berlin, in 1875, is, perhaps, all that can be done. He has reproduced, by lithography, the plates published in the first instance at the time the fragments were originally found, with notes by Bellori, and re-published in the fourth volume of the great collection of works upon ancient Rome, under the title of THESAURUS ANTIQUITATUM ROMANARUM CONGESSIT A J. G. GRÆVIO, MDXCVII., in folio. In this valuable work the Editor suggested the Regio to which each fragment probably belonged, and

That the portions of the Marble Plan of Rome in the sixteenth century were found on the same site as those that came to light in 1867, is evident from several passages in the writings of that period by persons who probably saw them when first discovered. The common opinion, that they formed part of the *pavement* of the temple, is evidently erroneous. The Plan was composed of a series of marble slabs fixed against the brick wall, at the foot of which some more of the fragments were found in 1867. These have the lines quite sharp; they have never been trodden upon or worn in any way, and this is equally the case with the other fragments.

A passage from Prudentius[u] is commonly cited by modern authors in proof that the TEMPLE OF VENUS AND ROME was on the site where S. Francesca Romana now stands, because he mentions them as *gemini*, or twins; but the temples on the site of SS. Cosmas and Damian are equally close together, and were probably under one roof. He also mentions the lowing of the cattle[x] sacrificed in these temples, and the incense used at their sacrifices. This temple was rebuilt by Maxentius, and completed by Constantine, and is mentioned by Aurelius Victor[y] among his buildings, along with his basilica adjoining.

The Templum Urbis [Romæ] and the Forum of Peace are mentioned together by Ammianus Marcellinus[z], writing in the fourth century. Cassiodorus, in his Chronicle written in the sixth cen-

supported his suggestions by passages from the Classics, or what by modern Roman writers are called, "*texts*." These are adopted by Professor Jordan, and arranged according to their respective Regiones. To these he has added the fragments found in 1867, of which Mr. Parker published photographs at the time, and has reproduced Signor Lanciani's drawing of the wall against which the Plan was placed, as mentioned above in note r.

[u] " Ac sacram resonare viam mugitibus ante
    Delubrum Romæ; colitur nam sanguine et ipsa
    More Deæ, nomenque loci, ceu Numen habetur,
    Atque Urbis, Venerisque pari se culmine tollunt
    Templa, simul geminis adolentur thura Deabus "
            (Prudentius contra Symmachum, lib. i. 214.)

[x] The cattle were probably in the great market-place called the Forum Pacis, to which the portico faced. Procopius mentions the driving of cattle into that Forum.

[y] " Adhuc cuncta opera quæ magnifice construxerat, Urbis Fanum, atque Basilicam Flavii meritis Patres sacravere." (Aurelius Victor de Cæsaribus, xl. 26.)

" . . . Quandoque trahet feroces
Per sacrum clivum merita decorus
    Fronde Sycambros."
        (Horatii Od. iv. 2, 34.)

"Intactus aut Britannus ut descenderet
    Sacra catenatus via."
            (Horatii Epod. vii. 7.)

From this it appears that there was a chain along the side of the slope, and the upper road on the bank of the lower, and parallel to it. Possibly the custom of having a chain across the road at the head of the Via Sacra, near the Arch of Titus, may be an ancient one.

[z] Ammianus Marcellinus, lib. xvi. c. 10—14.

tury, says that the Temple of Rome and Venus is *now* (that is in his time) called Templum Urbis.

The temple of Venus and Rome is represented on a coin of Hadrian, A.D. 128, as a lofty square temple; the portico, of ten columns, is presented to view, the central space left wider to shew a female figure. On the top of the pediment are the figures of Venus and Rome, with Cupid; at the lower angles, or *acroteria*, are trophies. The temple, standing on a platform, is raised on four steps, and at each end of the platform is a pediment, on which is a detached column carrying a figure. The legend is VRBS ROMA AETERNA S. C.[a] It is also represented on another coin of Antoninus Pius, with the legend ROMAE AETERNAE VENERI FELICI. This temple is considered to have been one of the most superb of Roman art; it was called by various names, TEMPLUM URBIS, TEMPLUM VENERIS, TEMPLUM ROMÆ ET VENERIS.

The circular temple which now forms the vestibule to the church of SS. Cosmas and Damian was the temple of Romulus, the son of Maxentius, dedicated by the Senate to Constantine after the death of Maxentius[b] (as has been said). De Rossi[c] has given a drawing by Ligorio of the ruins, as he saw them in the beginning of the seventeenth century, and as described by Panvinius with an inscription on the cornice:—

IMP . CAES . CONSTANTINO MAXIMO .
TRIVMPH . PIVS . FELIX . AVGVSTVS

This inscription is supposed to prove that the Temple of Rome, and the other temples erected by Maxentius, were dedicated (after his defeat and death) to Constantine by the Senate. The drawing also contains a plan of the two temples, with the church between them[d]; and the view represents the portico of the circular temple, with columns in front of the piers, between the arches, and four niches on each side of the door[e], two below and two above. Of

---

[a] See Plate XXVI.
[b] Chronographus anno 354, Maxentius Imper. an. vi., "Hoc imp. templum Romæ arsit et fabricatum est."
"Ad hæc cuncta opera quæ [Maxentius] magnifice construxerat Urbis fanum atque Basilicam Flavii [Constantini] meritis Patres sacravere." (Aurelius Victor de Cæsaribus, c. 40, s. 26.)
[c] Bullettino Cristiano for 1867, (pp. 66, 72).
[d] See Plates XXXI., XXXII.
[e] Statues supposed to have belonged to these niches were found, some in

front of the church, others near to it, with the inscription, FABIVS TITIANVS, V. C. CONSVL PRAE. VRBI . CVRAVIT. He was Prefect of the city from 339 to 341, and Governor of Rome under Constantine, and again in 350 and 351. It seems quite probable that he completed the decoration of the edifice left unfinished by Maxentius. (Vide Orellii, Inscriptiones, &c., n. 17.) Constantine himself, writing about this temple in his rescript, says, "Eidem Flaviæ hoc est nostræ gentis ut desideratis magnifico opere perfici voluimus ea obser-

this portico there are ruins on both sides of the door; on the north, remains of the brick vaults and niches; the marble columns are gone, but are mentioned by the writers of the seventeenth century as then remaining.

On the south side of the door the two marble columns remain erect in their places, with a portion of the cornice on one of them; both are buried to two-thirds of their length, and a modern chapel, called the Church of the Via Crucis, has been made behind them out of the ruins of the Portico[f]. Panvinius calls the chambers of the Porticus, on the north side, next the Capitol, the *Diaconia*, or the place where the poor were fed[g]. Joannes Diaconus, in his Life of Gregory the Great, mentions Felix IV. among his ancestors, and says that "he built the church of SS. Cosmas and Damian the martyrs in the Via Sacra, *against the Temple of Romulus*, as we now see it, of the ancient fabric[h]." In the Acts of the martyr Pigmenius, mention is made of the "Temple of Romulus on the *clivus of the Via Sacra*." The *clivus* began just in front of this church, and went up to the platform near the Arch of Titus; it is now (in 1876) all buried except the upper part, in front of the Basilica of Constantine, where the pavement has been excavated and left visible, and the slope of this leads down in a direct line to the front of the round temple; the fossway at the foot of the *clivus* or slope has been filled up to a depth of about thirty feet. Gregory the Great mentions this church in his Homilies as the *Basilica beati Felicis*, and in his second letter he mentions that the Litanies of the damsels began at this point[i], being the beginning of the Clivus Sacer, on which some martyrdoms took place, and which was the alleged site of the miraculous death of Simon Magus.

The church of SS. COSMAS ET DAMIANUS is described in Anastasius and in mediæval documents, sometimes as IN VIA SACRA, in other instances as IN TRIBUS FATIS, said to be from an image of the three

vatione perscripta ne ædis nostro nomini dedicata cujusquam contagiosæ superstitionis fraudibus polluatur." (De Rossi, Bull. Christiano, 1867, p. 69.)

[f] See Photos., Nos. 268, 418, 419; for the situation see the Plan, and the view from the Palatine, No. 784 A.

[g] "A latere ecclesiæ versus Capitolium erat diaconia nunc tota diruta, conjuncta pantheo ... ut de reditu eorum pauperes Christi reficerentur." (Panvinius, Lib. Pont. in Hadriano I., lxxxi.)

The use of the word Pantheum for the round temple is worthy of notice. Pantheum is a hall for men, here applied to a vestibule.

[h] "Basilicam SS. Cosmæ et Damiani martyrum via sacra juxta templum Romuli, sicut hactenus cernitur, ventissime fabricavit." (Joannes Diaconus in Vita S. Greg., i. 1.)

[i] "Litanea ancillarum Dei ab ecclesia beatorum Martyrum Cosmæ et Damiani." (Gregorii, Epist. ii.)

Fates, or the Sybils, which at one period gave a name to that part of the Via Sacra. It seems quite possible that *fatis* is an error of the scribe for *fanis*. It is also called IN SILICE, that is, on the pavement of the Via Sacra where Simon Magus fell, according to the apocryphal Roman legend—it is so called in the Register of Pope Innocent IV.[k]: and by modern writers, in Campo Vaccino, the modern name of the Forum Romanum and Via Sacra.

It was made into a church by Felix IV., A.D. 527[l], and is described as near the temple of Roma, which was behind or on the eastern side of that of Romulus[m], the son of Maxentius. The upper part of this circular temple forms a vestibule to the oblong church erected by Felix. The lower part of the temple, now part of the crypt of the church, is vaulted, but the vault to support the floor is a modern insertion. The fine classical doorway, with its columns and frieze and bronze doors[n], has been removed from its original site on the lower level, where it was buried by the filling-up of the street in front of it, and placed above its original site, now forming the fine entrance to the upper church. The apse, which was part of the work of Pope Felix, is filled with very fine mosaics of the sixth century[o], and the arch of triumph in front of it is also covered in the same manner.

This church was repaired by Pope Sergius, A.D. 687, who presented an ambo, a ciborium, and other donations. It was restored by Pope Hadrian I., A.D. 780. Leo III., A.D. 795, gave a silver corona and a coffer. A ciborium was presented by Innocent II., A.D. 1130. In the original apse, now part of the crypt, there is a good plain marble altar of the twelfth century, and some paintings on the walls, of apparently as early a period. Below the crypt is a small burial-chapel or cubiculum with the *arco-solia* on the sides, exactly like one of the cubicula in the Catacombs; this was the place where the bodies of the saints were deposited, when they were brought from the Catacombs in the eighth century, but even this has been rifled of its contents and left a ruin. The pavement of the crypt is a fine mosaic of the twelfth century, and in it is a tomb of the same period, with a fresco of the Madonna at the back. In the sacristy is a taber-

---

[k] Vide Maii Spicilegium, tomo ix. p. 300; Mezzadri, Disquisitiones Hist. de SS. Cosma et Damiano, pp. 52—54.

[l] "In loco qui appellatur Via Sacra juxta templum urbis Romae." (Anastasius, 90.)

[m] Two inscriptions were found during the excavation behind this church, nearly identical, with the name of the same Consul on each; they appeared to have been on the *portico*.

TIB. FABIVS . TITIANVS . V. C. CONS.
P. PRAEF. VRB. CVRAVIT.

Tiberius Fabius Titianus was consul A.D. 337, and prefect A.D. 340.

[n] Photos., Nos. 418, 419, 3250, 3251.

[o] Nos. 1441, 1442, 1443, 1444, 1445.

nacle for the Holy Eucharist, which is of the thirteenth century, and a chalice and paten said to have been given by Pope Felix in the sixth century, but which appears more like the work of the fourteenth or fifteenth.

The large central chamber, with the apse added by Pope Felix in A.D. 527, is described by Panvinius [p] as the site of a third temple; the construction of this apse is of the sixth century, and very good brick-work for that period. This chamber is built between the round temple of Romulus, the son of Maxentius, perhaps originally the Temple of Venus and the square "Templum Urbis." Canina has given a plan of this church divided into nave and aisles by columns, but this is a mistake; it never could have been so, the width of the apse, with the mosaic of the time upon it, proves the contrary. This plan for a church—a wide nave without aisles—was common in the fifth century; it occurs in the Santi Quattro Coronati, where aisles have actually been *inserted* in the twelfth century (just as Canina has drawn them here), and in other instances. In the present instance side-chapels have been added, instead of introducing arcades and making aisles. The addition of side-chapels was very common in France and other countries in the thirteenth century, when more altars were wanted for relics, generally sent from the Catacombs of Rome. The original plan of this church, and of others of the same period, was a large square chamber with an apse at the east end, in which is the mosaic picture, with the figure of Pope Felix holding a model of the church in his hand. The wall of the apse is, therefore, evidently part of the work of Felix; the flat wall at the west end is also of his period, but the side chapels have been added subsequently. The vault of the apse, with the mosaic picture upon it, made in the *cella* of the Templum Urbis, is carried on three arches, as may be seen in what is now the crypt of the church, with the altar standing in front of them on the chord of the apse, as usual. It is also evident that the apse was an addition to a wall previously existing; the wall of the apse is dated A.D. 526—530, by the inscription in the mosaic picture, from which it follows that the wall of the square temple is of an earlier period. This mosaic picture was evidently intended to be seen from below, and from a much lower level than it now is.

The circular temple was used as a vestibule to the church, and the bronze covering was probably stripped off this at the same time as that of the square temple behind, but the bronze doors were suffered to remain [q]. These were brought up from their original level,

[p] See ante, p. 70.

[q] The bronze was used to adorn S. Peter's, then rebuilding. The Pope applied to the Emperor Heraclius for permission to do this. (Anastas. 119.)

after the foss-way, called the Via Sacra, had been filled up, and the present floor and vault to carry it had been introduced into the church, and into the vestibule to it, to make it level with the present road. The bronze plates were replaced with lead by Sergius I., A.D. 695[r]. The word used is *trullum*, a name given at that period to a round building with a vault upon it, and this *trullum* was covered with lead. The present roof is of the seventeenth century, of the same period as the floor and vault, which divide the original height into two nearly equal parts. All this was done by the Franciscan friars, to whom the church was granted, in 1503, by Julius II. They *restored* the church in 1626, and to help towards the expense of it, they sold the travertine stone from the north end of the old *cella* of the Templum Urbis to the Jesuits for building their church of S. Ignatius Loyola, at the Roman College[s].

Pope Hadrian I. not only restored the church, but endowed it also "with land, vineyards, olive groves, labourers, money, and furniture, in order that from the returns the deacons might be enabled to supply the wants of the poor Christians[t]." At that period, A.D. 772—795, also the relics of the martyrs were translated from the catacomb in the suburbs, in which they had originally been deposited, and which had been damaged in the Lombard invasion. They were removed to this church, where a small crypt, called a catacomb, was made to receive them, in exact imitation of a *cubiculum* in one of the usual catacombs. This was painted in the same manner, and there are remains of the paintings on the wall of the staircase. The cave itself is made partly by excavating the rock, and partly by building brick walls, the character of which is of the eighth century. The relics of Felix II., A.D. 355, are said to have been found here in 1582. The catacomb in which the relics of a martyr had once been deposited was always considered as still sacred, and was restored and painted as before. The same history applies to many other churches and catacombs in Rome, but in this instance the new catacomb is visible, which is not usually the case. It is in the same miserable dilapidated state as all the other catacombs, stripped of all the tombstones and inscriptions.

[r] Liber Pontificalis, ap. Anastasius 163, in Sergio I., A.D. 696.
[s] Martinelli, Roma Ricercata, Gion vii., et Roma ex ethnica Sacra, p. 93.
[t] "Idem egregius praesul basilicam scilicet beati Hadriani martyris et sanctorum Cosmae et Damiani a novo restauravit, diaconias constituit, in quibus et multa bona fecit per suam sempiternam memoriam, concedens eis agros, vineas, oliveta, servos, ancillas et pecu lia diversa atque res mobiles, ut de reditu eorum crebris exactionibus diaconiae proficientes pauperes Christi reficerentur." (Pontif. Reg. in Hadriano I.)

In a *bulla* of Innocent II., of the date of 1139, this church is mentioned as *juxta templum Romuli*[u], literally, *against* the Temple of Romulus; and in the *Ordo Romanus* of Canon Benedict, of the same period[v], it is said, "The Pope went up before the asylum, on the pavement on which Simon Magus fell." In the *Mirabilia Urbis Romæ*[w], the church of SS. Cosmas and Damian is called "the Church of the Asylum."

About A.D. 760, "Paul I. dedicated a church to the two apostles Peter and Paul, on the Via Sacra, on the spot where Simon Magus fell[x]." This church was made in the north aisle of the great Basilica of Constantine, and was separated from the church of SS. Cosmas and Damian towards the east end by part of an ancient street, now a narrow courtyard, towards the western end. It is described in the *Liber Pontificalis* as *juxta templum Romuli* in some of the MSS., and *juxta templum Romæ* in others. Remains of mediæval paintings and other indications of a church have been found in that aisle; it was destroyed in the great earthquake in 1349. After this period, in 1375, the site of this miracle was transferred to the top of the *clivus*, to the church now called S. Francesca Romana, and the stone said to be marked by the knee of S. Paul on that occasion, was placed as a relic in the wall of the south transept of that church[y].

This apocryphal legend is of early date, but not earlier than the fourth century, if so early. It is not mentioned by Justin Martyr, nor Irenæus, nor the author of the *Philosopheumena* (usually supposed to be Origen), nor by the classical historians or poets of the period, Suetonius, Dion, Juvenal, and in so central and celebrated a part of Rome as the Via Sacra, if such an event had occurred in their time, they would hardly have been silent about it.

[u] Maii Spicilegium Rom., tom. ix. p. 399.

[v] "Ascendit ante asylum per silicem, ubi cecidet Simon Magus, juxta templum Romuli pergit sub arcu triumphali Titi et Vespasiani, qui vocatur Septem lucernarum; descendit ad Metam sudantem ante triumphalem arcum Constantini," &c. (Mabillon, Museum Italicum, p. 294.)

[w] Montfaucon, Diarium Italicum, p. 294.

[x] "Hic fecit noviter ecclesiam in via sacra juxta templum Romuli in honorem sanctorum apostolorum Petri et Pauli, in loco in quo ipsi beatissimi principes apostolorum tempore quo pro Christi nomine martyrio coronati sunt, dum Redemptori nostro funderent preces, propria genua flectere visi sunt. In quo loco usque hactenus eorum genua pro testimonia omnis in postremo venturæ generationis in quodam fortissimo silice, marmore scilicet, esse noscuntur designata." (Pontificale Romanum, ed. Vignoli, tom. ii. p. 130; ed. Bianchini, tom. i. p. 175; apud de Rossi, Bulletino, 1867, 4to., pp. 69, 70.)

[y] "Ibidem in uno altari est lapis signatus per genuflexionem S. Pauli, quando oravit in volatu Simonis Magi, qui ante eandem ecclesiam cecidit, ubi locus lapidibus est signatus." (Cod. Vat., 4265, p. 213, written A.D. 1375; ap. De Rossi, Bulletino, 1867, p. 70.)

Fulvius, writing in 1527, mentions[a] remains of the marble casing of the temple as existing in his time, when the church was rebuilding. These are probably the same fragments of a rich cornice, with foliage of the character of the third century, which were dug up with the fragments of the Marble Plan in 1867, and were, in February, 1868, preserved by the monks, together with the other fragments and the tiles found at the same time, which have the stamp of Domitian upon them[a]. The same facts are mentioned by Du Peyrac and Pompeius Ugonius[b], who also gives the inscription in honour of the saints to whom the church was dedicated in the sixth century, who were two medical officers of the imperial court, martyrs in the persecution under Diocletian[c].

The *restoration* of this church was completed under Urban VIII. in 1638, who refitted the nave and put in the present ceiling. A paschal candlestick supported by two lions, and a painted image of the Madonna, are of the twelfth century. The altar and the stalls bear the date 1638 and 1639.

The modern poor church called the VIA CRUCIS was part of the Temple of Romulus. It has nothing worth notice either inside or out, except two antique columns in front of it, one of which retains its Corinthian capital, the other has lost it; and both are buried deep in the earth owing to the filling-up of the foss-way. These originally belonged to the portico in front of the Temple of Romulus, now part of the Church of SS. Cosmas and Damian.

[a] Fulvii, Antiq. Urbis Romæ, 1527, p. lxxxii. 6.
[a] Photos., Nos. 782, 795, 798.
[b] P. Ugonii Stationi, p. 178 b.
[c] MARTYRIBVS MEDICIS POPULO SPES CERTA SALUTIS—VENIT ET EX SACRO CREVIT HONORE, LOCUS.

TEMPLUM PACIS AND BASILICA OF CONSTANTINE.

THE Templum Pacis, built or rebuilt by Vespasian, which gave its name to one of the Regiones of Rome, must have been an important building, and, in all probability, was on the site of the great Basilica, now called after Constantine. Suetonius[d] says it was *near to* the Forum Pacis[e], and this site would touch one corner of it. The two are mentioned together in the ancient catalogue of the Emperors, published by Eccard[f], as on the site of a great warehouse for pepper, which had been built there by Domitian. This temple was celebrated also for the extreme richness of its decoration, and the treasures taken from the Temple at Jerusalem were displayed there, but the greater part of these were said to have been destroyed by a great fire in the time of Commodus; and the contemporary writer, Herodian, in the history of his own time, says that it was the largest, the finest, and the richest temple in the city, with gold and silver ornaments[g].

Dio states that "when Vespasian and Titus were consuls, the Temple of Peace was dedicated," and "the Colossus as it is called was placed in the Via Sacra[h]; it is said to have been a hundred feet high, and to have had the head of Nero, or as some say of Titus." These two things are placed together by Dio as one event. Suetonius, in describing the Golden House or Palace of Nero, says that this Colossus stood originally in the vestibule of the Golden Palace[i]. This shews that the Basilica of Constantine is on the site of the Temple of Peace; the vestibule of the Golden Palace would include the sites both of that and of the Temple of Roma, now the eastern part of the Church of SS. Cosmas and Damian. The celebrated horses now in the Piazza dei Cavalli, in front of the Quirinal Palace, originally stood also in this vestibule, which must therefore have been of great extent, to correspond with the *porticus*, a mile long, which is mentioned by Suetonius in connection with it, and to which it was the entrance. This *porticus* extended to the Basilica of Constantine, as we see by the remains of it against the western cliff of the Velia.

The BASILICA NOVA of the *Curiosum* is the BASILICA OF CONSTANTINE of the Notitia. It is an enormous mass of building 320

---

[d] "Fecit et nova opera Templum Pacis foro proximum." (Suetonius in Vespasiani, c. 9.)

[e] "Limina post Pacis Palladiumque forum." (Martial, Epig., tib. i. Epig. 2.)

[f] "Horrea Piperataria ubi modo est basilica Constantinianam et forum Vespasiani." (Catal. Imp. Rom. ed. Eccard, in Domitiani.)

[g] Herodian's History, book i. c. 44.

[h] Dio Cassius, lxvi. 15.

[i] Suetonius, Nero, 31 : see also p. 93.

feet long by 240, consisting of three very large halls[j], or a central nave and two aisles, all of equal width, with an apse to the central one only, and arches between a grand vault of stucco ornament, and an upper storey, of which only some fragments remain. Within a stone's-throw of this building, on the other side of the Arch of Titus, are remains of the BASILICA JOVIS, the great state hall of the Emperors. This great hall on the Palatine was the type followed in the early Christian churches, and a restoration of this earlier type has been made in a drawing for the present work, to shew what a Basilica of that kind really was[k]. The vaults of the great Basilica of Constantine[l] are richly ornamented with stucco ornaments in sunk panels or caissons; exactly similar ornaments occur on the two apses back to back, near to this, between it and the Colosseum. This is one of the most remarkable buildings in Rome, and one perhaps more often referred to in England than any other. Its architecture was taken as a model by the Roman architects of the Renaissance school, and in England its plan is continually referred to as authority for that of a church, and yet it is perfectly certain that it never was a church at all; it was built for a law-court and market-hall. The building so frequently mentioned by Anastasius and other early ecclesiastical writers as the BASILICA CONSTANTINIANA, is undoubtedly the one now known by the name of the church of S. John Lateran; numerous passages could easily be referred to in proof of it. Aurelius Victor[m] mentions this and the Temple of Rome among the magnificent works of Maxentius.

It is a singular fact, that although the fourth Regio was called by Augustus TEMPLUM PACIS[n], the best Roman antiquaries are not at all agreed as to the site of the Temple of Peace. It is always identified by the populace with this magnificent ruin, now called the Basilica of Constantine[o]. Some consider that the Temple of Peace

---

[j] See No. 203.
[k] See Nos. 3912, 3913, and Plate iii.
[l] This was called the Temple of Peace until the time of Nibby (*Roma Antica*, vol. ii. p. 248), who had excavations made there, and found a medal or coin of Maxentius, with a view of the Temple of Venus and Roma, which was close to that site, as we have said.
[m] "Adhuc cuncta opera quæ magnifice construxerat Urbis fanum atque Basilicam Flavii meritis Patres sacravere." (Aurelius Victor de Cæsaribus, c. 40.)
[n] See p. 82.
[o] As this building is nearly in the centre of ancient Rome, and the platform on the top of its magnificent vaults is very easy of access, it is an excellent point for a panoramic view to give a general idea of the magnificence of the ancient city. The first person to point out that this great building was the Basilica of Maxentius and Constantine, was the late Professor Nibby, who relates, in his Roma Antica, (pars ii. pp. 247, 248,) that in 1828 a piece of the vault fell down, in which was a silver coin of Maxentius, with his head on the stone, and the legend MAXENTIUS P. F. AUG., and on the

was the same as the Temple of Claudius on the Cœlian, the name being altered after his death; but that is not in the fourth Regio, which Augustus called by the name of the Temple of Peace. It is certain that this was on or near the same site, although the present building is not on the plan of a temple, nor of a basilica of the ordinary type[p].

In the great earthquake of the year 1349, this great building was much damaged, and the north-east corner of the attic storey fell over on to the pavement in front of the Marble Plan of Rome (as before said). This is described in the Letters of Petrarch[q].

The walls were ornamented with fine fluted marble columns of the Corinthian order, some of which were remaining in the time of Poggio the Florentine, in the fifteenth century, under Martin V., A.D. 1420; he mentions one of large size particularly, this was removed by Paul V. [Borghese], A.D. 1620, and placed in front of the church of S. Maria Maggiore to carry a bronze image of the Virgin, where it now stands. Seven other marble columns were found during the excavations in the early part of the sixteenth century, and were used to form the triumphal car of Alexander Farnese, in the palace of his family. Colonettes of *giallo antico*, cornices, and other parts of the decorations were also found, but of a bad style of art; also some paintings, and an altar of the eighth century[r].

Ammianus Marcellinus[s], who lived in the latter part of the fourth century, and therefore after the present building was erected, calls it "Forum Pacis," which seems to agree with its being on the site of the temple of the same name, and its having been a market-hall.

---

reverse a building said to be the temple of Roma (?), with the legend P. F. AVG. CONSERV. VRB. SVAE.

[p] See Photos., Nos. 203, 204, 205, and a set of plates of the restoration of it in the great work of Canina on the Antiquities of Rome.

[q] "Ecce Roma ipsa insolito tremore concussa est tam graviter ut ab eadem Urbe condita supra duo annorum millia tale nihil acciderit. Cecidit ædificiorum veterum neglecta, civibus stupenda peregrinis moles. Turris illa toto orbe unica, quæ Comitum dicebatur, ingentibus rimis laxata dissiluit et nunc velut trunca caput superbi verticis honorem solo effusum despicit. Denique ut iræ cælestis argumenta non desint multorum species templorum atque in primis Paulo Apostolo dicatæ ædis bona pars humi collapsa et Lateranensis Ecclesiæ dejectus apex jubilæi ardorem gelido horrore contristant. Cum Petro mitius est actum." (Petrarch, lib. x. ep. ii. p. 873, ap. Nibby, p. 248.)

[r] The following inscription is said by Canina to have been dug up in or near this building, and if this can be depended on, it settles the question, that the Temple of Peace was on the same site:— PACI . AETERNAE . DOMVS . IMP. VESPASIANI . CAESARIS . AVG. LIBERORVMQ. EIVS . SACRVM . TRIB. SVC. IVNIOR. And another which relates the time of the dedication:—DEDIC. V. R. DEC. L. ANNIO COS. C. CAECINA PAETO.

[s] ". . . inter alia cuncta sperabat, Jovis Tarpei delubra, quantum terrenis divina præcellunt, lavacris in modum provinciarum exstructa, amphitheatri molem . . . et Urbis templum, Forumque Pacis et Pompeii Theatrum et odeum et Stadium, aliaque hæc decora Urbis æternæ." (Ammianus Marcellinus, lib. xvi. c. 10, s. 14.)

The winding staircase, at the south-east end, by which we ascend to the platform on the summit is very interesting; it is a brick staircase of the beginning of the fourth century, in very perfect preservation, with the central newel round which the stairs wind formed of circular tiles, the edges of which are polished: the stairs and the vault under them are of brick, faced with tiles. The doorways at the top and bottom of the stairs are well preserved, and by the side of the door at the top is a small window of the same period, with a triangular head faced with two tiles. There are remains of another staircase of the same kind at the opposite end, the upper part of which fell over on the pavement in front of the Templum Urbis Romæ, in the great earthquake of the fourteenth century, and still lies buried there. It was visible in the excavation of Tocco in 1867. There was an external roof, with a vault over the present brick-vaulted ceilings, with an external roof, as usual. Of this upper roof the piers and springings with the transverse arches to carry the vaults, are all that remain. The general effect of this ruin is grand and picturesque in the highest degree.

The apse in the present building is shewn by the construction to be an addition, but made soon afterwards. It seems probable that Maxentius rebuilt the Templum Pacis, and Constantine added the apse, and made it into a basilica. The plan is not the usual one, either for a temple or for a basilica. It is an enormous building, almost square, divided into three compartments of nearly equal size, with an apse added to the central compartment, and with an attic-storey over the vaults of the three compartments. Canina mentions having found in the cellars under this basilica remains of an earlier building of importance; these remains may have belonged to the pepper warehouses built by Domitian [t] on or near this site.

The principal spoils of Jerusalem brought to Rome by Titus were deposited by Vespasian in this Temple of Peace, and representations of them carved upon the arch opposite to it. The originals were carried into Asia by Genseric, or at least taken from Rome with that intention, and lost. But the sacred Ark was deposited in the church of S. John Lateran, and is said to have been of wood, but the authenticity of this is considered doubtful by Nardini [u]; it is not mentioned by Josephus, who enumerates the other spoils carried away from Jerusalem.

[t] "Domitianus . . . horrea Piperataria ubi modo est Basilica Constantiniana et forum Vespasiani." (Catalogus Imp. Rom., ed. Eccard.)

[u] That some of these trophies were at one period preserved in the Lateran, is mentioned on a mosaic inscription of the thirteenth century. They remained there until the sack of Rome by the Bourbons, when they disappeared.

PORTICUS LIVIÆ.

THE new fragments of the Marble Plan of Rome found in 1867[v], on the eastern side of the church of SS. Cosmas and Damian, have been mentioned, and amongst these fragments was one with the name of PORTICUS LIVIÆ upon it[w]; this was a very important discovery, as it shews us what *that porticus* was like. It was a double colonnade of large columns round the edge of an oblong platform, with the mark of a fountain at each corner, and some building in the centre marked by a thick square line, a smaller square within it, and within that a circle. At one end is a flight of steps leading up to it—assuming this was the north end, we have then on the eastern side a narrow street interrupted by a portico of four columns larger than the others. The only place in Rome that could fit such a colonnade is the platform on the Summa Sacra Via, on which the church of S. Francesca Romana now stands; and here the coincidences are very remarkable. It has the steps leading up to the platform[x], numbers of large columns lying about it on all sides[y], and four of the bases remaining in their original places, which can be identified with the Marble Plan[z]. There is a narrow passage on the east side, with a pavement of early character,—and it is intercepted in the middle by a recess, in which are four arches of the upper tier of a *porticus* or arcade of two storeys of the time of Nero, which may very well have had four columns in front of it. At the south end the level platform has been enlarged by carrying it out upon rude vaulted substructures beyond the natural cliff, as has been done in several other instances.

The streets towards the north are wanting, but we have historical evidence that streets and houses that stood here were demolished by the Popes in the seventeenth century, to make the open space, called the "Campo Vaccino" in ridicule by the wags of that day, which name it long retained. The pavement of the sloping street in the Palatine, excavated in 1869 by Signor Rosa, and left open[a], would agree very well for one of those westward, and the road up to the back gate, where the monastery of S. Bonaventura now stands, would agree well with another[b]. Strabo has been sup-

---

[v] Photos., No. 782.
[w] Photos., Nos. 816, 3227.
[x] Nos. 1060, 1061.
[y] Nos. 785, 1118.
[z] They are so marked upon the reduction of it, No. 1118, and in our plan of the Via Sacra.
[a] Photos., No. 3228, and Plate XII.
[b] Nos. 300, 1055.

posed to imply that the Porticus Liviæ was visible from the Forum Romanum, and this platform is the only site where such a colonnade would be visible from thence; his words do not necessarily imply this, but it is the most natural and the most probable interpretation of them :—

"If any one should visit the old forum and see the temples, basilicas, and porticoes, and should see the Capitol, with the great works on it, and those on the Palatine, *and the Porticus Liviæ*, each successive place would cause you speedily to forget what you have before seen. Such is Rome[e]."

The base in the centre of the plan of the Porticus Liviæ on the fragment of the great marble plan of Rome of the third century, has very much the appearance of being that of the great Colossus of Nero, dragged to this elevated spot up the Clivus Sacer, from the original site at the foot of that Clivus, where the church of SS. Cosmas and Damian now stands, with the wall on which the marble plan was placed, facing to the great "Forum Pacis," of the time of Nerva, now at the back of that church, the present entrance to which is from the Via Sacra; that entrance is through the round temple of Romulus, the son of Maxentius, which was built between the Temple of Venus and Rome and the Via Sacra. That temple was therefore not visible from that street when Apollodorus answered Hadrian, and said that the Emperor *ought to have* made it visible from that point. The modern theory, which places the temple of Rome on this platform, has no real foundation; the texts in the classical authors, which are quoted to support this theory, apply as much to the one site as the other. According to this theory, the elephants were employed by Hadrian to drag the Colossus *down hill* from this platform, to what they call the *Podium* or base for it under the wall of the Colosseum. This base is faced with brickwork of the third century, and is not large enough for a colossus of that height. The feet of a Colossus 120 ft. high must have been twenty feet long; it is also mentioned that the head was visible from the (gulf?) or central passage in the substructures of the Colosseum, which has been found 21 ft. below the level of the arena, and on a direct line with this platform. If the Colossus had stood on the brick basement close to the great building, it would have been under the shadow of it, and hardly visible from the Forum Romanum, and could not have been said to have its head in the skies or in the stars, as the poets describe. The most probable site for the Colossus is nearly where the tall campanile of S. Francesca Ro-

[e] Strabo, lib. v. c. iii. s. 8.

mana now stands, a most conspicuous object from the Forum and all the neighbourhood, and on the great platform which has the bases of the double row of columns round the edge of it.

One objection taken to this opinion is, that the buildings now remaining within that double colonnade do not agree with the marble plan of this *porticus;* but those buildings commonly, but erroneously, called the "Temple of Venus and Rome," are of the time of Constantine, at the beginning of the fourth century, and the brick-stamps of Maxentius were found by Nibby in the walls [d]. The marble plan was made thirty years *before* these buildings were erected, and we do not know what was there before. The plan represents a single column (?) or statue (?) standing on a large square base. The ruins have not the usual character of a temple or temples; the vaults which stand back to back are of the same character as the vaults of the great basilica of Constantine close by, which was built by Maxentius, and only named after Constantine by the senate after the death of Maxentius. It is probable that the two other halls were also basilicæ for some public purpose, and not for temples. Probably—for the use of the three markets, which were held on the site of the Summa Sacra Via from a very early period (as has been shewn)—three great halls called basilicæ were built. The basilica of Constantine, on the side of the Clivus Sacer, and on the level of the Summa Via Sacra, was one of these, the site for it was cut out of part of the Velia. It is quite possible that the two other great halls, *miscalled* the temple of Venus and Roma, on the Summa Sacra Via itself, were also great market-halls. Both these, and the one called after Constantine, were built or rebuilt by Maxentius, or *soon after* his time; and the construction is exactly the same, with the same kind of vaulting in all the apses. These two halls were built in the beginning of the fourth century, within a large double colonnade, probably, as we have said, the Porticus Liviæ.

Further light has been thrown on this interesting point by the excavations of 1873-4 [e], under the south end of the great platform, which is supported by rude rubble walls and vaults of the time of the Republic. These, when excavated, were found in so rough a state, that they could not have been used at all. There does

---

[d] See Nibby, Roma Antica, parte ii. p. 732. He also found in *the drains under it* bricks with the stamps of the Consuls Petinus and Apronsanus—Servianus III. and Varus, all of the time of Hadrian, but these were found in the substructure only, and have nothing to do with the buildings on the surface, which have evidently been erected on older foundations. He describes this drain as a very fine one, of travertine, 9 ft. high and 3 ft. wide; such drains would be required for the fountains above, and the construction is described as of the time of Hadrian.

[e] Photos., Nos. 3191 A and B.

not appear to have been any original entrance to them, but it is to this space that Apollodorus alluded when he said that if the Temple of Rome had been built on that high ground, which at this lower end is 28 ft. above the level of the pavement in front of the Colosseum, the space under it *might have been* used for the scenery or apparatus of the Amphitheatre, *but was not*. Upon this wall is a small aqueduct, which turns the corner at both ends from the south-east, to run up the two sides of the platform, and seems evidently to have supplied the fountains at the corners represented on the Marble Plan. If Hadrian had built his temple on this platform (as is commonly said) he would also have rebuilt the substructure, as Apollodorus suggested.

The platform was lengthened to build the great house of Vedius Pollio upon it in the time of the Republic, and the substructure has not since been rebuilt. Vedius Pollio, at his death, bequeathed his large property to Augustus; this large house, which he had built, therefore reverted to Augustus, who building a *porticus* round it, inscribed it not to Pollio, but to Livia. This was dedicated to Caius and Lucius Cæsars in A.U.C. 765, A.D. 12 [f]. Trajan administered justice there, as in the Forum of Augustus, and in other places [g]. Vedius Pollio had been a great libertine and gourmand, and Augustus had found it necessary to forbid his feeding his fish (lampreys) on human flesh [h]; but instead of resenting this, he respected the justice of the emperor, and left him a considerable part of his property, which was very large [i]. The sumptuousness of his house, and its prominent and conspicuous position, had given offence to the republican feeling of the Romans, and Augustus thought it better to destroy it and erect a public building on the site, which is mentioned by Ovid, who says that where the *porticus* of Livia then stood had been a house with an immense roof; that one house was the work of a city, and the space it occupied was enough for the walls of a town [j]; that its luxury gave great offence, and that when Cæsar

---

[f] Dio Cassius, lvi. 27.
[g] Ibid., lxviii. 10.
[h] Plinii Nat. Hist., ix. 39 and 78.
[i] Dio Cassius, liv. 25.
[j] "Disce tamen, veniens ætas; ubi Livia nunc est
porticus, immensæ tecta fuere domus.
Urbis opus domus una fuit: spatiumque tenebat,
quo brevius muris oppida multa tenent.
Hæc æquata solo est, nullo sub crimine regni,
sed quia luxuria visa nocere sua est.
Sustinuit tantas operum subvertere moles
totque suas heres perdere Cæsar opes.
Sic agitur censura, et sic exempla parantur;
quum judex, alios quod monet, ipse facit."
Ovidii Fasti, vi. 638—648.

became heir to it he entirely destroyed it. One cause of this offence seems to have been that it was a conspicuous object from the Forum.

The objection to this site is, that the Colossus was in Regio IV., Templum Pacis. It is possible that the division of the Regiones crossed the middle of the great platform. The northern line of Regio III. may very well have been the ridge on which the northwest end of the colonnade stood on the rock; and the *portico* at the south-east end, on the raised substructure, may have been the only part called Porticus Liviæ, and not the whole colonnade on all sides of the platform. It is on this part of the marble plan that the name occurs. The Meta Sudans was in Regio IV. TEMPLUM PACIS, which also included the Via Sacra, and this is on the Summa Sacra Via; but the Arch of Constantine was in Regio XI., also the Circus Maximus, and is much further from that circus than the Meta Sudans is from the Basilica of Constantine. There was also a *Templum Solis et Lunæ* in Regio XI. This Temple is close to the Arch of Constantine, and the same Regio may very well have included both.

It is certain that the old fortifications were frequently the boundaries of the Regiones; some were in *the city*, others outside of it, and in this instance the cliffs of the Palatine at the southeast corner, and of the Velia opposite to it, were the forts to protect the principal gate, near the Arch of Titus. This is the natural plan of a fortification, and we find the same plan followed at the Porta Capena, between the western side of the Cœlian and the Aventine, and at S. Clemente between the eastern side of the Cœlian and the Esquiline, and there can be little doubt that the Porta Mugionis would be protected in the same manner. Regio XI. would then extend nearly to the ridge on which the Arch of Titus stands. The boundaries of the Regiones are only the conjectures of the learned men of the seventeenth century; we really know nothing more about them than what the catalogue tells, and this puts the Porticus Liviæ in Regio IV. There is no other site in Rome that would fit the plan of the *porticus* found in 1867, and the place here assigned to it fits all the requirements in a remarkable manner. It seems impossible that these can only be accidental coincidences. On carefully examining the ground on which the monastery stands, Signor Cicconetti, the architect and surveyor employed, found what appeared to him to be remains of the *podium*, or large basement, on which the Colossus stood. It was large in proportion to the enormous statue. The head of the Colossus, placed on this basement, would then stand up clear against the sky above the great colonnade, and it was quite natural for Martial to say that the head "was in the stars." As the Colossus was that of Apollo or the Sun, this colonnade, with the statue in the centre and an altar in front, would become a Temple of Apollo or the Sun.

On the eastern side of this platform is a narrow street, or rather path, the pavement of which is of the Early Empire, and this again agrees very nearly with the Marble Plan: this street, or path, is interrupted on the plan by a portico of four large columns; and we have now remaining on the corresponding spot four arches of the Porticus of Nero. But the word *porticus* has two meanings: the Porticus of Livia was a colonnade, as we have seen; the Porticus of Nero was an arcade, and a mile long, extending from the vestibule in which the Colossus originally stood, on the site where the church of SS. Cosmas and Damian now stands, to the Esquiliæ or public burial-ground. There are remains of it at the south end near the Lateran, and at intervals, against the cliff of the Esquiline in several places. Perhaps the most perfect part of it is just that near the great Basilica of Constantine, and in the narrow street, or path, before mentioned. That *porticus*, like several others in Rome, was a double arcade, one over the other; and there are here four of the upper arches remaining, the construction of which is very evidently of the time of Nero[k]. It is extremely probable that four large columns stood in front of these, (as shewn on the Marble Plan,) and that this is the reason why these four arches have been preserved, while the rest have been destroyed. There are remains of four marble columns of a larger size than the rest. The back wall of this arcade remains for a considerable distance, and supports the cliff of the Velia; it has evidently been cut through when the Basilica of Constantine was built, the site of which was cut out of part of the Velia. The foundations of this platform were uncovered by the Pontifical government in 1828 and 1830. Near the Arch of Titus some of the marble steps leading up to the platform have been preserved; they were originally five hundred feet long in one uninterrupted line on the two sides of the platform, and three hundred at the end next the Via Sacra.

On the opposite side of the platform, between the Arch of Titus and the Colosseum, great excavations were made in 1873 and 1874, bringing to light several things that were previously unknown[l]. They consist of three distinct parts.

1. Close under the eastern cliff of the Palatine is a series of guard-

[k] Photos., Nos. 796, 1062, 3161, 3162. [l] Nos. 2727, 2728.

chambers, between these and the road which is called the Clivus Triumphalis, similar to those on the western side of the hill, which are of the second century. This was the line of march of the army in the triumphal processions, when they passed through the triumphal arches of Constantine below [m], and of Titus [n] above.

2. In front of these are bath-chambers of the third century, considered to be the Lavacrum of Heliogabalus, which was a building for gratuitous washing-places for the poor (corresponding nearly to the public baths and wash-houses of modern times), begun by him and finished by Alexander Severus. These are mentioned by Lampridius [o] in connection with the restoration of the amphitheatre, after the burning of the upper storey, as the temple of the Sun (a name given to the Porticus Liviæ after the colossal figure of Apollo or the Sun was placed by Hadrian in the centre of that magnificent double colonnade). Of these baths there are considerable ruins, but they had become ruins before the ninth century.

3. In these ruins a church was made at that time. It was begun under Leo III. [p], A.D. 800. At first a small church was built on the plan of a Greek cross, the four arms nearly equal, but with an apse at one end, in which stand (in 1875) the remains of the altar, which is hollow, making a sort of sarcophagus for relics in it, with a marble pavement in the path round it, the walls also lined with marble [q]. In front of the flat end, opposite to the altar, are remains of a portico; two of the columns have the lower part standing. This small church had a long nave added to it in the time of Benedict III., A.D. 855, and at the further end of this nave is another apse, with another hollow altar similar to the other, or perhaps a baptistery (?). The semicircular structure in the apse being hollow, may be a font for baptism by immersion, made out of an old bath. The construction of the walls of both parts of the church is rough stone-work of the ninth century, but where the brick walls of the third conveniently remained, they were used and adopted by the builders as part of the plan. In front of the portico of the original small church a steep flight of steps descends to a deep well, which is under the nave and

---

[m] No. 808. [n] No. 303.

[o] "Opera publica ipsius (præter ædem Heliogabali dei quem Solem alii, alii Jovem dicunt, et amphitheatri instaurationem post exustionem et lavacrum in vico Sulpicio quod Antoninus Severi filius cœperat) nulla extant: et lavacrum quidem (Antoninus) Caracallus dedicaverat et lavando et populum admittendo, sed porticus defuerant, quæ postea ab hoc subditicio Antonino exstructæ sunt et ab Alexandro [Severo] perfectæ." (Lampridius — Antoninus Heliogabalus, ap. Script. Hist. Aug., c. 17.) Photos., No. 2727.

[p] "Pariter et ecclesiam sanctæ Dei Genitricis semperque Virginis Mariæ dominæ nostræ, sitam in Fonticana quæ per obitana marcuerat." (Anastas., 362.)

[q] This marble lining was nearly all carried away in 1875.

near the entrance. There is a holy well in the same position in the church of S. Prassede, which is of about the same period. It is said in that case to have been used as a secure place for some of the most precious relics of the martyrs brought from the Catacombs. Both Leo III. and Benedict IV. brought many relics from the Catacombs into Rome for security, and several churches were built at that period to receive them, with crypts under part of them, called Catacombs, because the relics of the martyrs were placed in them [r].

This church was dedicated to S. Mary; and as another church, also dedicated to S. Mary, was made close to it a short time afterwards, this was called S. Maria Antiqua [s], and the other was called S. Maria Nova; but the name of the latter was afterwards changed to Santa Francesca Romana.

A basso-relievo was found at Cento Celle, on the Via Labicana, in 1849, having a representation of an arch with the words—

ARCVS AD ISIS.

By the side of this, on the same piece of sculpture, is another arch, with the inscription—

SVMMA SACRA VIA.

This sculpture is of the second century, it is now in the Lateran Museum, and belonged to the tomb of the Aterii; it appears most probable that it was the tomb of an architect of that family, from the number of buildings represented, and a machine for raising stones and placing them on a high wall, resembling a modern crane or a fire-escape, such as are used in London [t].

There are also figures of the three *Parcæ* or Fates, which were said to have given the name of IN TRIBUS FATIS to this part of Rome, mentioned in Anastasius, when the church of SS. Cosmas and Damian was founded, and by Procopius [u] in speaking of the bronze Janus.

The *Colossum altum* of the Regionary Catalogue is usually called the Colossus of Nero. This gigantic statue is described as 110 ft. in height, and it had round the head seven rays of glory, each 22½ ft. long; other authorities say 120 ft. high and the rays 12 ft. It was erected c. A.D. 65. As this Colossus was dedicated to the Sun, Hadrian ordered Apollodorus to make a second, to be dedicated to the Moon, and a temple of the Sun and Moon is mentioned in

---

[r] See our Chronological Table, A.D. 772-810; Photos., No. 3248, 3249, and Plate XXXVI.

[s] In the time of Nicolas I., A.D. 858-867, Anastasius, 592.

[t] See our Chapter on the Construction of Walls, and Plate XXIX., and Photo. No. 1500.

[u] Procopius De Bello Gothico, lib. i. c. 25.

Regio XI.* The Colossus is described by Pliny as cast in bronze in his time by Zenodorus. He mentions its dedication to Sol, and gives the height as 110 ft.*

"But all the vastness of statues of that time, Xenodorus in our age surpassed, having made a Mercury in a city of Gaul for the Auvergnats, (that engaged him) for ten years, the price 40,000,000 sesterces. After he had proved his skill there, he was summoned to Rome by Nero, where he made a colossus 110 feet high, intended to represent that prince, (but) it was dedicated to the worship of the Sun (or Apollo), (when) the crimes of that prince (met with) condemnation. We admired in the workshop, not only (a striking model) in clay, but also, from very little (studies), what the first sketch of the work was. That statue shewed that the art of casting in bronze was not lost, since Nero was prepared to lavish both gold and silver, and Xenodorus is considered second to none of the ancients in the art of designing metal-work *."

This was originally placed in the vestibule *y* of Nero's Golden House, by the architect, Decrianus, under Vespasian, and was moved by Apollodorus, under Hadrian, to make room for the TEMPLUM URBIS. This is particularly described by Dion Cassius *z* and Spartianus.

"When Vespasian was consul for the sixth time and Titus for the fourth, the Temple of Peace was dedicated, and the Colossus, as it is called, was placed in the Via Sacra, which is said to have been a hundred-and-twenty feet high, and to have been the image of Nero, or, as some say, of Titus *a*."

"Vespasian gave a handsome gratuity to the artist who repaired the Colossus *b*."

"Hadrian removed the Colossus, standing and suspended or (kept upright) by Decrianus the architect, from that place where the Temple of Rome now stands, an immense undertaking, so that twenty-four elephants were required for the work. And he dedicated the image to the Sun or Apollo, which before had been called after Nero, whose likeness it bore. Another similar to this, which Apollodorus the architect had made, he dedicated to the Moon *c*."

---

v "Transtulit et Colossum stantem atque suspensum per Demetrianum Architectum de eo loco in quo nunc templum Urbis est ingenti molimine, ita ut operi etiam elephantos viginti quattuor exhiberet. Et cum hoc simulacrum post Neronis vultum, cui antea dicatum fuerat, Soli consecrasset, aliud tale Apollodoro architecto auctore facere Lunae molitus est." (Spartianus in Hadriano, c. 19.)

w Plinii Nat. Hist., lib. xxxiv. c. 18.

x "Zenodorus .... Postquam satis ibi artem approbaverat, Romam accitus est a Nerone, ubi destinatum illius principis simulacrum, colossum fecit, cx. pedum longitudine, qui dicatus Solis venerationi est, damnatis sceleribus illius principis. Mirabamur in officina non modo ex argilla similitudinem insignem, verum et ex parvis admodum surculis, quod primum operis instar fuit. Ea statua indicavit interisse fundendi aeris scientiam, cum et Nero largiri aurum argentumque paratus esset, et Zenodorus scientia fingendi cœlandique nulli veterum postponeretur." (Plinii Nat. Hist., lib. xxxiv. 18.)

y "Non in alia re tamen damnosior, quam in ædificando. Domum a Palatio Esquilias usque fecit, quam primo *Transitoriam* mox incendio absumptam restitutamque *Auream* nominavit. De cujus spatio atque cultu suffecerit hoc retulisse. Vestibulum ejus fuit, in quo colossus centum viginti pedum staret ipsius effigie." (Suetonius in Nerone, c. 31.)

z Dion Cassius, lib. lxix. c. 4.

a Dion Cassius, lib. lxvi. c. 15, (A.U.C. 828, A.D. 75).

b Suetonius in Vespasiano, c. 18.

c Spartianus in Hadriano, c. 18.

The Colossus was moved by Hadrian to make room for the temple of Roma, and on account of the enormous weight of this great bronze statue, the twenty-four elephants were employed to drag it up to the top of the Clivus Sacer, on the spot where the church of S. Francesca Romana now stands, in front of the Colosseum, between that and the Forum Romanum. This is a very lofty spot. The present campanile or belfry-tower of S. Francesca Romana, is nearly on the site once occupied by the Colossus, and is of about the same height, a very conspicuous object [d]. This agrees with the notice of it by Martial [e], and with all the other passages from Classical authors on the subject. To this platform the sloping roads or inclines (*clivus*) ascend both from the north and from the south, and it is on the boundary between two Regiones. There is no authority for the exact line of the boundaries of the Regiones, we know only what the Catalogue tells us.

It seems almost certain that the place where the Colossus originally stood was in the vestibule of the Golden House, and that this was near the south-east end of the Via Sacra [f]. The third of the three temples out of which the church of SS. Cosmas and Damian was made agrees well with this site. The fact is now thoroughly established, that the Marble Plan of Rome was fixed upon the eastern wall of that temple; that wall still stands, with remains in it of the metal hooks by which the marble slabs had been attached to it [g]. The great Basilica of Maxentius and Constantine, which stands against the south side of that church, was not built until long after the time of Nero and of Hadrian; and the arcade of the time of Nero built against the cliff of that part of the Palatine, called the Velia, extends to that Basilica, and is cut off by it. There is no improbability, therefore, in supposing that the arcade or *porticus* extended to the vestibule, in which stood the Colossus and the colossal horses, that were fit companions to it; these were removed in the time of Constantine to his thermæ on the Quirinal, near to where they now stand. Flaminius Vacca [h] observed, at the time they were again moved, that on that part of the base which had been built into the wall of the thermæ, there were mouldings of the time of Nero, of the same character as on other buildings well known to be of his time.

[d] See Plate XXXIV.
[e] "Hic ubi syderius proprius videt astra Colossus
Et crescunt media pegmata celsa via."
(Martialis, Ep. de Spectaculis, ii.)
[f] See p. 84, Basilica of Constantine.   [h] Flaminius Vacca, Memorie, No 10,
[g] See Photos., No. 783.   ap. Fea, lviii.

The *podium* or pediment in front of the Colosseum, usually shewn as that on which the Colossus was placed by Hadrian, is not nearly large enough for a statue of that height. It is also faced with brick-work of the third century, which is the date of the medal of Gordianus of the Colosseum, in front of which is represented a colossal figure, but only about fifty feet high. The fragments of a bronze statue, of from forty to fifty feet high, are now preserved in the courtyard of the palace of the Conservatori on the Capitoline Hill. These are said by F. Vacca[i] to have been found near the Meta Sudans, between that and this pediment or *podium* on which they stood. The head, and a foot and a hand are preserved; the head is not that of Nero, and has no marks of rays round it.

This great bronze Colossus is said in the *Mirabilia*[j] to have been destroyed as an idol of Apollo or the Sun, by order of Pope Silvester, in the time of Constantine. That Nero was represented in the character of the Sun is evident from the rays round his head, each twenty feet long; and after the Colossus was placed in the centre of the great colonnade of Livia, that became the sacred enclosure with the statue of the god, and probably an altar at the foot of it. A temple of the Sun in front of the Colosseum is mentioned in several of the Acts of the Martyrs.

A Colossus is represented on a coin[k] of Gordianus I., in the third century, resting on such a base as the *podium* before-mentioned, with the inscription over it—MUNIFICENTIA GORDIANI AVG.; this figure stands in front of, and under the shadow of, the Colosseum, not extending to the summit[l]. Fragments of a colossal bronze statue were found near this podium or base, or between that and the Meta Sudans, and are now preserved in the Museum on the Capitol, and a measurement of these fragments shews that the figure of which they formed a part could not have been more than fifty feet high. The character of the sculpture is that of the third century, and would agree very well with the time of the Gordians, but not at all with the time of Nero. There is also the legend already cited, that the great bronze Colossus was destroyed as an idol of the Sun, by Silvester, in the time of Constantine, after the celebrated edict for the Peace of the Church.

[i] Flaminius Vacca, Memorie, No. 71, ap. Fea, lxxxv.
[j] Mirabilia Civitatis Romæ ap. Codex Urlichs, p. 136.
[k] On some bad impressions of this coin there appear to be two figures, one considerably shorter than the other, and these have been supposed to be father and son; but on better impressions it is seen that what appears to be the shorter figure is the Meta Sudans, with the one figure behind it.
[l] See our Plate of Coins or Medals, with ruins of the Colosseum.

TEMPLE OF THE SUN.

A Temple of the Sun was built by the Emperor Heliogabalus, and it is mentioned by Lampridius[m] in connection with the Amphitheatre and the Lavacrum; this porticus, with the Colossus in the middle of it, would be a Temple of the Sun, and it is between the other two buildings. This is most probably the temple intended, rebuilt by that emperor; the massive columns of Egyptian granite are more likely to have been erected in the third century than in the time of Augustus, although the name of PORTICUS LIVIÆ seems to have been retained for the portion of it towards the Colosseum, as shewn in the fragment of the Marble Plan.

In the *Descriptio plenaria totius Urbis* of the twelfth century, the Temple of the Sun is placed "in front of the Palatine and before the Colosseum, where the ceremonial worship was performed before the image that stood on the slope in front of the Colosseum[n]." In the *Graphia aurea Urbis Romæ*, of the thirteenth century, the same words are repeated[o]. In the anonymous Itinerary of the fifteenth century, known by the name of *Anonymus Magliabecchianus*, which is to a great extent a reproduction of the *Mirabilia Urbis Romæ* of the thirteenth, it is also stated that there was a temple of the Sun in front of the Colosseum (*ante*[p]), where ceremonies were performed, standing in front of the image in the middle of the same temple[q]. In the corresponding passage in the *Mirabilia*, the word *ante* before *Colosseum* is omitted, which makes it nonsense[r]. It is stated

---

[m] Script. Hist. Aug., Lampridii Antoninus Heliogabalus, c. 17.

[n] "... in fronte Palatii templum Solis. . . . *Ante* Coloseum templum Solis, ubi fiebant cerimoniæ simulacro quod stabat in fastigio Colosei." (Descriptio plenaria Urbis, ap. Urlichs, p. 110.)

[o] Graphia Urbis, ap. Urlichs, p. 121.

[p] "*Ante* Colliseum fuit templum Solis, ubi fiebant cerimoniæ simulachro adstanti in medio dicti Collisei cum corona in capite aurea et palla in manu ad representationem totius orbis, ut supra dictum est." (Anonymus Magliabecchianus, ap. Urlichs, p. 167.)

[q] "(*Ante*)Coloseum fuit templum Solis miræ magnitudinis et pulchritudinis, diversis camerulis adaptatum, quod totum erat coopertum æreo celo et deaurato, ubi tonitrua fulgura et coruscationes fiebant et per subtiles fistulas pluviæ mittebantur. Erant ibi præterea signia supercelestia et planetæ Sol et Lunæ quæ quadrigis propriis ducebantur. In medio ejus Phebus i.e. deus solis manebat, qui pedes tenens in terra cum capite celum tangebat, qui pallam tenebat in manu, innuens quod Roma totum mundum regebat. Post vero temporis spatium beatus Silvester jussit ipsum templum destrui et alia palatia, ut oratores qui Romam venirent non per edificia profana irent, sed per ecclesias cum devotione transirent, caput vero et manus prædicti ydoli ante palatium suum in Laterano in memoriam fecit poni, quod modo palla Samsonis falso vocatur a vulgo. Ante vero Coliseum fuit templum, in quo fiebant cerimoniæ prædicto simulacro." (Mirabilia Urbis Romæ, ap. Urlichs, p. 136.)

[r] The word *ante* was wanting in one of the MSS., but there was a damaged part of the parchment, with space for that word, which is supplied by the other MSS., as above cited.

that the head of the statue of Phœbus, the God of the Sun, *touched the skies*, and stood in the middle of it (*in medio ejus*), this is the true reading. The whole passage may be then translated or paraphrased.

"*Before* the Colosseum was the Temple of the Sun, of a wonderful size and beauty, surrounded by various small vaults, all covered with a gilt bronze ceiling, whereby they would make (an imitation of) thunder, and flashes of lightning, and send rain by means of small pipes [supplied by the aqueduct]. There was besides an imitation of the celestial signs, and the planets (*Sol et Luna*), who drove their own carriages and four (*quadrigæ*). In the middle stood Phœbus, that is, the Sun-god (or Apollo), who holding his feet on the earth touched the sky with his head, and held in his hand a Pallium, to intimate that Rome governed the world. But after a short space of time the blessed Silvester ordered the temple to be destroyed, with many others, that the orators who went to Rome should not go to profane buildings, but should go with devotion to the churches. But he caused the head and the hands of the said idol (or Colossus) to be placed before his palace in the Lateran as a memorial, which, however, the common people called the 'pallium of Samson;' but before the Colosseum was the temple in which the ceremonials (worship) to the said image were performed."

Putting these medieval traditions together, and comparing them with the recent excavations and the fragments of the Marble Plan of Rome, found in 1868, with the name of Porticus Liviæ upon it, there can be no doubt that this magnificent double colonnade of the time of Augustus was made into the Temple of the Sun and Moon by the Emperor Hadrian, who placed the great Colossus of Nero in the character of Phœbus, or Apollo, or the Sun, "on the slope of the Palatine, in front of the Colosseum," and ordered another Colossus of the Moon to be made. This agrees with the tradition of the Pilgrim. A deep slope would be very inconvenient either for a fine colonnade, or for the house of the time of the Republic that was pulled down by Augustus to erect this colonnade; the ground was therefore made level by cutting off some of the tufa rock on the summit of the ridge, called the SUMMA SACRA VIA, and by making a substructure of rubble-stone under the platform at the lower end, opposite to the Colosseum (excavated in 1873-4), by which it was brought up to a level, and had an aqueduct upon it to convey water to the four fountains at the four corners. This agrees also with the account given by Strabo, that it was visible from the Forum Romanum; and with Martial, who says that the head of the Colossus was among the stars. Also with the account of the Pilgrim, that an imitation of rain was made by water conveyed in small pipes (with holes in them) carried in the bronze vault over the double colonnade.

S. Francesca Romana.

The Church and Convent of S. Francesca Romana, formerly called S. Maria Nuova, which occupy a part of the site of the great platform between the Colosseum and the Forum, is on a plan very usual in the early churches of Rome, a T cross, with an apse at the east end, and a porch of three bays at the west, and side chapels added in 1615. The walls of the nave are still those of the ninth century, with the double-brick arches over the windows (now blocked up), as at S. Prassede and other works of that period. The transept was rebuilt in 1216. The campanile belongs to the latter period, and the mosaic pavement in the chancel and transept; also a painting of the Madonna and infant Christ on a gold ground, in the apse. It was again almost rebuilt and reduced to its present form by Paul V. in 1615, and the carved ceiling is of that time; on it is represented the history of S. Francesca Romana. In the transept there is another painting of the Madonna, of the sixteenth century, inscribed, SINIBALDUS . PERUSINUS . D. INSTIT. M. D. XXIIII. Sinibaldus was a native of Perugia, and a pupil of Perugino.

Some modern writers have considered this church to be the same as that of SS. Peter and Paul, built by Pope Paul I. in A.D. 760, but De Rossi has shewn that this is a mistake; that church was made in part of the great Basilica of Constantine, and near to the church of SS. Cosmas and Damian. Others have considered it to be the same as that of S. Maria Antiqua[l], mentioned before the eighth century; but that older church, built by Leo IV.[n], was not quite on the same site, though very near to it. The road on the *clivus* passes between them. The remains of this church of S. Maria, afterwards called Antiqua, when another church of S. Maria

---

[l] Rione I.—Monti.

[l] This church, dedicated to S. Peter and S. Paul, was made by Pope Paul I., A.D. 760, as recorded by Anastasius:—"Hic fecit noviter Ecclesiam infra hanc civitatem Romanam in Via Sacra, juxta templum Romæ in honorem Sanctorum Apostolorum Petri et Pauli, ubi ipsi beatissimi Principis Apostolorum tempore quo pro Christi nomine martyrio coronati sunt, dum redemptori nostro funderent preces propria genua flectere visi sunt." Some editions read "Templum" Romuli for "Romæ;" the mention of the Via Sacra identifies it with this. The legends respecting the place of martyrdom of these Apostles are contradictory. This church was made in part of the great Basilica of Constantine.

[n] "Ecclesiam autem Dei Genitricis semperque Virginis Mariæ, quæ primitus Antiqua, nunc autem Nova, vocabatur, quam domnus Leo quartus papa a fundamentis construxerat; sed picturis eam minime decoraret, iste beatissimus præsul pulchris ac variis fecit depingi coloribus augens decorem, et plurimis corde puro ornavit speciebus." (Anastasius 592, Nicolaus I., A.D. 858.)

was built close to it, were excavated in 1873 by Signor Rosa, for the Italian Government. It was made out of some of the chambers of the Lavacrum of Heliogabalus, of which the ruins were also brought to light at the same time[v]. The church of S. Francesca Romana was restored or rebuilt by Nicolas I., A.D. 860, and the mosaic picture in the apse is attributed to that period. It represents a cross on a Calvary, between the palm-trees and the monogram of Christ. A hand coming out of the clouds puts a crown on the head of the Blessed Virgin, on her right are the figures of S. Peter and S. Andrew, and on her left those of S. James and S. John. The ancient painting of the Madonna is said to have been brought from Troia by the Cavaliere Angelo Frangipani, on his return from Palestine about the year 1100.

The tomb of S. Francesca was made by Bernini in 1643, with bronze figures ornamented with precious stones, with colonettes of jasper, a balustrade and lamps. There are also tombs of Cardinal Alamanno, of the Aduman family of Pisa, who died in 1122; and of Cardinal Vulcani, of Naples, who died in 1322; and that of Antonio Rido, of Padua, who was commandant of the fortress of S. Angelo in the time of Eugenius IV., and General of the Pontifical army under Nicolas V., he died in 1475, and is represented on horseback, and in armour. The tomb of Gregory XI. was erected in 1384 by the senate and people, to commemorate the return of the Pope from Avignon in 1377. This return is represented on a fine alto-relievo by Paul Olivieri.

THE CAMPANILE is quite of a different construction from the nave, regular brickwork of the thirteenth century, and it cuts right through the old wall with a straight vertical joint, passing through two of the old arches, and cutting off a portion of them. It is very tall, and perhaps the finest campanile in Rome[w]. The three upper storeys are remarkably open, with windows of three lights, separated by marble shafts only; these, with the entablature, or cross pieces, which they carry, are cut out of antique marble tombs, with portions of the old carving left, and the shafts are slightly of the baluste form, as is the case in several other campaniles in Rome. The surface of the wall is ornamented as usual with small round paterae of majolica ware, chiefly green; some of these have patterns upon them—one a spread eagle; another, a trellis-work pattern in yellow, on a green ground; an-

---

[v] See p. 75.

[w] This campanile was considered by Mr. Gally Knight as of the ninth century, and Sir George Head falls into the same mistake, which is indeed commonly entertained; but an examination of the construction compared with that of the church adjoining, or with that of S. Prassede and several others, clearly shews that this is an error.

other, a sort of star: all these are in the style of the twelfth century, which in Rome is continued in the thirteenth.

THE CLOISTER of the adjoining convent, and the entrance porch, were built in the fourteenth century by Gregory XI. (Roger de Beaufort of Limoges, 1370—1378), as recorded on an inscription over the inner door. The cloister is of two storeys, with rather large and wide semicircular arches, quite plain and square-edged, resting on octagonal piers, with very short capitals of foliage, and bases moulded, a style of architecture which was never used in England after the twelfth century. The cloister is much defaced, and the arches filled up with a modern wall, but the porch is tolerably perfect, and affords a curious proof how much Rome was behind England in the changes of style during the Middle Ages. The outer cloister of *Ara Cœli* is of the same style and the same period, and there the bases have the foot-ornament at the angles also, a sort of rude imitation of what we have in England at St. Cross, near Winchester, in the middle of the twelfth century.

The Temple of JUPITER STATOR[x] is supposed by some authors to have been the small temple on the Palatine, by the side of the *clivus*, and nearly behind the Arch of Titus, (the foundations of which were excavated by Signor Rosa in 1865); and the *Cella Lavernæ*, named in an inscription, printed by Dodwell, to have been another small temple near the Forum. The position thus assigned to the Temple of Jupiter Stator agrees with the description of Plutarch in his life of Cicero, as being "at the head of the Via Sacra." Dionysius mentions this temple as being on the Palatine, " Romulus consecrated the Temple of Stator of the Forum, near the Porta Mugonia, leading from the Via Sacra into the Palatine." The site of this gate is a matter still undecided, but the most probable one is that left open by Signor Rosa, near this spot.

---

[x] Plutarch in his Life of Cicero mentions this temple as at the head of the Via Sacra, where we ascend into *the Capitol*, but this must mean the *capitol* of the Romans, or Roma Quadrata, not the capitol of the united people on the hill of Saturn, afterwards called the Capitoline Hill, which is not consistent with its being on the Palatine. There was a *clivus* or steep ascent at each end of the VIA SACRA, which has caused a confusion of ideas, this street being considered by some to have extended along the Forum to the foot of the *Clivus Capitolinus*. The CAPUT VIÆ SACRÆ would in that case apply to either end. This is, however, supposed to be an error of Plutarch, as Dionysius mentions this temple as on the Palatine : " They built temples and consecrated them to those gods to whom they had addressed their vows during their battles, Romulus to Jupiter Stator, near the gate called Mugonia, which leads to the Palatine hills from the Holy Way." (Dionysius Hal., book ii. c. 50.) Festus says that this gate was named from Mugius, the person who had the charge of protecting it.

The Arch of Titus is not mentioned either in the *Curiosum Urbis* or the *Notitia* as in any Regio, it is just outside of the old gate of the Palatine, which is in the boundary line of Regio X. The site on which it stands was on the Summa Sacra Via. It was erected by the senate and people of Rome in the time of Domitian, in honour of the Emperor Titus, the son of Vespasian, as recorded on an inscription on the south front [y]; and the chief object was to record the conquest of the Jews by Titus. The trophies of that war are carved upon it, and among them the most faithful representations of the well-known seven-branched candlestick and the ark of the covenant.

In the Middle Ages this archway was converted into a tower and gateway of the castle of the Frangipani, which was entirely destroyed about 1830 [z]. Some remains of masonry of the time of the Kings, which had been used in it, remain near to it. When the arch was destroyed it was found to be so much damaged, that considerable repairs were necessary, so that the greater part of the existing fabric is modern imitation, but in travertine instead of marble. It had been stripped of much of its original ornament by Paul III. at the same time (A.D. 1534—1550) with the temple of Antoninus, the temple of the Sun and the Colosseum, in order to provide marble and travertine and ornament for his family palace, the Farnese. Yet this same pontiff forbade the exportation of antique marbles, and appointed a commissioner to superintend ancient monuments and their conservation.

[y] SENATVS POPVLVSQVE ROMANVS.
DIVO . TITO . DIVI . VESPATIANI . F. VESPASIANO AVGVSTO.

Another inscription published by Faunus, Panvinius, and Gruter, is said to have been on the north side, which is quite possible; but it is said by the anonymous author published by Mabillon, to have been on another Arch of Titus in the Circus Maximus:—

S. P. Q. R.
IMP. TITO . CAESARI . DIVI . VESPASIANI . FILIO
VESPASIANO . AVG. PONT. MAX.
TRIB. POT. X.
IMP. XVII. COS. VIII. P.P.
PRINCIPI SVO QVI
PRAECEPTIS . PATRIAE . CONSILIISQVE . ET
AVSPICIIS . GENTEM . IVDAEORVM . DOMVIT
ET . VRBEM . HIEROSOLYMAM . OMNIBVSANTE . SE
DVCIBVS . REGIBVS . GENTIBVSQVE . AVT . FRVSTRA
PETITAM . AVT . OMNINO . INTENTATAM . DELEVIT.

[z] In a picture by Claude, of about A.D. 1650, this arch is represented, and a building connecting it with the monastery of S. Francesca Romana, which looks like a barrack for soldiers. Another painting, by Hermann Swanrett, c. A.D. 1680, represents the Arch of Constantine, and a building on which is a Guelphic forked battlement, connecting it with the Colosseum. These seem to be remains of the great fortress of the Frangipani. Both of these pictures are now in the Dulwich Gallery.

REGIONARY CATALOGUE.

REGIO IV.ᵃ—TEMPLUM PACIS or VIA SACRA.

Contents according to the " Notitia" and the " Curiosum Urbis."

Continet.

Porticum Absidatum . . . 104	Templum Faustinæ . . . 66
Aream Vulcani . . . . *ib.*	Basilicam Pauli ¹ 109
Aureum Bucinum . . . 106	Forum Transitorium . . 40, 109
Apollinem Sandaliarium ᵇ . . *ib.*	Siburam ʲ 110
Templum Telluris . . . *ib.*	Balneum Dafnidis ᵏ . . . 112
[Horrea Chartarea ᶜ] . . . 108	Vici viii. . . . . . *ib.*
Tigillum Sororium ᵈ . . . *ib.*	Ædes viii. [Ædiculæ octo.] . *ib.*
Colossum altum pedes cii. s. [cen-	Vico-Magistri xlviii.
tum duo semis] habet in capite	Curatores ii.
radia [numero] vii., singula	Insulæ iidcclvii.¹
pedum xxii. semis . . . 93	Domus lxxxviii. [Domus octoginta
Metam Sudantem . . . 108	octo.]
Templum Romæ [et Veneris ᵉ] . 75	Horrea xviii.
Ædem [Jobis] [Jovis Statoris] ᶠ . 101	Balnea lxxv. ᵐ
Viam Sacram 66	Lacus lxxxiii. [lxxviii., lxxix.]
Basilicam Novam et Pauli ᵍ . . 109	Pistrina xv.
———— Constantinianam ʰ . 83	Continet Pedes xiii. [tredecim millia.

Modern Contents.

Churches and Convents of—
  S. Francesca Romana.
  SS. Cosmas and Damian.
  S. Hadrianus.
  S. Quiricus.
  S. Lorenzo (in miranda).
  SS. Domenic and Sixtus.
  S. Maria de' Monti.
  S. Francesco di Paola.
  S. Agatha in Subura.

ᵃ In the same manner as it has been found convenient to incorporate the information which has been collected to explain the Regionary Catalogue for Regio VIII., with the topographical description of the Forum Romanum, so in this instance the materials collected to illustrate the Regio IV. are more conveniently applied here as supplementary to the topography of the Via Sacra.
ᵇ Sandaliarum, in MSS., *vide* Codex ed. Urlichs.

ᶜ In *Notitia* only.
ᵈ Vigilum, in MSS.
ᵉ et Veneris, in *Notitia* only.
ᶠ Jobis, in *Curiosum*; Jovis Statoris, in *Notitia*.
ᵍ In *Curiosum*.
ʰ In *Notitia*; MS. B. adds "et Pauli."
ⁱ In *Notitia*.
ʲ Suburram, in MSS.
ᵏ Daphnidis, in MSS.
ˡ iidcclvii. in *Notitia*.
ᵐ lxxxv. in *Notitia*

The fourth Regio contains the Via Sacra, and extends from the Area of Vulcan on the eastern side of Regio VIII., the Forum Romanum, and the Forum Transitorium on the north-west, to the Meta Sudans, the Colosseum, and Regio III. on the south, with the cliff of the Palatine (Regio X.) or the foss-way under it for its western boundary. On the east, it includes a part of the Esquiline Hill believed to be the part called by Varro the Oppia, extending to the valley between the Viminal and this part of the Esquiline, and southward to the Suburra. It there touches Regio VI., Alta Semita, and Regio V., Esquilina. It includes the Velia of the Palatine, with the great Basilica of Constantine.

Porticus Absidata. This is supposed by Canina and the Roman antiquaries to have been an ancient *street* from the Via Sacra, on the eastern side of the platform on the higher level (the Summa Sacra Via), and passing by the apse. But a *porticus* is not a street; it is either an arcade or a colonnade. If this view of the site is correct at all, it is most likely to be the building with two apses (*apsidata*), which they miscall the Temple of Venus and Roma. This structure is not a temple, but two basilicas or market-halls, standing within the magnificent double colonnade, which seems to correspond with the Porticus Liviæ.

Area Vulcani. This is supposed to have been a space at the foot of the Capitol or Campidoglio, on the east side of the Forum Romanum, dedicated to Vulcan from the earliest period of Roman history, and the place where probably in ancient times the blacksmiths worked. It is mentioned by Dionysius, Plutarch, Livy, and Festus, who says that—

"A statue was ordered by the senate to be erected in this area in honour of Ludius (probably a favourite actor, called *the* player), who was killed by a stroke of lightning in the Circus, and was buried on the Janiculum; his bones were believed to work miracles and give oracular answers; they were therefore ordered to be translated and buried under the base of a statue in this place, which is on a higher level than the Comitium [a]."

A Temple of Concord was erected in the Area of Vulcan by Cneius Fabius, who was *Ædilis Curulis*, or magistrate of the public temples and games (A.U.C. 303, B.C. 450), which serves to identify the site, with the help of other passages, as being at the foot of the

---

[a] "Statua est Ludii ejus, qui quondam fulmine ictus in Circo, sepultus est in Janiculo. Cujus ossa postea ex prodigiis, oraculorumque responsis Senatus decreto intra Urbem relata in Vulcanale, quod est supra Comitium, obruta sunt, superque ea columna cum ipsius effigie posita est." (Festus in voce Statua.)

Capitol, just within the boundary-wall of the Forum, but on a higher level than the Comitium[o]. Livy mentions among the prodigies (B.C. 181) that blood fell in the areas of Vulcan and Concord[p]. A statue of Horatius Cocles, said to have fallen from heaven, was placed at an early period in the Comitium, and was removed, which caused a riot, and it was eventually restored to a higher place in the Vulcanale, or area of Vulcan[q]. The narrow space between the temples of Concord on the east, and of Saturn on the west, is now called by this name.

The temples of Vulcan and of Mars made by Romulus were outside of the original city, or the Roma Quadrata, according to Plutarch[r]. This shews that the boundary of the Roma Quadrata was the foss at the foot of the scarped cliff of the Palatine Hill, but this locality became within the city when the hill of Saturn, afterwards called the Capitoline Hill, was added to it, and this temple is mentioned as in the city by Dionysius[s]. A lotus-tree is said by Pliny to have been planted in the Vulcanale by Romulus, which grew to so large a size that the roots of it extended into the Forum of Julius Cæsar, passing by the stations of the municipality (*municipium?*). There was also in the Vulcanale a cypress-tree of equal size, which was destroyed from neglect in the time of Nero[t], towards the end of his reign.

Part of this Area touched the foot of the Capitolium, as the Temple of Concord stood in part of it, which is northward of the Arch of Septimius Severus, and on higher ground, separated from the Forum Romanum by the wall against the lower cliff, or bank, and the foss-way which passed under the Arch, and was subsequently made into a paved street, on the eastern side of the Forum Romanum (see p. 55). The Church of S. Hadrian, or Adrian, is in the Area Vulcani, which was originally of considerable extent, and must have passed along the whole length of the Forum to reach this Regio; it was gradually curtailed by being built upon. It

[o] "Eo anno Cn. Flavius . . . ædilis curulis fuit. . . . . Ædem Concordiæ in area Vulcani summa invidia nobilium dedicavit." (Livii Hist. ix. 46.) See also Forum Romanum, Temple of Concord, in this work, and Plates III., IV., V.

[p] "In area Vulcani et Concordiæ sanguine pluit." (Ibid., xl. 10.)

[q] "Eam statuam in locum editum subducendam atque ita in area Vulcani sublimiori loco statuendam." (Aulus Gellius, iv. 5.) See also the sculpture in the Comitium, Plates XIV., XV., XVI.

[r] Plutarchi Quæst., c. 47 ; Romulus 24, and 27.

[s] Dionysius, ii. 50 ; see also vi. 63, vii. 17, xi. 30.

[t] "Verum altera lotos in Vulcanali, quod Romulus constituit ex victoria de decumis, æquæva Urbi intelligitur, ut auctor est Masurius. Radices ejus in forum usque Cæsaris per stationes municipiorum penetrant. Fuit cum ea cupressus æqualis, circa suprema Neronis principis prolapsa atque neglecta." (Plinii Nat. Hist., xvi. 86.)

was probably named from a blacksmith's forge being there; and it is a singular coincidence, that there still is a blacksmith's forge and a wheel-wright's factory close to the church of S. Hadrian.

Aureum Bucinum. Probably a bronze horn gilt, perhaps in connection with the Porta Mugionia, which was so named from a bronze figure of a bull.

Apollinem Sandaliarium. This is supposed to have been a bronze figure of Apollo with remarkable sandals, mentioned by Suetonius in the life of Augustus [u]. There was also a Vicus Sandaliarius, which had the statue in it: an inscription relating to the *Vicus Sandaliarius* is preserved by Panvinius [v]. This street was occupied by booksellers' shops, as we learn from Aulus Gellius [x] and Galen [y], and it was a favourite lounge in the time of the Empire. The shops were probably under a *porticus*, either an arcade or colonnade, and the titles of the books were attached to these columns. This custom is alluded to by Horace [z].

On one of the fragments of the Marble Plan of Rome is a portion of a street, with the letters .... DLARIVS, which is supposed to be the Vicus Sandaliarius; it is a short street between two other streets, running across from one to the other. This fragment is placed by Canina to the east of the Colosseum, between the Esquiline and the Quirinal.

Templum Telluris. This is said to have been founded in the early years of the Republic (A.U.C. 268, B.C. 486), on the site of the house of Spurius Cassius [a]. The senate and people were so furious against Cassius that they demolished his house, and built this temple on the site of it [b]. A statue of Spurius Cassius, which had been placed here by himself when he strove to obtain the chief power,

---

[u] "Equites Romani natalem ejus sponte atque consensu biduo semper celebrarunt. Omnes ordines in lacum Curtii quotannis ex voto pro salute ejus stipem jaciebant; item Kalendis Januariis strenam in Capitolio, etiam absenti: ex qua summa pretiosissima deorum simulacra mercatus vicatim dedicabat, ut Apollinem Sandaliarium, et Jovem tragoedum, aliaque." (Suetonius in Augusto, c. 57.)

[v] GERMANICO . CAESARE = C. FONTEIO CAPITONE = COS = KAL. JVN. SEIAE FORTVNAE . AVG = SACR = SEX. FONTEIVS C. L. TROPHIMVS = CN. POMPEIVS . CN. L. NICEPHORVS = MAG. VICI = SANDALIARI . REG. IIII. = ANNI. XVIII. DD. =

[x] "... In Sandaliario forte apud librarios fuimus." (Aulus Gellius, xviii. 4.)
[y] Galen, De Libris suis, iv. 361.
[z] "Nulla taberna meos habeat neque pila libellos." (Horatii, Sat. l. 4. 71.)
[a] "Cassius, quia in agraria largitione ambitiosus in socios ... damnatumque populi judicio, dirutas publice ædes. Ea est area ante Telluris ædem. ..." (Livii Hist., lib. ii. c. 41.)
[b] "Senatus enim populusque Rom. non contentus capitali cum supplicio afficere interempto domum superjecit, ut penatium quoque strage puniretur. In solo autem ædem Telluris fecit." (Valerius Maximus.)

was burned by order of Lucius Piso, along with many others round the Forum; those only were saved that had been ordered by the senate and people [e]. This probably shews that the early statues in Rome were of wood. The account given by Dionysius and Suetonius of the site of the house of Cassius is, that it was in the street leading to the Carinæ [d], under the *divus*, and outside of the Templum Telluris, which the people had built on part of the area [e].

The Carinæ are believed by some authorities to have been in nearly the same district that is now called *de Pantani*, near the modern Suburra [f]. The *divus* mentioned by Dionysius is said to be the steep road up the south end of the Quirinal, facing the street called Cyprius, which is the same as before mentioned, leading to the Carinæ. This incline was called *Clivus Ursi*, from the figure of a bear. There was a temple of Pallas near the Templum Telluris. This site was the scene of some of the martyrdoms of the early Christian saints, as mentioned in the *Acta S. Gordiani*. Clementianus ordered his head to be cut off before the Templum Telluris, and his body to be thrown before the temple of Pallas [g]. The Templum Telluris was restored or rebuilt in the time of Cicero, who mentions it in one of his Epistles to Quintus, and says he has placed the statue of his friend there [h].

In one of the fragments of the Marble Plan of Rome are two temples united together with arcades, and the words IN TELL[*ure*]. One of these temples was probably that of Tellus or Terra, and the other that of Laverna, which is recorded to have been built near that of Tellus, at the expense of some butchers, who had sold meat without the permission of C. Titimus ædilis plebis, which they ought to have obtained. This appears from a fragment of the ancient Pontifical Books published by Dodwell [i]. In the Plan of Rome by Bufalini (A.D. 1551) an ancient church, now destroyed, is given by the name of S. Salvatore in Tellure, near the church of S. Quirico et Giullattæ. This probably indicates the site of the Temple of Tellus and Laverna, opposite to the Temple of Pallas,

[e] Plinii Nat. Hist., lib. xxxiv. c. 14.
[d] "Lenæus .... schola se sustentavit, docuitque in Carinis ad Telluris ædem, in qua regione Pompeiorum domus fuerat," &c. (Suetonius de Illustris Grammaticis, 15.)
[e] Dionysius, lib. viii. c. 79.
[f] Nardini and Nibby, vol. i. p. 315, Roma, 1818.
[g] Acta S. Gordiani, and Anastasius in S. Cornelio, 22.
[h] "... In qua de æde Telluris et de portica Catuli me admones. Fit utrumque diligenter: ad Telluris quidem etiam tuam statuam locavi." (Cicero ad Quintum Fratrem, lib. iii. epist. 1, c. 4.)
[i] C. TITINVS AED *dis* PL *ibis* MVLTAVIT LANIOS QVOD CARNEM VENDIDISSENT POPVLO NON INSPECTAM DE PECVNIA MVLCT ATITIA CELLA EXTRVCTA AD TELLVRIS LAVERNAE. (Dodwell, Prædict. Acad., Appendix, p. 665.)

in the Forum Transitorium[k]. Suetonius also mentions a temple of Tellus in Carinis, where was a school in which Lenacus taught. The small church of S. Maria in Carinis is in the Via del Colosseo, No. 62, near the Conservatorio de' Mendicanti. The present church or chapel is modern, and built into a modern palace, but the name indicates an ancient site. The street runs from the Colosseum into the Forum of Augustus, and the church is not far from the Temple of Pallas, though in a different street.

Horrea Chartaria. A number of various readings of this item in the Catalogues occur in different manuscripts or printed versions of it (*Cartaria, Cautharia, Testaria, Tastaria*), but no explanation is afforded by any one, and the most probable account of it seems to be that it was a great paper-warehouse; as the rest of these names are all unmeaning, they were probably errors of the scribes only.

Tigillum Sororium. The sister's gate or beam. This is said to have been near to the TEMPLUM TELLURIS, in a narrow street leading from the CARINÆ to the VICO CIPRIO. But this does not seem to agree with Livy's account of the origin of the name[l], which implies that the gate was put across the street where the murder was committed, outside of the Porta Capena. Dionysius says that the beam was supported by two walls, Festus by two other wooden beams or posts. It was long kept in repair or renewed at the public expense, and Livy says it was in existence in his time. In this place were two altars, one of which was dedicated to JUNO, surnamed also SORORIA[m], the other to Jupiter Curiatii.

Meta Sudans[n]. This is a hollow cone of brickwork which belonged to the great fountain, and was so called from its resemblance to the *meta* or goal of a circus, and the water trickling over it. This fountain was erected by Domitian in front of the Colosseum, at one end of the Via Sacra; and the arch of Constantine stands very near to it. The fountain must have been originally of considerable height, and was probably damaged when the upper storey of the Colosseum was burnt, and then rebuilt by Commodus. It is

---

[k] Palladio gives an engraving of the remains of a temple on this site in his *Antichita di Roma*, lib. iv.

[l] "Horatius ibat, trigemina spolia præ se gerens; cui soror virgo, quæ desponsata uni ex Curiatiis fuerat, obvia ante Portam Capenam fuit, ... Id hodie quoque publice semper refectum manet: Sororium tigillum vocant. Horatiæ sepulchrum, quo loco corruerat icta, constructum est saxo quadrato." (Livii Hist., lib. i. c. 26.)

[m] See Dionysius, lib. iii. c. 22; Festus in Sororium Tigillum.

[n] There is an early representation of a *Meta Sudans* engraved on a marble slab in the Gallery of Inscriptions at the Vatican.

mentioned by Seneca[o] and Cassiodorus, and other ancient authors, and in inscriptions given by Gruter and Muratori; and there are representations of it on coins of Vespasian and of Commodus, the latter gives it separately, the former only along with the Colosseum. The remains of it are well known; they are of historical interest, but no longer ornamental. A bronze colossus stood opposite to it, and the square basement of this is faced with brickwork of the third century.

Templum Romæ [*et Veneris*], (see p. 75).

Basilica Pauli Æmilii. This is mentioned by Cicero[p] in his letters to Atticus as building in his time, with ancient columns in the middle Forum. It is supposed to have been a restoration of that of Fulvius, and is mentioned by several classical authors. Others consider the passage in Cicero to mean that Paulus was building two basilicas or market-halls at the same time; one a restoration of an old one in the Forum Romanum, the other entirely new, in the street leading from it, afterwards made into the Forum Transitorium. On one of the fragments of the Marble Plan there is part of a basilica shewn near the Forum of Trajan, with part of the name EMILI . .; this is in the eighth Regio, and would not be the same as the one in the fourth, unless possibly it was on the borders of both, part in one, and part in the other[q]. It seems hardly probable that Paulus Emilius would build two so very near together at the same time, and the passage in Cicero does not necessarily mean that there were two basilicas, but one basilica between two forums.

Forum Transitorium. This is supposed to have been named from the great traffic which passed through it. The form of it was long and narrow, with colonnades. It was originally built or begun

---

[o] Senecæ, Ep. 57.

[p] "Paulus in medio Foro basilicam jam pæne texuit iisdem antiquis columnis: illam autem quam locavit facit magnificentissimam. Quid quæris? nihil gratius illo monumento, nihil gloriosius. Itaque Cæsaris amici, (me dico et Oppium dirumparis licet) in monumentum illud quod tu tollere laudibus solebas, ut forum laxaremus, et usque ad atrium Libertatis explicaremus, contempsimus sexcenties sestertium." (Ciceronis Epist. ad Atticum, lib. iv. ep. 16, s. 14.)

In medio foro does not mean in the middle of the Forum Romanum, but in the middle of the eastern side of it, and near the hall of Liberty.

[q] During some excavations in 1870, in making a new drain from the Capitol to the Cloaca Maxima, and across the east end of the Forum Romanum, in front of the church of S. Hadrian, the basement of some large building parallel to the front of the church was brought to light, with bases and part of a column upon it. This was chiefly medieval, but appeared to be on foundations of the time of the Empire belonging to some great building, probably the Basilica Pauli Æmilii (?). This is just at the north end of Regio IV., and very near to the Forum Transitorium.

by Domitian, and probably finished by Nerva[r], as it was often called by his name[s], (see p. 40).

Suburram. This was the name of one of the four divisions of ancient Rome in the time of Servius Tullius. It is supposed to have been partly on the northern slope of the Cœlian, and partly on the southern side of the Esquiline Hill, with the valley between, which in the time of the Empire was covered with fine buildings, as shewn upon one of the fragments of the ancient marble plan of Rome, but its limits are not well defined[t]. The church of S. Peter in Vincula is always described as in the Suburra, but it is in the third Regio of Augustus. Probably a part of the Suburra only was in this Regio in the time of the Empire. Suetonius mentions it as the original residence of Cæsar. It is mentioned also by Juvenal[u], and frequently by Martial[x].

The Suburra is mentioned as in the fourth Regio, both in the *Curiosum* and the *Notitia*. The limits of this Regio are not very well defined in that direction, but it seems probable that in it is the church of S. AGATHA IN SUBURRA.

Portions of this church are very ancient, and we have records of a mosaic picture made by Flavius Ricimer, a general in the time of the Emperor Valentinian III., and consul, A.D. 459, in which are said to have been representations of Christ and the Apostles, with an inscription[y]. The interior of the church is divided into nave

---

[r] IMP. NERVA . CAES. AVG. PONT. MAX. TRIB. POT. II. IMP. II. PROCOS.

[s] "Cassiodori Cronica," published by Eccardus, in Domitiano.

"Novam autem excitavit ædem in Capitolio Custodi Jovi, et forum, quod nunc Nervæ vocatur." (Suetonius in Domitiano, c. 5.

"Statuas colossas vel pedestres nudas, vel equestres, divis imperatoribus in foro Divi Nervæ, quod Transitorium dicitur, locavit." (Lampridius, in Alexander Severo, c. 28.)

[t] "Prima est scripta regio Suburana, secunda Esquilina, tertia Collina, quarta Palatina. In Suburanæ regionis parte princeps est Cœlius mons. . . . Eidem regioni attributa Subura quod sub muro terreo Carinarum, in quo est Argeorum Sacellum sextum. Subura Junius scribit ab eo, quod fuerit sub antiqua urbe, quod testimonium potest esse, quod subest ei loco qui Terreus murus vocatur." (Varro de Ling. Lat., lib. v. s. 8.)

[u] Juvenal, lib. i., Sat. iii. v. 5.

[x] "Dum tu forsitan inquietus erras clamosa, Juvenalis in Subura." (Martial, lib. xii., Ep. 18, ii. 17, vi. 66, vii. 34, ix. 19, c. 38, x. 94, xii. 3, c. 21.)

[y] FL. RICIMER, V. I. MAGISTER VTRIVSQVE MILITIÆ PATRIONIS ET EXCONS. ORD. PRO. VOTO. SVO. ADORNAVIT.

This mosaic was only destroyed in 1589, in a *restoration* of this church, and a coloured drawing of it is preserved in the Vatican Library; this was made by F. Penna, and is mentioned in Doni (Class. ii. n. 157).

Muratori (Thes. Nov. Inscript., p. cclxvi. and mdccclxvii., n. 1) has published another inscription found in this church, which was engraved on a copper-plate, with letters of silver inserted :—

SALVIS . DD. NN.
ET . PATRICIO
RECIMERE
PLVTINVS
EVSTATHIVS V. C.
P. VRB. FECIT.

Plutinus Eustathius was prefect of Rome, A.D. 470.

and aisles by two rows of antique columns, sixteen in number, of granite of the kind called *bigio*, with Ionic capitals. In a tomb in this church are the remains of the celebrated Daniel O'Connell, who died in Rome. The bas-reliefs are by M. Benzoni.

The *Carinæ* are believed to have been partly in the Suburra. Augustus was educated in a house in the Carinæ, as we learn from the *scholia* of Servius on the Æneid of Virgil[t], and the place was then celebrated for its fine houses. Servius also tells us that *carinæ* were houses built after the fashion of keels (that is, with gable ends). We are told by Livy that Flaccus with the army entered the city by the Porta Capena, and passed through the Carinæ to the Esquiline[u]; that is, the army marched through the street between the Cœlian and the Palatine, and through the gate where the Arch of Constantine now stands, into the large square then surrounded by houses called the Carinæ. In one corner of this area or place stood the Meta Sudans.

There were various other streets leading into this place; on the south the Via Labicana and the modern Via di S. Giovanni in Laterano, meeting at the east end of the Colosseum, and carried round the north side of it under the Thermæ of Titus, into this place; the Via de Santi Quattro Coronati, passing along the south side of the Colosseum; another street from the north passes under the east end of the Thermæ of Titus from the Esquiline and the Suburra; both this street and the place itself were called *Carinæ*, from the number of gabled houses (*keels*) in them. This large area or place was in the very centre of the city, and was often called *in Medio Urbis*. The south-east corner of this place touched the Cœlian, with the Palace of Claudius upon it. The north-east touched the Esquiline, with the Thermæ of Titus upon it. Immediately to the north was the Velia, a detached part of the Esquiline, on one corner of which the Basilica of Constantine has been built. On the south was the Palatine, with the *clivus* or slope up this side of it, against the scarped cliff. The house of Pompey and several other houses of importance are mentioned as being in the Carinæ and on the Esquiline, but as that name seems to be applied not only to this place, but to the streets leading from it, there is some doubt in which Regio they were situated.

[t] "Lautas autem dixit, aut propter elegantiam ædificiorum, aut propter Augustum, qui natus est in curiis veteribus, et nutritus in lautis Carinis. Carinæ sunt ædificia facta in Carinarum modum, quæ erant infra Templum Telluris." (Servius in Æneid, viii. 361.)

[u] "In hoc tumultu Fulvius Flaccus porta Capena cum exercitu Romam ingressus media urbe per Carinas Esquilias contendit." (Livii Hist., xxvi. 10.)

Balneum Daphnidis. The site of this is not known. Dafne is supposed to be the name or nickname of the keeper of the bath-house in the time of Martial[b], and Pliny[c], and Aurelius Victor, all of whom mention him.

Vici viii. The Catalogue of the *Curiosum* and *Notitia* gives the number of streets only; the one attributed to Rufus supplies these names:—

a.	Vicus Sceleratus.		e.	Vicus Trium Viarum.
b.	,, Eros.		f.	,, Anciportus Minor.
c.	,, Veneris.		g.	,, Fortunatus Minor.
d.	,, Apollinis.		h.	,, Sandaliarius.

a. The *Vicus Sceleratus* is the same that was previously called Cyprius, and had the name changed in consequence of the murder of King Servius. It must therefore have led from the Forum Romanum towards the Esquiline, and is probably the same street which now leads to S. Pietro in Vincoli[d]. That church and monastery is on the site of an important fortress of the time of the Kings of Rome. It stands on a lofty scarped cliff, with a flight of steps up to it, through an arch, which appears to have been the gate of the fortress in the time of the Kings. This appears to have been the *arx* or citadel of the Esquiline, when that was a separate fortress, in the early period, before the union of the seven fortified hills into one city. It continued in use as a castle to the time of the Empire, and in the Middle Ages.

Ædes viii. The Catalogue attributed to Rufus for this Regio enumerates also eight *ædiculæ*, that is, small temples, but without any further particulars respecting them, and all traces of them seem to be lost. They may have been merely way-side altars, or niches for images, such as are still common in Rome, or perhaps with altars under them:—

Musarum.	Lucinæ Valerianæ.
Spei.	Junonis Lucinæ.
Mercurii.	Mavortis.
Juventutis.	Isidis.

[b] "Julius, assiduum nomen in ore meo.
　　Protinus hunc primæ quæres in limine Tectæ;
　　Quos tenuit Daphnis, nunc tenet ille, Lares."
　　　　　　　(Martialis Epigram., lib. iii. ep. 5.)

[c] Plinii Nat. Hist., lib. vii. c. 39.

[d] "Fit fuga regis apparitorum atque comitum. Ipse prope exsanguis quum sine omni regio comitatu domum se reciperet, pervenissetque ad summum Cyprium vicum, ab iis, qui missi a Tarquinio fugientem consecuti erant, interficitur. . . . A quo facessere jussa ex tanto tumultu quum se domum reciperet pervenissetque ad summum Cyprium vicum, ubi Dianium nuper fuit; flectenti carpentum dextra in Urbium

AQUEDUCTS IN THIS REGIO.

We learn from Frontinus that this Regio was supplied with water from the Anio Vetus, the Marcia, and the Tepula; afterwards, the Claudia and the Anio Novus united, were distributed here as in other parts. But these different streams of water were always kept separate, being intended for different purposes. The Marcia was always the best for drinking. The water of the Claudia and Anio Novus united was more abundant than any of the others, and was used to supply their place when they failed, which was sometimes the case in time of drought. This water was not of equally good quality, and was generally used for washing and for irrigation, excepting when the better water failed. The Tepula was always brought with the Marcia, though in a different pipe or *specus*. The Anio Vetus was always underground, but not very deep; it is most probable that one branch of this came straight on from the Porta Maggiore, where it entered Rome, to the great reservoir on the highest ground, where the Trophies of Marius were afterwards hung, and from thence was distributed, one branch going to the other great reservoir, called the Sette Sale, in this Regio.

The small branch of an aqueduct under the south end of the Porticus Liviæ, and opposite to the Colosseum, probably came from the Marcia or Tepula from its level, which is considerably below that of the Anio Novus, on the Cælian, and the Palatine, and above that of the Anio Vetus in the Forum Romanum. The levels of the aqueducts were always carefully attended to, so that the continuous running streams might always flow along gently. This branch seems to have come from the Thermæ of Titus, on the Esquiline, as on that side the platform of the Summa Sacra Via touches the Velia, or the bank on which the road is carried in a line from these great thermæ. Towards the Colosseum and towards the Palatine, the space is too large for the aqueduct to pass, unless over a bridge or in a syphon, neither of which would have been convenient here.

clivum, ut in collem Esquiliarum eveheretur, restitit pavidus atque inhibuit frenos is, qui jumenta agebat, jacentemque dominæ Servium trucidatum ostendit. Fœdum inhumanumque inde traditur scelus, monumentoque locus est (Sceleratum vicum vocant)," &c. (Livii Hist., i. 48.)

CHURCHES IN THIS REGIO.

CHURCH OF SS. QUIRICUS [OR CYRIACUS, MARTYR] AND GIULITTA OR JULITTA[e].—The first mention that we find of this church is in the time of Pope Hadrian I., A.D. 772—795, who restored it. Benedict III., A.D. 855, gave a vestment for the altar in this church. In the *Mirabilia* of the thirteenth century it is mentioned: "Ubi est Sanctus Quiricus (fuit), Templum Jovis." But nothing is known of this temple of Jupiter, and there is supposed to be some confusion on the part of this writer, who makes many errors. We do not find any further notice of it until the fifteenth century, but the campanile is partly of the twelfth. It was restored by Sixtus IV. in 1475, as recorded by an inscription on the lintel of the door[f], and again in 1580, by Cardinal Alexander de Medici.

Paul V., A.D. 1606, restored the pavement after an inundation of the Tiber, and also restored the vault[g]. Urban VIII., in 1680, ornamented it with some pilasters. It was at first a collegiate church, but was given to the Dominicans by Clement XI., A.D. 1680. Benedict XIII. modernized it and embellished it A.D. 1728. There is a good painting over the altar of SS. Quiricus et Giulitta by an unknown hand; and there are other modern paintings. The interior was again restored in 1856.

This church is so closely surrounded by houses, and the walls are so carefully plastered over, that it is impossible to see whether there are any parts of the early walls remaining or not; the only part visible that has any character, is a piece of cornice on the south side, which is of the twelfth century. There is an ancient crypt under the church, but inaccessible, so that the date of it could not be ascertained. There is also the lower part of a tower of the twelfth century, but the upper part is modernized.

The church and nunnery of SS. DOMINICUS ET SIXTUS, on the cliff of the Quirinal, was established here in 1570 by Pius V., who transferred to this situation the establishment of the same name on

---

[e] RIONE I., MONTI.
[f] INSTAURATA VIDES QUIRICVS CVM MATRE JULITTA
QUAE FUERANT LONGA DIRUTA TEMPLA DIE
PRINCIPE SUB SIXTO DELUBRIS NULLA VETUSTAS,
HIC REFICIT PONTES, MOENIA, TEMPLA, VIAS.
[g] PAVLVS V. PONT. MAX.
ECCLESIAM HANC TITVLO VACANTE EX
DEPRESSIORI LOCO ET AQVARVM INVN
DATIONIBVS EXPOSITO IACTIS FORNICI
BVS STRATO PAVIMENTO IN ALTIOREN
MELIOREMQ. FORMAM. RESTITVIT ANNO
SAL. HVMANAE MDCVI. PONTIFICATVS I.

the Via Appia, this being considered a more convenient and more healthy situation. The buildings of the old establishment were then deserted, and are now known by the name of *S. Sisto Vecchio*. The present one has nothing to interest the archæologist except the site, which is evidently that of an ancient fortress of considerable extent. There are remains of the upper row of shops of the Forum of Trajan under part of this building, which is now (in 1875) a barrack.

The neighbouring church of S. Maria de Monti, was founded by Gregory XIII. in 1580, and therefore has no archæological features. Its frescoes are esteemed.

The church and convent of S. Francesco di Paola was established on this site in 1623, in the palace or castle of the Cesarini, which had been bought for that purpose by G. Pizzullo, a priest. It contains nothing archæological, but has some modern fresco paintings, said to be of merit. A medieval tower of the castle serves for a campanile.

APPENDIX.

DURING the spring of the year 1876, the Italian Government excavated the basement of the Temple of Antoninus and Faustina, with the remains of the steps as described by Palladio; but the marble had been all carried off as part of the building-material for the great church of S. Peter in the Vatican, as we are informed by Ligorio, who was living at the time, in a work still in manuscript, and now preserved in the Bodleian Library in Oxford[a]. The whole of the building-material for that enormous structure is said to have been taken from the temples, and thermæ, and palaces of the Empire, considerable ruins of which had remained until that time. Palladio has preserved drawings of some of them; he had more respect for antiquities than his contemporaries, and wrote a short guide to the antiquities of Rome, which is printed at the end of a "Guide to the Churches and the Relics of the Martyrs," published under the sanction of Pope Sixtus V.[b], and which contains also an account of his aqueduct.

Part of the pavement of the Via Sacra has been also brought to light; this shews that it went along on the eastern side of the Forum Romanum, under the modern road, and that the Arch of Septimius Severus was built over it; the paved road down the middle of the Forum must therefore be the Via Nova, coming from the Porta

[a] B. B. MSS. Canon. Ital. 138.
[b] Le Cose Maravigliose dell' Alma Citta di Roma, &c.

Romana on the Palatine, the upper part of which Via was in steps, and was destroyed by Signor Rosa about 1870. Some fragments of the pavement of it were also visible in 1875, behind the Temple of Vesta, and in front of S. Maria Liberatrice, but at the low level of the old Forum. The side walls of the cella of the temple, now the church of S. Maria in Miranda, are built of large blocks of tufa and peperino, of the character usually of the time of the Kings, and were probably taken from the second wall of Rome, which enclosed the two hills in one city, and must have passed close to the back of this temple. This old tufa, from long exposure to the weather, has very much the appearance of travertine, so much so that it was long considered to be travertine; it was only when a piece was broken off that it could be ascertained to be tufa, as this is a soft sandstone of volcanic origin, and travertine is a hard limestone; the difference can be clearly seen when a piece is broken, but on the surface it is sometimes difficult to distinguish one from the other. It is well known that tufa was always used in the time of the Kings, and travertine not till near the time of the Empire.

ALPHABETICAL INDEX.

FORUM ROMANUM. — VIA SACRA.

Ædes Jobis, or Jovis, 101.
Ærarium in Capitolium, 5.
Ambones in Ara Cœli, 62.
Ancus Martius, Ædes, or House of, 67.
Ancyra, Inscription at, called Monumentum, 53.
Antoninus and Faustina, Temple of, 65.
Apollodorus, speech of, to Hadrian, 70, 87.
Apollo Sandaliarius, 106.
Aqua Cernens, quatuor Scaurus, 49.
Aqueducts in the Forums, 34; the lines by which they were brought, *ib.*; tunnel through rock of Palatine, 35; over bridge of Caligula, *ib.*; remains at foot of Capitoline, *ib.*; western part of Ærarium made a reservoir, *ib.*; this made in the third century, *ib.*; remains of bridge of Caligula, *ib.*; in this Regio, 113.
Ara-Cœli, Church of, 59; Convent of, A.D. 1250, 62.
Arch of Constantine, sculpture of Rostrum, 12; sculpture of Forum has a row of tall columns, 18.
—— of Titus, 102.
—— of Janus, or Arcus Quadrifrons, in the Velabrum, 27.
Area of Saturn included site of Temple of Concord, 6.
—— Vulcani, 104.
Aterii, tomb of the, 93.
Atrium Libertatis, now the site of the churches of S. Martina and S. Hadrian, 19.
—— —— Caci, 49.
—— —— Minervæ, 40.
Augurs, procession of, 68.
Aureum Bucinum, 106.

Balneum Dafnidis, 112.
Base of an equestrian statue, 19.
Basilica Æmilia (?), 19.
—— Argentaria, 46.
—— Julia of Julius Cæsar, 19.
—— Julia of Augustus, 20; early buildings on this site, *ib.*; had the Temple of Saturn at one end, and of Castor and Pollux at the other, *ib.*; the celebrated three columns belonged to Temple of Castor and Pollux, *ib.*;

the construction of the early part is of travertine, 21; this agrees with the Monumentum Ancyranum, *ib.*
Basilica Pauli Æmilii, 109.
—— of Constantine, 83; marble columns removed in fifteenth century, 84; one placed in front of S. Maria Maggiore in 1620, *ib.*; seven form the triumphal car of the Farnese, 85; spoils of Jerusalem placed in, *ib.*; apse an addition to the building, *ib.*
—— three markets on Summa Sacra Via, 88; the building with two apses is not a temple, *ib.*; substructures of rubble walling, *ib.*; aqueduct to supply the fountains made upon them, *ib.*; substructures to lengthen platform of the time of Vedius Pollio, 89; became the Temple of Apollo when the Colossus was put in it, 90; was a double colonnade, 91; foundation excavated in 1830 and 1874, *ib.*
Boundaries often the old fortifications, 90.
Brick structures down the middle of the Forum hollow, and likely to be wine-shops, 18.

Cæsars, Palaces of, public offices after first century, 27.
Caligula, Palace of, 23.
Campidoglio, piazzo or place on Capitoline Hill, pavement of, much raised, 33.
Capitolinus Clivus, pavement of, 6; in front of Schola Xanthi, 11.
Capitolium, 5, III.; on the slope of the Hill of Saturn, 5; at north end of Forum, *ib.*
Carinæ, the, 111.
Castor and Pollux, Temple of, 23.
Church of Ara Cœli on Capitol, 59; Ambones, Cosmati-work, 62; Convent built A.D. 1250, *ib.*; favourite burying-place, 60; relics of S. Helena, 61; south porch, mosaics, 60; Tombs of the Savelli, A.D. 1306, of Honorius IV., 1286, 61.
—— SS. Cosmas and Damian, 95; Marble Plan of Rome fixed against east wall, *ib.*

Alphabetical Index.

Church of SS. Dominicus and Sixtus, 114.
—— S. Francesca Romana, 99; formerly called S. Maria Nuova, *ib.*; not the same as SS. Peter and Paul, nor S. Maria Antiqua, 100; rebuilt A.D. 860, *ib.*; Tombs and Sculpture contained in, *ib.*; Campanile of the thirteenth cedtury, *ib.*; Cloister built in 1370, 101.
—— S. Francesco di Paola, 115.
—— S. George and S. Sebastian, or S. Giorgio in Velabro, 55; classical portico of thirteenth century, 56; Campanile, *ib.*
—— S. Hadrian, or Adrian, 55.
—— S. Maria di Monte, 115.
—— S. Maria Antiqua, on Summa Sacra Via, 91.
—— S. Martina and S. Luca, 54.
—— SS. Peter and Paul, on Via Sacra, made in Basilica of Constantine, 80; legend of Simon Magus, *ib.*
—— SS. Quiricus and Giulitta, 113.
—— SS. Sergius and Bacchus, built A.D. 790, destroyed 1540, 14.
—— S. Theodorus, 58.
Churches in Forum Romanum, &c., 53—64.
Clivus Sacer, line of, 66.
Cloaca Maxima drained the Curtian Gulf, 4; three streams which now run into it had supplied the lake, 24.
Cohors vi. Vigilum, 46.
Colosseum, *podium* in front of, 96.
Colossus Altus pedes [M.]XIII. is that of Nero, 93.
Column of the Emperor Phocas, 14.
Comitium, the open space for the assembly of the people, 14.
Concord, Temple of, founded B.C. 303, rebuilt B.C. 26 and A.D. 11, 5; therefore often called the Senate House, 6; was the vestibule to the Senate House, *ib.*; Emperor Pertinax sits in, to wait for the key of the Curia, 8.
Constantine, Basilica of, 84.
Cosmas and Damian, Church of, on site of three temples, 95.
Cosmati-work in Ara Cœli, 62.
Curia in Capitolium, 5.
Curtian Gulf, or lake, site of Forum, 4, 24; drained by Cloaca Maxima, 4.

Dei Consentes, Temple of, 5.
Dioscuri, fountain of, 22.

Elefans Herbarius, 47.
Equus Constantini, 19.
Excavations throw a new light on the history of the City of Rome, 3; absolutely necessary, *ib.*
—— in 1874, between platform on Summa Sacra Via and cliff of Palatine, 91; three objects found by these,—1. Guard chambers; 2. Lavacrum of Heliogabalus; 3. Church of S. Maria Antiqua, *ib.*

Fasti Consulares, fragment of, 25.
Forum of Augustus and Temple of Mars Ultor, 39.
—— Boarium, or cattle-market, 42.
—— of Cupid, on the Upper Via Sacra, 36.
—— of Julius Cæsar, 37.
—— of Nervæ, or Transitorium, 40; figure of Pallas or Minerva there, *ib.*, 109.
—— Olitorium, remains of, 36.
—— Piscatorium, or fish-market, 36.
—— Pistorium, or of the Bakers, 36.
—— Romanum Magnum, 44, XIX.; belongs to earliest period of history of Rome, 3; length and breadth, 4; the name has a double meaning, general and special, *ib.*; steps at south end, 25; previous history based upon conjecture, 27; extent of, exaggerated by these conjectures, *ib.*
—— Sallustii, near House of Sallust, 36.
—— Suarium, or pig-market, *ib.*
—— Trajan, 42.
—— Vespasian, or Forum Pacis, 41.
Fountain of Juturna, 25.
—— of the Dioscuri, 22.
Fragment of Fasti Consulares, 25.

Gate of Saturn a double gate, 6; foundations remain, *ib.*
Genius Populi Romani aureus, 46.
Græco-Stadium, or Græcostasis, 7; on a platform, on the side of Temple of Concord, 8; space exactly suited for the purpose, 9; site covered by path of Michael Angelo, *ib.*
Guard-chambers on Palatine, 91.

Hadrian, House of, near Thermæ of Caracalla, 26.
—— and Apollodorus, 87.
Heliogabalus, Lavacrum of, 91; rebuilt the Temple of the Sun, 97.
Honorius III., Tomb of, A.D. 1286, 61.
Horrea, Germanica et Agrippinæ, 49.
—— Chartaria, 108.
House of Ancus Martius and Ædes, 67; called Sacellum Streniæ, *ib.*
—— Hadrian, near Thermæ of Caracalla, 26.
—— Trajan, on the Aventine, 26.

Janus had originally two faces, afterwards four, 28; one kind made of bronze, *ib.*; one in each of the four-

teen Regionaries, 29; these were small structures of bronze, *ib.*; one at the junction of the four principal Forums, 30.
Julia, Basilica of, 20.
Jupiter Capitolinus, Temple of, 31.
Jupiter Stator, Temple of (?), 101.
Juturna, fountain of, 25.

Lake of Curtius, 24.
Lavacrum of Heliogabalus, 91.
Line of the Via Sacra, Clivus Sacer, Summa Sacra Via, 66.
Livia, Porticus of, 86.

Marble Plan of Rome, 71; fragments all found on same spot, near east wall of church, *ib.*; excavations made by Tocco, *ib.*; work of Professor Jordan on, 72.
Marcus Aurelius, statue of, 33.
Marforio, or Mars, statue of, 33.
Markets, three held on Summa Sacra Via, 67.
Mars Ultor, two temples, the round one in the Forum, 18.
Meta Sudans, 108.
Milliarium Aureum, 13, XI.
——— and Umbilicum Urbis, 13; streets of Rome measured from it, but not the roads, 14.
Monumentum Ancyranum, 53.
Municipium in Capitolium, 5.

Nero, Golden House of, 94.
——— Colossus of, 93; first placed in the vestibule of Golden House of Nero, 94; moved by Hadrian to make room for the Templum Urbis Romæ, *ib.*; elephants dragged it up the Clivus Sacer, 95; the site where it stood is part of the church of SS. Cosmas and Damian, *ib.*; destroyed by Pope Silvester, as an idol of the Sun, 96.

Old fortifications are often the boundaries, 90.

Pacis, Temple of, 82; antiquaries not agreed upon the site, 83.
Palace of Caligula, 23.
Palaces of the Cæsars, public offices after first century, 27.
Palatine, guard-chambers, 91.
Panvinius on the site of the Templum Urbis, 70.
Peace, Temple of, 82.
Phocas, Emperor, column of, 14.
Photography of great use, 3.
Piazza del Campidoglio, pavement much raised, 33.
Plan of Rome on marble plates, 71.

Podium in front of Colosseum not large enough for the great Colossus, 96; used for a smaller one of Gordianus, *ib.*; basement of the time of Gordianus, *ib.*; smaller Colossus represented on a coin of Gordianus, *ib.*
Porta Saturni, foundation of old wall, 5; ground within on a higher level, *ib.*; wall destroyed at an early period, *ib.*; remains of all three periods, *ib.*; back wall touches the Ærarium, *ib.*
Porticus Absidata, 104.
——— Liviæ, 86—91; this name upon the Marble Plan, 86; platform on Summa Sacra Via the only place that fits this, *ib.*; mentioned by Strabo, 87; base shewn on the Plan was for the great Colossus, *ib.*; the platform is that on which Apollodorus said that Hadrian *ought to have* placed the Templum Urbis, *ib.*

Regiones, divisions of uncertain, 90.
Regio VIII., continet pedes
M. XIIII. LXVII., 48.
Restorations, probable, 26.
Roma and Venus, Temples of, 69, 72.
Rostra, three in Forum, 11; one by the arch of Septimius Severus, *ib.*; another near the Temple of Antoninus, 12; third not yet excavated, *ib.*
Rostral columns, 13; that of Duillius, A.D. 14, represented on a medal, *ib.*
Rostrum represented on Arch of Constantine, 12.

Sacellum Streniæ, 67.
Sacra Via Summa, or Caput, 66; three markets held in, 67.
Saturn, Temple of, 5.
——— gate of, a double one, 6.
——— area of, included site of Temple of Concord, 6.
Savelli, Tombs of the, 61.
Schola Xanthi, on the lower level, 10; discovered in the sixteenth century, *ib.*; colonnade restored by Canina, 11.
Screen walls of marble in the Comitium, with sculpture of the time of Hadrian, 15; on the inner side of each wall are the *suovetaurilia*, 16; on the outer side groups of figures, *ib.*; on both the figure of Marsyas, *ib.*; the same object represented on coins of Hadrian, 17; Pliny mentions the fig-tree as near this site, *ib.*
Sculpture from Tomb of the Aterii, 93.
Senaculum, or Curia, in Capitolium, 5.
Senate House behind the Temple of Concord, 6; can be traced, *ib.*;

Via Sacra.

Description of Plate XXX.
Church of SS. Cosmas and Damian.
Longitudinal Section.

This Church is made out of three Temples, as recorded by Panvinius.

A. The round Temple of Romulus, the son of Maxentius; this forms the vestibule of the present church. It is divided into two storeys, as shewn in the Plate, by the insertion of a floor supported by a vault, in the seventeenth century.

B. Portico, as shewn in the Codex Vaticanus, 3439, f. 40, and of which some of the columns remain half buried.

C. The present Church, built by Felix IV., on the site of the Temple of Venus.

D, D. The subterranean Church or Crypt, originally the floor of the two temples, before the level was altered.

E. The Apse added A.D. 530, with the Mosaic picture.

F. Brick wall of the façade of the Temple of Roma, on the eastern side, upon which the marble plan of Rome was fastened by metal hooks, in the third century.

G. South wall of the Temple of Roma, built of large square blocks of tufa, with a doorway of the time of Hadrian.

H. Excavation in 1867, in which the fragments of the marble plan of Rome were found, with architectural details of the third century.

I. Another excavation, made at the same time, in which was found on the marble pavement of the Portico, a great mass of the north-east corner of the attic storey of the Basilica of Constantine.

K. Basilica of Constantine.

L. The Velia.

a. Present level of the road.
b. Filling-up of the old foss-way.
c. Ancient level of the pavement.
d. A well, said to have held the blood of martyrs (?).
e, e, e. Modern buildings.

CHURCH OF SS. COSMAS AND DAMIAN. LONGITUDINAL SECTION.

VIA SACRA.

PLATE XXXI.

CHURCH OF SS. COSMAS AND DAMIAN.

Plans.

VIA SACRA.

DESCRIPTION OF PLATE XXXI.

CHURCH OF SS. COSMAS AND DAMIAN.

PLANS.

1. The Church in use on the present level of the ground.
A. Temple of Romulus, now the Vestibule.
B. Portico of the same.
C. Temple of Venus, now the Church.
E. Apse, added A.D. 530.
F. East wall on which the marble plan was placed.
G. Doorway of the time of Hadrian, in the south wall, excavated in 1868.
H. Excavations of Signor Tocco in 1867.
I. Fragment of the attic storey of the Basilica of Constantine.

2. Plan of part of the Basilica of Constantine.
K. The Apse.
L. The Velia.

3. Plan of the Substructures, now the Crypt of the Church, with the same letters of reference.

4. Plan of the Subterranean Chapel, under the floor of the Temple of Romulus, now the Crypt of the Vestibule, called a Catacomb.

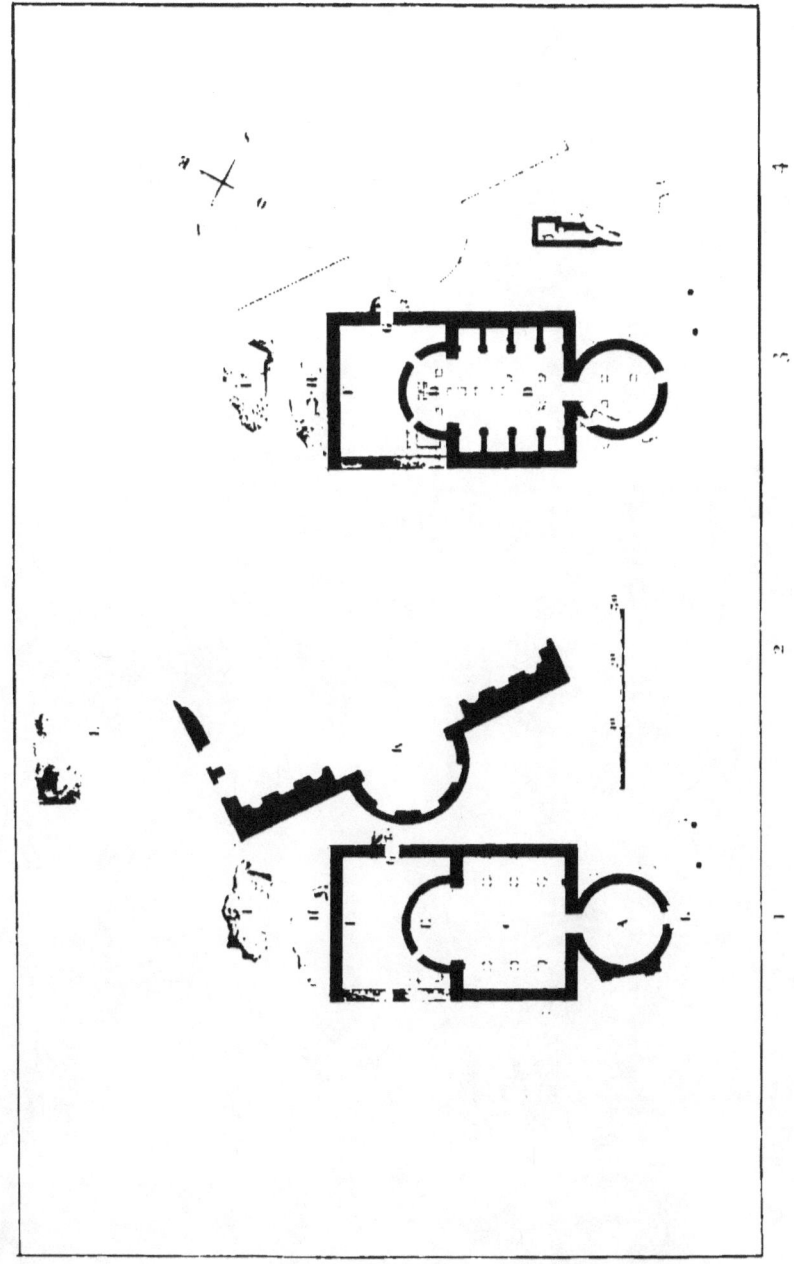

CHURCH OF SS. COSMAS AND DAMIAN, &c. PLANS.

VIA SACRA.

PLATE XXXII.

TEMPLE OF ANTONINUS AND FAUSTINA,

And Church of S. Lorenzo in Miranda.

Section and Plan.

Description of Plate XXXII.

TEMPLE OF ANTONINUS AND FAUSTINA,
And Church of S. Lorenzo in Miranda.
Section and Plan.

The excavations made in front of this temple in 1876, shew that it stands upon the tufa rock, and not merely on a *podium*, or basement built for it, as in other instances. The flight of twenty-one steps up to it, described by Palladio in the sixteenth century, can still be traced, although the marble was carried away as part of the building-material for S. Peter's in the Vatican; the foundation of the seven lower steps still remains, and the measurements, *c*, shew that, if completed, they would exactly rise to the level of the bases of the great monolithic columns marked *a a*. The pavement of the Via Sacra remains at the foot of the steps, and indicates that this street was continued along the eastern side of the Forum, and passed under the arch of Septimius Severus, and that the paved street down the centre of the Forum must be the Via Nova, which was a new street in the time of Augustus. The *cella* of the temple, *b b*, is built of large blocks of tufa and peperino, probably taken from the second wall of Rome, which enclosed the two hills in one city, and must have passed very near to the east end of this temple. The church made in it is marked *f* in the diagram; the roads or streets on the east and north side are marked *g g*; the floor of the church is made at the level of the streets, which is nearly ten feet above the original level of the temple; the roof of the church is also carried twenty feet above the level of the cornice of the temple. A burial-place has been made under it in the space marked *b b*. The columns are monolithic blocks of cipellino marble, 46 ft. high.

TEMPLE OF ANTONINUS AND FAUSTINA

VIA SACRA.

PLATE XXXIII.
BASILICA OF CONSTANTINE.
Front View.

Description of Plate XXXIII.

BASILICA OF CONSTANTINE.

Front View.

This is the largest basilica that remains in Rome, and only about one-third part of it is still standing; it extended to the pavement in front, and had wings on each side, as well as an attic storey over the present vaulted ceiling; it was very richly decorated, but has been thoroughly stripped, the niches for statues remain in the apse, which is an addition to the original building; the ceilings have the caissons, in which bronze or stucco ornament has been inserted. The niches and the vaulted ceilings of the two apses, back to back, on the Summa Sacra Via, are exactly similar to these[a]. This large building was begun in the time of Maxentius, and finished in that of Constantine[b]. Of the attic storey very little is left; it was almost destroyed in the great earthquake in the fourteenth century. The pavement seen in front of the building is that of the Clivus Sacer, where, according to the Church legends, Simon Magus fell dead at the feet of S. Peter. The steps seen in the right of the picture go up to the modern entrance of the Church of S. Francesca Romana. Trees growing on the Velia are seen through the openings in the place of windows, which have been destroyed, if there ever were any. The plan is not at all the usual one of a basilica; here we have three parallel aisles, all of the same height and width; usually we have a lofty and very wide nave, with low and narrow aisles, as in the Basilica Jovis. On the left hand, or north-west side, a small church was made in the Middle Ages. The corner of the attic storey, in which was a newel staircase (*cochlea*), fell down in an earthquake on to the pavement in front of the Marble Plan of Rome (just beyond the limits of this picture), and by the crash of the fall of that great mass caused the marble plates also to fall on to the pavement below, and to be broken to pieces.

---

[a] See Plate XXVII.

[b] The two smaller basilicas were built in the time of Constantine, after the great Colossus had been melted down by order of Pope Silvester, as an idol that was worshipped by the people. This is mentioned in the *Mirabilia Urbis*; see Codex Urlichs, pp. 110, 136.

BASILICA OF CONSTANTINE — VIEW OF FRONT

VIA SACRA.

PLATE XXXIV.

BASILICA OF CONSTANTINE.

Back View, and Interior of Apse.

DESCRIPTION OF PLATE XXXIV.

BASILICA OF CONSTANTINE.

1. VIEW OF THE BACK.

1. This side of the building was originally in the FORUM PACIS, and the arch which is here seen open, was the communication from the market-place to the Basilica, both being the largest in Rome. This arch was walled up by Signor Rosa about 1870, thereby destroying an important part of the history of the building [c]. To the left of the picture is seen the wall against the cliff of the Velia; the wall on the right hand shuts out the view of the east front of the Temple of Rome, where the Marble Plan of Rome was hung. The upper part of the Basilica on this side is made to accommodate itself to the levels of the ground, and part of a modern villa (now an Orphanage) is built up against it.

2. VIEW IN THE INTERIOR WITH THE APSE.

2. This apse was added on to the original building very soon after that was built; probably added in the time of Constantine to the large square building of Maxentius. It seems probable that this was intended originally for a rebuilding of the Temple of Peace, and the apse was added when it was made into a basilica; a temple never has an apse, and a basilica always has. The details of this apse, of the time of Constantine, are exactly the same as those of the two apses back to back on the Summa Sacra Via. (See Plate XXXVII.)

---

[c] The object of Signor Rosa was to shut out the low and bad population of the district behind; that this was not without reason is proved by the fact, that in the year 1874 an elderly English archæologist, who was quietly taking notes in this basilica, was attacked and robbed in the middle of the day.

BASILICA OF CONSTANTINE

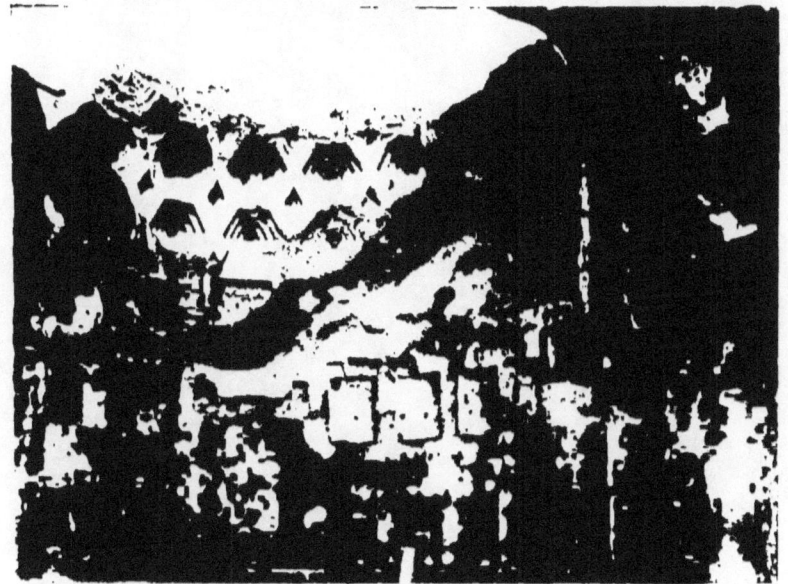

A. VIEW OF THE BACK WITH PART OF THE VELIA
B. VIEW IN THE INTERIOR, WITH THE APSE

VIA SACRA.

PLATE XXXV.
BASILICA OF CONSTANTINE.
Sections.
A—B. Longitudinal.
C—D. Transverse.

Description of Plate XXXV.

BASILICA OF CONSTANTINE.
Sections.

A—B. Longitudinal, looking eastward.

C—D. Transverse, looking north.

a a a a. Part of the east wall of the Temple of Rome, against which the Marble Plan of Rome was fixed.

b b b. South wall of the same temple.

c. North aisle of the Basilica.

d. Central part of the Basilica.

e. South aisle of the Basilica.

f f. The Velia.

g g. Restoration of the vault of the attic storey.

h. Excavations made in 1870 by Mr. Parker, in search of the south door of the temple, which was found [d].

i. Pavement of the Summa Sacra Via.

k. Pavement of the Clivus Sacer.

l l. Foss of the Velia.

m m. Level of the modern road and houses.

n. Level of the pavement of the old road in the foss.

o o. The Esquiline Hill.

y. Newel stairs (*cochlea*) to ascend to the attic storey.

[d] See Photos., No. 850.

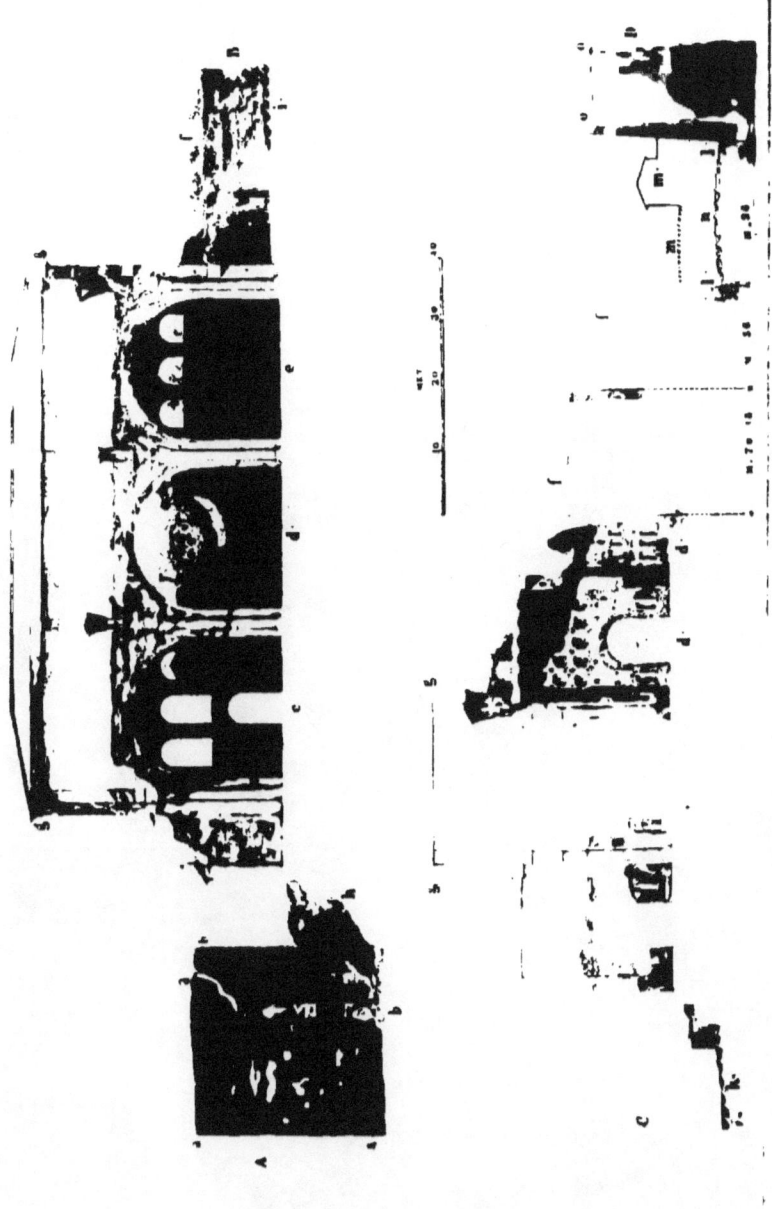

A–B. LONGITUDINAL.   C–D. TRANSVERSE

VIA SACRA.

PLATE XXXVI.
BASILICA OF CONSTANTINE.
Plan.

Description of Plate XXXVI.
BASILICA OF CONSTANTINE.
Plan.

A—B. Line of Longitudinal Section.
C—D. Line of Transverse Section.
a a. East wall of Temple of Roma.
b b. South wall of the same.
c. North aisle of the great Basilica.
d. Central part, with the apse *added.*
e. South aisle of the Basilica.
f f f. The Velia.
h. Excavations in 1870, to shew the south door of the temple.
i. Pavement of the Summa Sacra Via.
k. Pavement of the Clivus Sacer.
l. Foss of the Velia.
m m m m. Modern road and houses.
o o. The Esquiline Hill.
y. *Cochlea,* or newel staircase.

BASILICA OF CONSTANTINE - PLAN

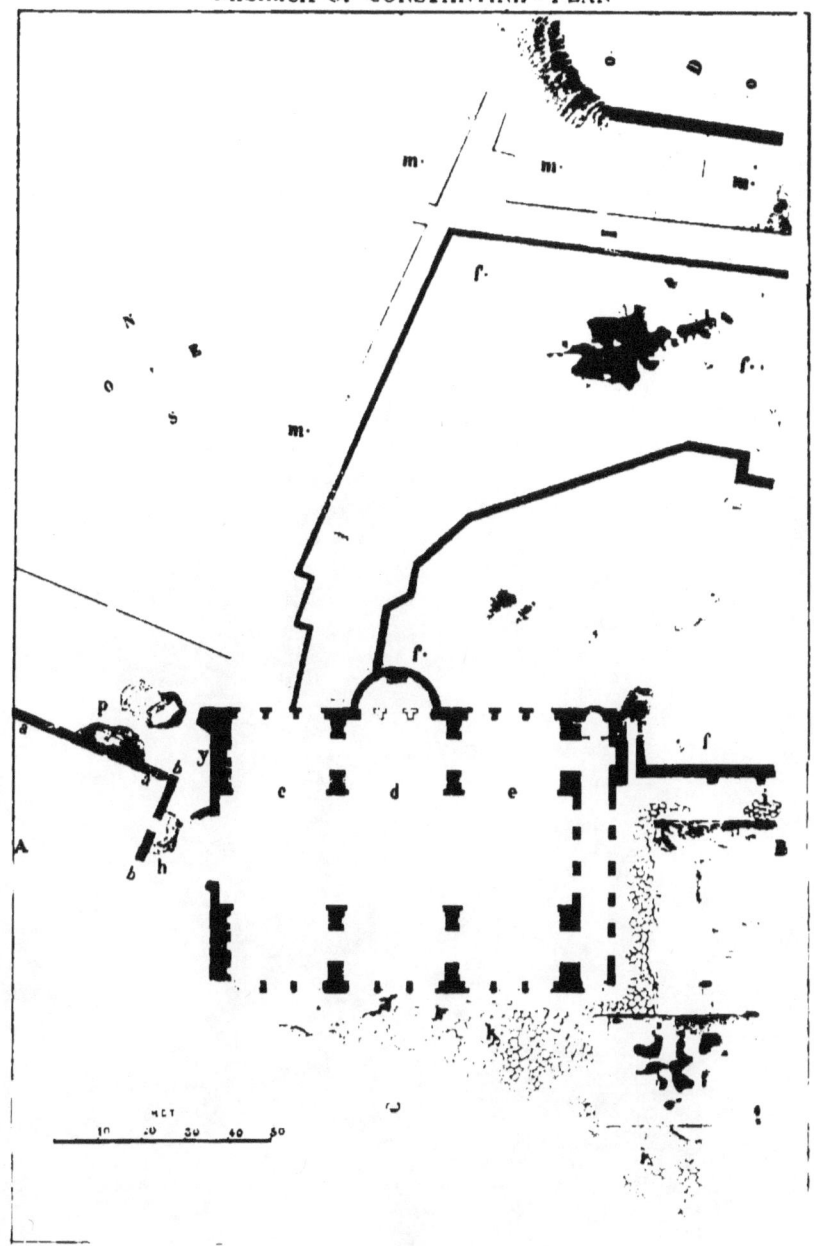

VIA SACRA.

PLATE XXXVII.
SUMMA SACRA VIA.

DESCRIPTION OF PLATE XXXVII.

SUMMA SACRA VIA.

1. APSE, now in the Monastery of S. Francesca Romana, from the north, with the Colosseum in the distance.

2. The same double apse from the south, with the monastery and campanile in the background, and the substructure of the platform in the foreground; the two apses are back to back, and each has formed one end of a large hall, of which there are remains.

The object of these two views is to shew that the construction of the apse agrees exactly with that of the great Basilica of Constantine, which is close to this apse (one corner of it is visible on the right of the lower view). The platform on which the apse stands is on the Summa Sacra Via, and it is recorded that *three* markets were held there. The Basilica of Constantine was long called the Temple of Peace, and is on the site of it; the present building certainly was not a temple, but a hall connected with the Forum of Peace, in the same manner as the Basilica Julia was connected with the Forum Romanum.

The old error, which has been corrected in the case of the Basilica of Constantine, has been continued in the others; these two market-halls are still, in 1876, called the Temple of Venus and Rome, although they were more usually called by Palladio the Temple of the Sun and Moon, as they are on the site of that temple; they have none of the character of a temple, and that double temple stood on the site of the present church of SS. Cosmas and Damian, (see Plate XXX.). All the texts of the Classical authors usually cited to prove this to be the Temple of Venus and Rome, apply quite as well to the one site as the other. *Both are between* the Forum Romanum and the Colosseum. The Colossus of Apollo, or the Sun, was placed on that platform by Hadrian, within the Porticus Liviæ, which was a double colonnade of the time of Augustus. It was rebuilt by Heliogabalus, and fragments of large columns of Egyptian granite are lying about on the platform in all directions. The apses were built in the middle of that colonnade, in the place of the Colossus, the base of which is represented on the Marble Plan of Rome, of the time of Aurelian, or fifty years before the two halls with the double apse were built.

APSIS IN MONASTERIO _ S. FRANCESCÆ ROMANÆ

VIA SACRA.

PLATE XXXVIII.

PORTICUS LIVIÆ AND COLOSSUS OF NERO.

Restoration.

Description of Plate XXXVIII.

PORTICUS LIVIÆ AND COLOSSUS OF NERO.

Restoration.

The Platform on the Summa Sacra Via, looking east, with steps up to it at the north end, and a substructure at the south end, agreeing with the Plan of the Porticus Liviæ, in the Marble Plan of Rome of the third century, with a probable restoration of it.

Longitudinal section, and a side view of the Colossus of Nero, placed in the middle of it.

A. Basilica of Constantine, south-west corner.

B. Part of the Velia of the old Palatine fortress, the earth or cliff supported by remains of the Porticus of Nero.

C. Porticus of Nero. Four arches of the upper storey seen through the columns.

D. The Colossus of Nero, on its podium or basement, as it is shewn on the Marble Plan.

E. The Substructure of vaults of rubb'e stone, with an Aqueduct upon it to supply the four fountains at the corners.

F. Pavement in front of the Colosseum.

G. The Velia of the old Palatine fortress, a triangular promontory, cut off from the Esquiline Hill by the wide and deep foss, now called the Via del Colosseo.

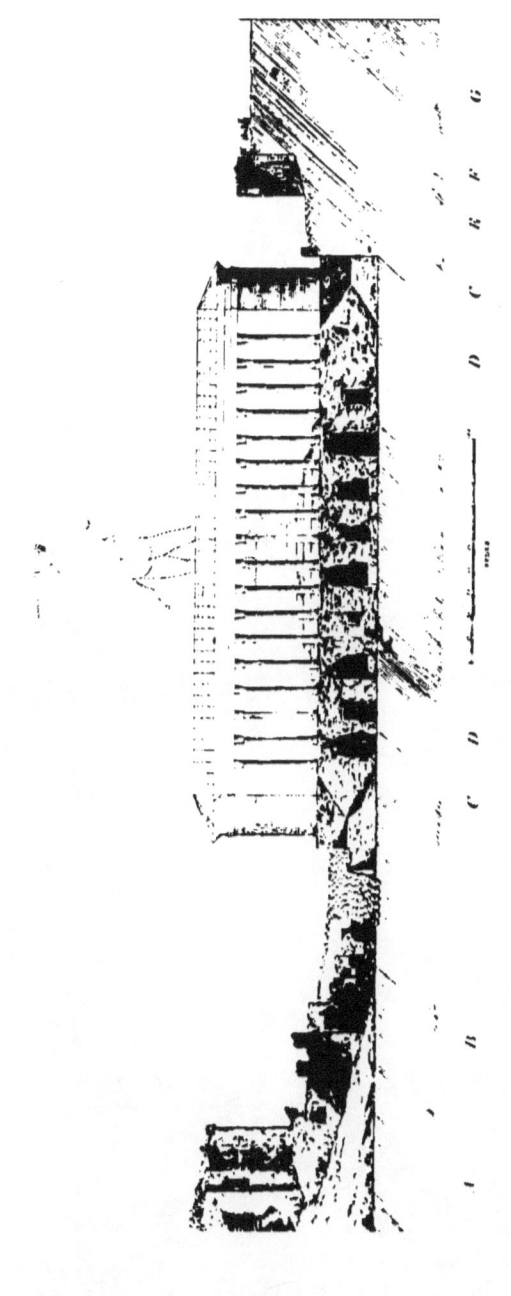

VIA SACRA.

PLATE XXXIX.

SUMMA SACRA VIA.
Church of S. Maria Antiqua.

Description of Plate XXXIX.

SUMMA SACRA VIA.

Church of S. Maria Antiqua.

The remains of this interesting church were excavated in 1874. It was built in the ninth century on the ruins of the Lavacrum of Heliogabalus, and with much ingenuity the old walls of the third century, which are of excellent brickwork, were used wherever they could be brought into the plan of the church, which was not built all at once, but at two different periods, though the latter was not very long after the former. The original church, of A.D. 847, was a small cruciform church on the plan of the Greek cross, the four arms of the same length, and with an apse in the eastern arm, which remains, and is of the same construction of rubble usual at that period; in the centre of the apse are remains of the altar, with the opening for the relics under it, (the *confessio* had not then been introduced). At the west end of the cruciform church was a portico, of which two of the marble columns remain in their original places, and under the portico, or just outside of it, is a steep staircase descending to a holy well, which is under the church near the west end, in the same situation as a similar well in the church of S. Prassede, of about the same period. This small church was not found large enough, and a large nave was added to it a few years afterwards, in A.D. 855[e].

At the west end of the nave was another apse, of which we have also the lower part of the walls remaining, of the same rude construction, and in the centre of it another altar (?), but it is hollow, and perhaps was a font for baptism by immersion. On both sides of the nave the walls are in part the old brick walls of the third century, wherever they could be used, in other parts the rubble walling of the ninth century. All these walls were veneered with marble, of which there are considerable remains, especially round the altar at the east end, on the wall behind it, and on the floor of the path round the altar, but the greater part of the marble has been stolen, either before or in part since it was excavated.

The church was originally dedicated to S. Mary, but another church, also dedicated to S. Mary, having been built soon afterwards very near to it, this church was then called S. Maria Antiqua; the name of the other has been changed from S. Maria Nova to S. Francesca Romana.

[e] Anastas., 592.

CHURCH OF S. MARIA ANTIQUA

A. EXTERIOR — B. INTERIOR OF APSE

VIA SACRA.

PLATE XL.

CHURCH OF S. MARIA ANTIQUA, A.D. 847—855.
PLAN.

Description of Plate XL.

CHURCH OF S. MARIA ANTIQUA, A.D. 847—855.

Plan.

This is in the Lavacrum of Heliogabalus, on that part of the Palatine Hill also called the Sub-Velia, or the Summa Sacra Via; it is between the Arch of Titus and the Colosseum, under the eastern cliff of the Palatine. The history of this church has been given in the text on the authority of Anastasius, the librarian of the Vatican, who was authorized to publish the Pontifical Registers, which in a matter of this kind are excellent authority, and the plan agrees with the history perfectly. The rubble walls of the ninth century are of the rude rough stone walling used at that period, as is seen in the two apses and some of the side walls; but the old brick walls of the ruins of the Lavacrum were used whenever they could be brought in with the plan of the church, which is evidently of two periods, though one soon after the other. The original small church, of the plan of a Greek cross, is seen on the right of the plan, with the remains of the altar, which has a hollow opening in it for the relics of the martyrs; opposite to this altar two columns of the portico are seen, and a flight of steps going down to a well, passing under the original west front of the church. To this small cruciform church a long nave has been added soon afterwards, the construction being the same, and here also the old brick walls are used as far as they could be. At the opposite end is another apse, and what may have been a second altar, or as some say a baptistery, or font for baptism by immersion, which seems not improbable. The brick wall is distinguished by a lighter tint in the plan; it will be seen that some of the old brick walls do not belong to the church at all, but are suffered to remain where they were found, having belonged to the earlier building.

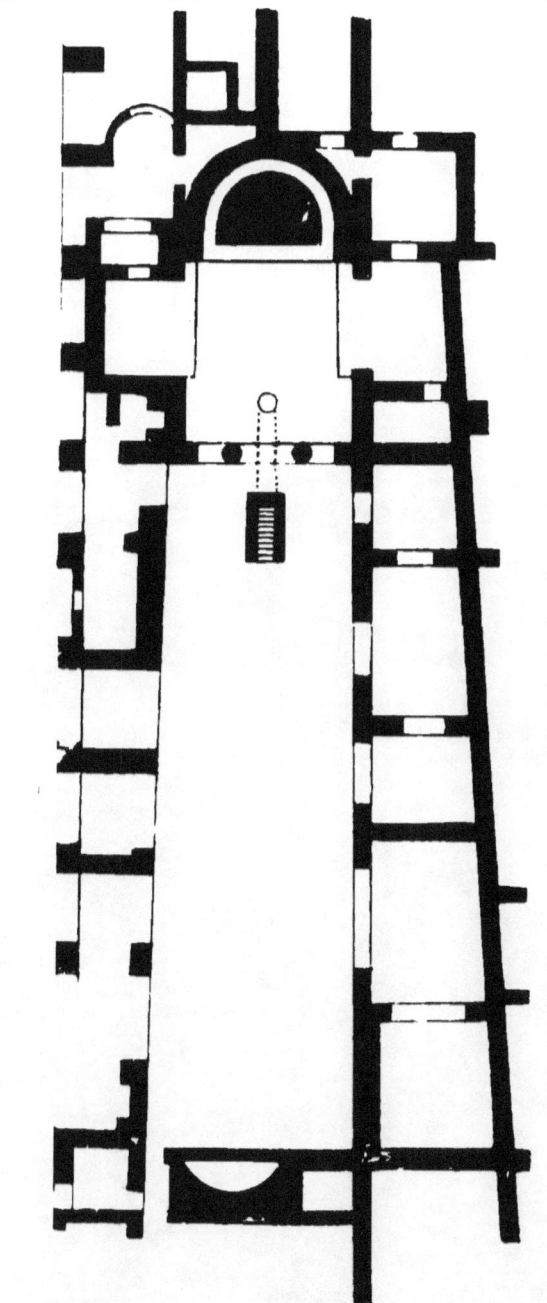

CHURCH OF S.ᴬ MARIA ANTIQUA A.D. 847-855. PLAN

IN THE LAVACRUM OF HELIOGABALUS ON THE PALATINE HILL.

VIA SACRA.

PLATE XLI.
THE ARCH OF TITUS.

Via Sacra.

Description of Plate XLI.

THE ARCH OF TITUS.

This arch stands on the Summa Sacra Via, on the ridge, with a steep incline up to it from the Arch of Constantine and the Colosseum. The Porta Mugionis, the original entrance into the Palatine fortress, or Roma Quadrata, must have been near to it. The remains of a gateway shewn in another Plate are at a short distance behind it, that is, to the left of the present view. The buildings seen in the view are, on the left, part of the Villa Farnese, now the residence of Signor Rosa; on the right, the small museum built by him to contain and exhibit the statues that *were to be found*, before they were sent to Paris; it now contains a small collection of fragments, &c., not without interest.

The arch had been built upon by the Frangipani, in the eleventh and twelfth centuries, as part of their great fortress on the Palatine; the remains of this great fortification were destroyed about 1820, under Pius VII., and the arch restored as we now see it with travertine, but left plain, so that the restoration can be readily distinguished from the original work. It was originally erected by Vespasian, after the death of Titus, to commemorate the conquest of Jerusalem, and the sculpture under the arch represents the triumphal procession carrying the spoils of Jerusalem, including the celebrated seven-branched candlestick. The inscription seen over the archway is:—

SENATVS
POPVLVSQVE ROMANVS
DIVO TITI DIVI VESPASIANI F.
VESPASIANO AVGVSTO.

ARCH OF TITUS

VIA SACRA.

PLATE XLII.
THE ARCH OF TITUS.

Via Sacra.

Description of Plate XLII.

THE ARCH OF TITUS.

PART of the procession of the Jewish captives, under Titus, carrying the celebrated seven-branched candlestick from the Temple at Jerusalem in triumph through the streets of Rome. A priest, with the long trumpet, leading the way.

SUMMA SACRA VIA — SCULPTURE FROM THE ARCH OF TITUS A. D. 83

SCULPTURE OF THE SPOILS OF JERUSALEM WITH THE CANDLESTICK

VIA SACRA.

PLATE XLIII.

EAST WALL OF THE
TEMPLUM URBIS ROMÆ,
On which the Marble Plan was fixed.

Via Sacra.

Description of Plate XLIII.

East Wall of the
TEMPLUM URBIS ROMÆ,
On which the Marble Plan was fixed.

THE wall is here shewn with the pit in front of it, as excavated by Signor Tocco in 1868, in which several fragments of the celebrated Marble Plan of Rome, of the third century, were found, and it was ascertained that all the fragments called the Capitoline Plan, because they are placed on the wall of the Capitoline Museum, were found on the same spot. That this plan was made of marble plates of about a yard square is also evident, and that these plates had been broken to pieces by falling on a marble pavement;—there can be little doubt that this was caused by the great earthquake of the fourteenth century, of which Plutarch has given a vivid account in his letters; nor can there be any longer a doubt that this wall was the east wall of the Temple of Roma, which faced to the Forum Pacis of Vespasian, the largest market-place in Rome, and had behind it, under one roof with it, the Temple of Venus. To this Maxentius added a third, in honour of his son, whom he also named Romulus, and by this means he connected these temples with the Via Sacra, which had not been the case originally, though they were very near to it. This was the mistake of Hadrian, pointed out by Apollodorus, and the emperor was so much vexed at his mistake, and angry at having it pointed out to him rather rudely, that he ordered the architect to be put to death.

WALL ON WICH WAS FIXED THE MARBLE PLAN OF ROME

VIA SACRA.

PLATE XLIV.

DETAILS OF THE WALL OF THE MARBLE PLAN.

Via Sacra.

Description of Plate XLIV.

DETAILS OF THE WALL OF THE MARBLE PLAN.

In this plate the upper part shews a small portion of the wall, with remains of the metal hooks by which the slabs of marble, with the plan engraved upon them, were attached to the wall. The shafts of these hooks can still be seen in the holes in the brick wall of the third century; the hooks were broken off by the vibration of the marble plates caused by the earthquake, and the shock of the great mass of the Basilica of Constantine falling on to the marble pavement in front of the wall. One corner of that enormous fabric, with a corkscrew staircase in it, remains buried on the pavement where it fell.

The lower part of the Plate shews a fragment of a cornice of the third century, with brick-stamps of the same period, and the fragments of the Marble Plan then found, the most important of which is the Porticus Liviæ, with that name upon it.

DETAILS OF WALL OF MARBLE PLAN

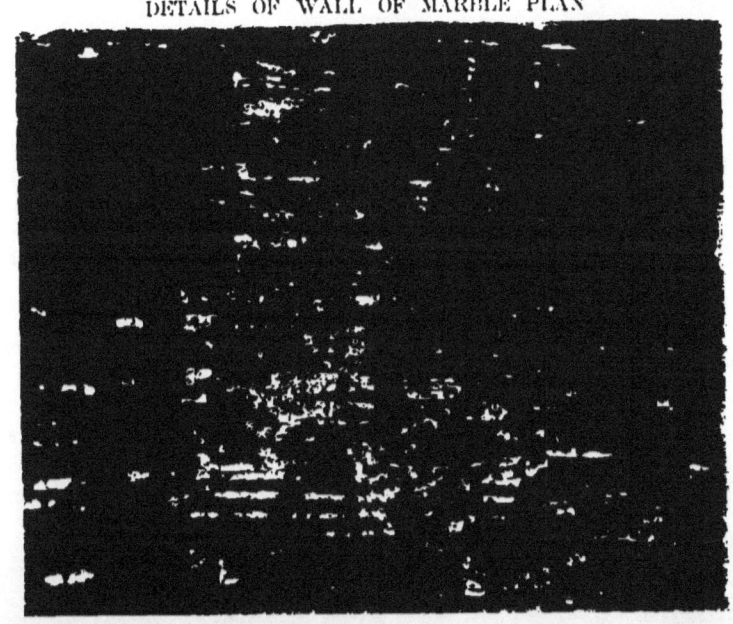

VIA SACRA.

PLATE XLV.

TEMPLE OF ANTONINUS AND FAUSTINA,

As Excavated in May, 1876.

Via Sacra.

Description of Plate XLV.

TEMPLE OF ANTONINUS AND FAUSTINA,

As Excavated in May, 1876.

In this view the remains of the steps are now made visible for the first time for centuries past, and the whole height of the building is now also made distinct. The monolithic columns come out in all their grandeur, and the hideous modern church inserted in the fine old temple is distinctly brought to light. On the right is seen the present level of the streets, and the lower part of the columns were buried to the depth here shewn for some centuries, until the excavations were made in 1876. A pit had been made in order to look down upon the bases by the French, in 1812, but no proper idea of the height of the magnificent columns could be formed. The difference of level between the old Forum and the modern streets is also brought out clearly, and there is no denying that the Forum was at the level of the old foss-ways. In the centre is the *podium*, or basement for an altar, and at each end one for a statue, no doubt those of Antoninus and Faustina.

TEMPLE OF ANTONINVS AND FAVSTINA
AS EXCAVATED IN 1876.

www.ingramcontent.com/pod-product-compliance
Lightning Source LLC
Chambersburg PA
CBHW030320240426
43673CB00040B/1230